W9-ABH-951

THE LAST IVORY HUNTER

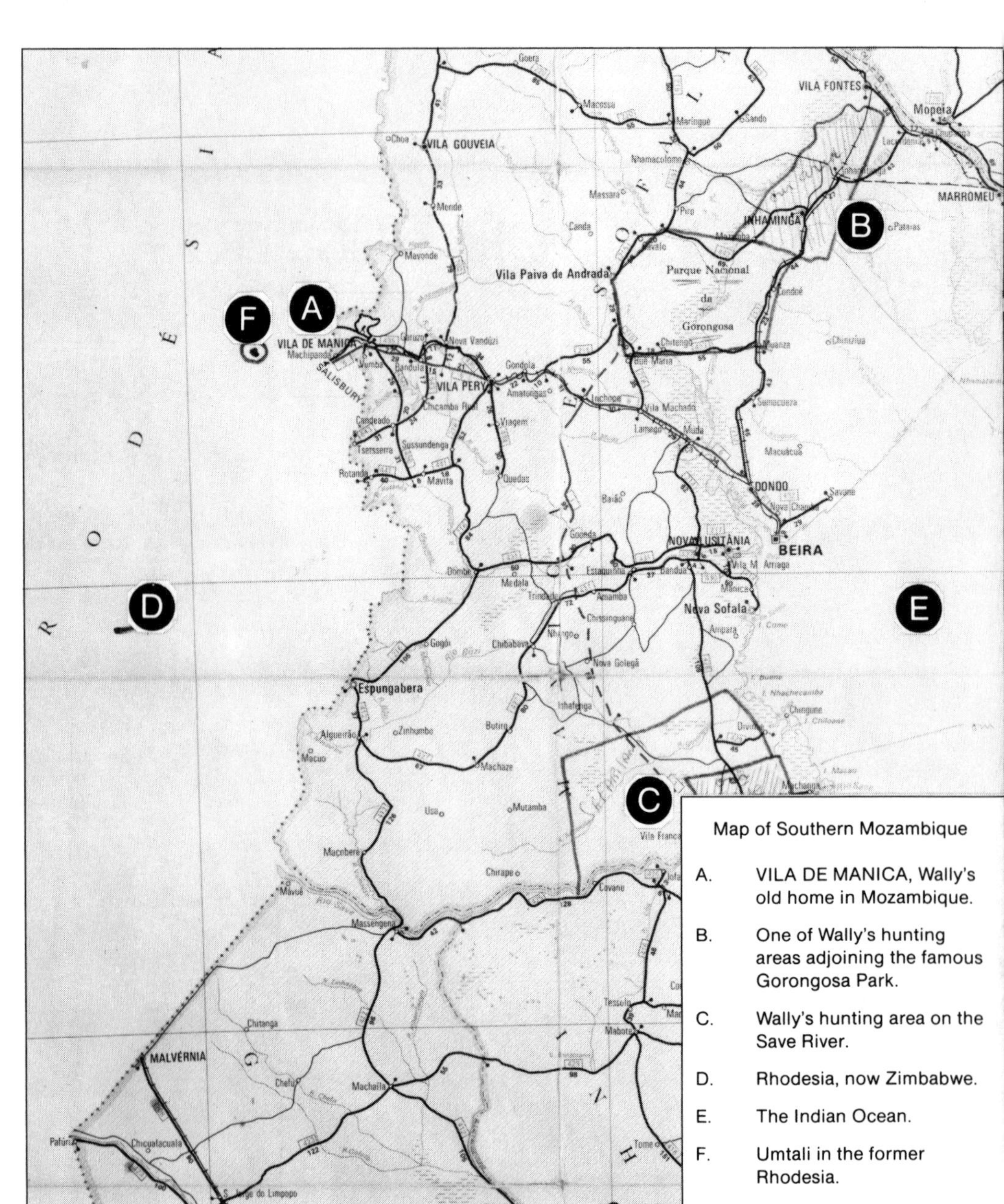

Map of Southern Mozambique
A. VILA DE MANICA, Wally's old home in Mozambique.
B. One of Wally's hunting areas adjoining the famous Gorongosa Park.
C. Wally's hunting area on the Save River.
D. Rhodesia, now Zimbabwe.
E. The Indian Ocean.
F. Umtali in the former Rhodesia.
VILA FONTES
Mopeia
MARROMEU
VILA GOUVEIA
INHAMINGA
Vila Paiva de Andrada
Parque Nacional da Gorongosa
VILA DE MANICA
VILA PERY
DONDO
NOVA LUSITÂNIA
BEIRA
Nova Sofala
Espungabera
MALVÉRNIA

THE LAST IVORY HUNTER

The Saga of Wally Johnson

PETER HATHAWAY
CAPSTICK

St. Martin's Press • New York

THE LAST IVORY HUNTER

Copyright © 1988 by Peter Hathaway Capstick. All rights reserved. Printed in the United States of America. No part of this book may be used or reproduced in any manner whatsoever without written permission except in the case of brief quotations embodied in critical articles or reviews. For information, address St. Martin's Press, 175 Fifth Avenue, New York, N.Y. 10010.

DESIGN BY DEBBY JAY

Library of Congress Cataloging-in-Publication Data

Capstick, Peter Hathaway.
The last ivory hunter / by Peter Hathaway Capstick.
p. cm.
ISBN 0-312-00048-0
1. Big game hunting—Africa. I. Title.
SK251.C273 1988
799.292'4—dc 19 87-38266
[B] CIP

10 9 8 7

In abiding memory of my wife, Lilly,
and for my children, Erika and Walter,
who shared and loved my vanished Africa.

WALTER WALKER JOHNSON

"The generation to which I belong has seen Africa yield up her secrets; and the survivors of this generation, who have witnessed the passing away or transformation of many of the great game regions, alone can tell of what our generation has done and seen, and which those who come after can never do or see again."

The Book of the Lion
by Sir Alfred E. Pease, Bart.
(London, John Murray, 1913)

CONTENTS

LIST OF ILLUSTRATIONS

PREFACE

The story of Walter Walker Johnson will be one of the last to emerge from the old Africa of classic big game hunting and high adventure, when elephant could be hunted on an unlimited commercial basis and when a man could still explore vast areas of an Africa all but untouched by Western sophistication and progress.

This book is not a biography in the true sense. Rather, it is a collection of incredible stories told by an old friend and veteran professional hunter, who has earned the respect of everyone who has ever known him. Wally—as he will be known throughout this book—will be seventy-six years old by the time you settle down to read these lines. He is one of the last living legends of an Africa that has in many ways sadly succumbed to the Soviet bloc and its surrogates, as you will see. His Africa, the limitless plains, forests, marshes, and savannas of Mozambique on the east coast of Africa, has undergone a frightening transformation and has become a battleground where human beings are starving and where the game that remains faces annihilation. Elephants, once the scourge of the country because they were so prolific, are fast becoming a memory. Poachers and guerrilla warfare have seen to that.

A hunter since 1926, Wally Johnson conducted his last professional safari in Zambia, with my good friends Lew and Dale Games, when he was over seventy. (His client, Hank Williams, Jr., the well-known recording artist, had the privilege of sharing Wally's company and experience.)

The Last Ivory Hunter is certainly not an arbitrary title. On a simple chronological basis, Wally probably *was* the last commercial hunter of ivory. He certainly had contemporaries, but almost everyone of note is already dead. Nobody, I think, who is still alive, has spent the sheer years Wally has in pursuit of "white gold." He is the doyen of that noble band of adventurers who lived the hard, hungry, weary way in the malaria-ridden expanses of Africa. His story bears witness for posterity to African hunting and the men who lived the life that can no longer be known. And, as you learn of Wally's adventures in this book, you will marvel that he is alive at all, let alone that he was able to record his amazing life before it was too late.

Wally's life has been one of unique excitement and danger. According to the best of our information, Wally is one of only two people known to have survived a full bite of a mature gaboon viper, surely one of the most lethal snakes in Africa. He survived a near-fatal goring by a Cape buffalo. He and a couple of pals stood off several hundred armed poachers in a totally isolated part of Mozambique, where they could have been overwhelmed and murdered in a flash—their bodies never recovered. He has killed nearly a hundred lions, many with the American deer rifle, a lever-action .30-30, and has shot some 1300 elephant, all bulls except for perhaps 5 percent cows, which he was forced to take in self-defense. He has been victim to all kinds of tropical diseases and has known privations we only read about—all this quite apart from being a professional hunter and safari host to many outstanding personalities of the day, including Robert Ruark, and from having survived a communist revolution, where he was shot up by RPGs, assaulted, arrested, stripped of everything he owned, and thrown out of the country he had called home for over half a century. Wally is a survivor. His story is one of survival, of surmounting often frightening odds and of coming through with spirit intact and memories still fresh of an Africa now relegated to one of the more tragic chapters of human history.

Wally's birth presaged an unusual life to come. He was born on the high seas between Australia and Durban, South Africa, on January 8, 1912 to parents in the racehorse business. I got a kick out of his answer when I asked him the name of the ship: "I don't recall. I was just a little baby, you know."

He and his two sisters lived in South Africa for a time, Wally having been sent to a convent school just north of Durban where the nuns scared him half to death. The family then moved to Southern Rhodesia, now Zimbabwe. Although Wally left school at fourteen, he is a great reader, a marvelously articulate raconteur, and has a wealth of life experience.

At fourteen years of age, Wally traveled to Mozambique, where he joined his brother-in-law, August Wood, as a shipping clerk in the quaint, ancient port town of Lourenço Marques, a Portuguese possession since the dawn of the sixteenth century. Wally had arrived in what was a truly unspoiled, wild part of the world, where game teemed on the doorstep of the harbor town and where the whiff of African adventure was constantly in the air. That same year Wally started the lifelong apprenticeship of the hunter, but more of that later.

This book is the result of more than 150 hours of taped interviews with Wally, starting with the memorable safari we enjoyed together in 1985 in the Luangwa Valley of Zambia, where we planned the project in detail. We then met many times in my home, where I helped Wally chip away at the treasure house of memories and often extraordinary experiences that fill this book. I had the pleasure of speaking at length with his son, Walter, Jr., and with his daughter, Erika, who both contributed a great many details to the fund I eventually amassed. I met two of Wally's grandchildren in the process and was given valuable documents, photographs, and other memorabilia. Such addenda took on a new significance when I learned that the illustrations you see in this book were but a minute fraction of what we could have used had the communist-backed FRELIMO government of the new Mozambique not stolen practically every possession Wally had. It is thanks to Wally's daughter, who had some copies of photographs, that we have any illustrations at all. Wally's beautiful home at Vila de Manica, just across the border from the then-Rhodesian town of Umtali, is now a memory, a home he last saw in 1975.

The story unfolds largely in Wally's voice. I have included some of my own experiences and comments in order to better highlight Wally's tale. Wally does not handle dates well—after more than half a century in the bush, experiencing traumas that nearly cost him his life, who could?

Wally Johnson is a professional bushman, a man of his hands and his eyes. So, if you reckon that the occasional "hell" or "damn" or the somewhat frequent invocation of the deity are offensive, put down this book. Wally is a rough and ready soul who has been to hell and back several times, often bringing along souvenirs. I absolutely refuse to tell his story in any way other than that in which it was told to me—Portuguese invectives and all. This is the true story of a man and an era, told accurately and to the best of my ability.

What you are about to read is the story of one of the great African hunting personalities. His tale is testimony to a time and place that are irrevocably gone. It is a story I immediately recognized as significant and worthy of recording because of its sweep, truth, and high drama. With this book, Wally has surely sidestepped oblivion and has left for posterity a document that will be treasured. It has been a great privilege for me to chronicle the tales of the African world as it used to be. We shall see no more of it.

ACKNOWLEDGMENTS

The author wishes to express his appreciation and that of Wally Johnson to the following people:

Erika Soffe, Wally's daughter, for making available so much true Africana and for records from her father's life. Walter, Jr., for his many enticing tales, information, and memorabilia of his father's life as an ivory hunter and professional safari operator.

Andrew Soffe, Wally's grandson, who was of great help and company to his grandfather in the creation of this book. Lew and Dale Games, so mentioned in *Peter Capstick's Africa,* for the part they played in jogging Wally's memory as we sat those many nights about the leadwood and mopane campfires on the Mupamadzi River of Zambia.

Gordon James Petch Cundill, Esq., for the many courtesies that made this book eventually possible. Mozambique-born Manuela Bruno, our good friend, who gave excellent insights into language usage and significant events in her old country.

Thomas McCormack, President of St. Martin's Press, Inc., who had the foresight to see the importance of preserving the true story of *The Last Ivory Hunter.*

Michael Sagalyn, my editor, for his invaluable assistance.

Dave and Hazel Dawson of Texas for getting Wally and me together, resulting in this book.

Paul Kimble for his usual expert photography.

My wife, Fiona Claire Capstick, my constant companion on safari, a professionally trained linguist and African herself who, with her knowledge of Africa and the languages involved, researched details and typed to perfection the final draft.

To Wally, thank you, old friend of the long grass with the wounded leopards at night.

INTRODUCTION

It is no accident that Peter Hathaway Capstick is the author of my life story. As a former professional hunter and an established writer on African hunting adventure, Peter was known to me, and he, in turn, had heard of me many years ago through my son, Walter. We have also hunted in Botswana at the same time. A mutual friend, Dave Dawson of Houston, Texas, persuaded us to get together in order that my fifty-five years of hunting and bush adventures would not be lost to my family and to all those who may never have the privilege of hunting in Africa and of enjoying a way of life that is disappearing.

Peter and I spent a memorable safari together in Zambia during July 1985, where our hosts, Lew and Dale Games, shared our evenings by the campfire on the banks of the Mupamadzi River as we reminisced about old friends and planned this book. Listening to Peter's laughter and observing him in the bush during a follow-up after a wounded leopard in extremely dense cover, I could not help being reminded of my late friend and client on many safaris, Bob Ruark. The only thing missing was the gin, but the two men shared a similar courage and capacity to enjoy life in the bush. And they both knew how to tell a story.

Peter was lucky to be there at all, as he had just completed a hunt in Botswana with Gordon Cundill where Gordon's double-barreled .500 Nitro Express insurance gun malfunctioned on four shots during a charge by a record-size lion, which Peter managed to put down with his .375 H & H at the last moment. It was a very close thing indeed, but it illustrates that Peter does not sit at a desk all day. He gets out there and stands his ground. My story needed someone who knows what it is to confront dangerous game and keep his nerve under the worst hunting circumstances.

Over many days of taped interviews—and after referring to whatever material I was able to salvage from Mozambique in the wake of the revolution in that country in 1975, when I lost everything except one vehicle and the clothes on my back—my story emerged. Perhaps this is a suitable place to explain that the Africa of my youth was a very different place from the continent it is today. When I first started hunting for ivory, elephant were so numerous and caused such terrible damage to the crops of villagers in Mozambique that the herds had to be drastically thinned out. Peter understood this as he was cropping elephant in Zambia decades later to help curb their numbers and the destruction of habitat. Politics, poaching, and population explosions have changed all that now.

It has often been difficult recalling exact details, because a great deal has happened to me since I arrived as a young boy in Mozambique in 1926. I have known so many people during my years in the bush that it is not easy to sift through my memories and single people out. But Harry Manners, author of *Kambaku,* occupies a special place as my hunting partner of the very early days, and I can never forget Luis, my gunbearer of some twenty-five years, and the other Africans, black and white, who became part of my life, sharing good times and often very bad times. I recall dozens and dozens of clients with whom I enjoyed splendid hunts and who came back for more. Many of them keep in touch to this day. Peter helped me remember a great deal, as he has lived the safari life, knows the African bush, and has long fallen under the spell it has cast over both our lives.

Looking back now, with the perspective that only age can bring, there are indeed some experiences I wish I had never had to endure, and there are incidents I wish I could have handled differently. But, given the choice, I would live my life again as a professional hunter in Africa where my home was the bush and my days were filled with adventure. I hope this story helps you share some of that magic.

WALLY JOHNSON
On safari—Mupamadzi River, Zambia
July 1985

1

GABOON

"For God's sake, Luis, help me! I'm dying!"

The Mozambican Shangaan looked at Wally with penetrating eyes, eyes whose quickness had saved lives time and again over the twenty years he had been with Wally, hunting in Mozambique. The head gunbearer's gaze was as bloodshot as usual, testimony to malaria, safari, and long hours after game. Though he was a good man—reliable as most to whom one entrusts one's life—he wanted nothing to do with this.

His patrão was going to cash in and he wanted no part in the proceedings.

"No, Baas, you're going to die. We have been together a long time, and I don't want to be there when you die. You must die alone. It is the way of things."

"My old friend of so much danger, help me! I don't want to die on a lonely road and the hyenas take my body. Help me! *Vou morrer!*"

"I can't, Baas. What if the authorities find out when you die? And you *will* die, because that is the worst snake. They will accuse me and the other men of killing you. What will I do then? You know they will then kill me. . . ."

"Help me! You can do no less!"

Oh yes, he could do less. Odd chap, Luis.

On the day Wally was bitten by a massive Gaboon viper in 1957, it had been nearly a year since he had captured another snake, which he thought at the time to be a young python. He kept it in a wire cage and fed it mice, the snake apparently enjoying the easy life. Then, one day, Wally took it down to show his chums at the local sawmill. Much to his shock, the manager called him an unadulterated idiot and advised him that it was a Gaboon viper, one of the most feared snakes in Africa, and from whose bite only one person had been known to recover. Wally, however, told the manager that it was he *who was the idiot. Clearly it was a young python.*

"You madman! That thing is deadly poisonous! Are you some kind of nut?"

"No, man," answered Wally. "It's a python. I've even had my fingers in its mouth!"

"You've what?*"*

"Sure. No fangs [he not realizing that they fold up against the roof of the mouth and that the snake had somehow tamed down]. I keep it in a wire pen as a pet. Give it frogs and mice and stuff."

"Well, get it the hell out of here or I'll kill it. Now!"

The cocking clicks of his revolver were ominous in the silence, the other strong and able men having scrambled onto the dining-room table when Wally threw the snake on the floor for exhibition.

"Don't touch my bloody snake! You don't want him, I'll take him home."

And with that, he grabbed the snake by the back of the head and dropped him into a sack, the deadly reptile as docile as a pussycat.

But Wally was wrong. It was *a Gaboon. . . .*

The Gaboon viper is certainly one of Africa's most dangerous snakes, possibly because of its lethargy, much like that of the puff adder, rather than because of great activity or aggressiveness. The

Gaboon, happily, is a fairly rare snake. Its coloring closely resembles the colors of the Napier Clan tartan, the body pattern being a complex geometric of primarily tan, blue, and black, some colors having a white edge to them. It has nasal "horns" that, together with the striking colors, make it surprisingly difficult to spot in long grass. So Wally found out. . . .

Bitis gabonica *probably has the longest fangs of the vipers. It is a thick, short snake, the longest recently recorded Gaboon viper being from Sierra Leone and measuring 6 feet 8½ inches. But it's one very bad bastard if it loses its sense of humor.*

After several months in its wire cage, being ogled at by the local kids, the snake was found one morning with blood on its back, just as Wally was about to feed it. One of the children had jabbed the snake with a piece of wire and it died soon afterward. Wally pitched it into the bush and gave the matter little more thought. He should have.

It was almost a year later to the day when Wally was nearly killed twice. But let him tell you the story. . . .

"I was down in the same area where I had caught what I thought was the baby python. I was staying for a couple of months to hunt for ivory, and I decided to take along a new cook my wife had just hired. The old guy had to leave for some reason or another and she got this new man. My wife insisted that he come along with me in the bush as I never seem to eat. She wanted somebody to look after me. She told him to pack up a chopbox with pots and pans, canned food, and anything else he thought he might need.

"Well, we got down to the spot within twenty miles of where I had been the year before, and I went out hunting with Luis on the first day we were there. As there wasn't much doing, I came back at about eleven in the morning. The cook didn't expect me back at that hour and hadn't prepared any food for lunch. I asked him what he had, and he said he was sorry that he had only expected me that evening.

"'*Patrão,* look in that box there and maybe you'll find something I can cook for you, spaghetti or something. You must find something, *patrão*; there's a lot of tinned food.'

"He opened the box and I had a look through and pulled out a tin of spaghetti or bully beef or something. Then I happened to notice another tin there, picked it up, and found out it was a snakebite kit. My wife used to carry this outfit. She always had it at home, as she did a lot of gardening and was scared as hell of snakes. I turned to the cook and said, 'Hey, where'd you get this thing from?'

"'*Na casa de banho.* From your bathroom.'

"'But did the *senhora* give it to you?'

"'No, *patrão.* I just saw it and took it.'

"'Do you know what it is?'

"'*Sim, senhor!* Yes, I do. It's snakebite *muti.* I know about these things from the mission school.'

"'Hell,' I said, 'I'm going to be in trouble if the *senhora* finds out this thing is missing, because she doesn't like to be without this medicine in the house. Ah, on second thought, *não faz mal.* Don't worry about it. You did very well to bring the snakebite kit. I just hope that my wife doesn't notice you've taken it.'

"'Baas, you never know when you may be bitten by a bad snake.'"

This book exists because of the forethought of that cook.

"While I was having something to eat, my headman and gunbearer, Luis, came to me and said, '*Patrão,* can I borrow one of your rifles? I want to go down to the river to catch some fish. There are a lot of big crocs down there, and I'd like a rifle for protection.'

"'Yeah, sure, take that 9.3mm Mauser. There are four shots in the magazine and one more in the chamber. Go ahead and take that rifle, but *cuidado*! Just watch out!'"

Luis went off and Wally was still eating lunch when, maybe ten or fifteen minutes later, he heard a shot.

"I thought to myself, well, Luis has seen some crocs. But then I heard another one, and in all, he fired off the whole five shots. When this happened, I thought, hell, this can't be a crocodile he's shooting at—with five shots, there's something wrong. I immediately grabbed my .375 Holland & Holland Magnum and started running in the direction of the shots, along the riverbank on the path.

"I hadn't gone very far when I saw some native women washing some clothes in the river and I asked if they had heard some shots going off just about where they were. 'No, we heard nothing.' I said to myself, hell, that's damned strange. Then I asked: 'Well, did you see a man come along this path with a gun—you know, *uma espingarda?*'

"'No,' they answered. 'We never saw a man with a gun.'

"That's goddamn funny, thought Wally. Seemed to be just about here somewhere."

Wally encountered the reluctance of rural women in Africa to speak to strangers.

"There was a deep little dry river that fed into the main river, a steep embankment that could only be done on foot if one ran at top speed down the near side to gain momentum that would carry one halfway up the other side. It was surrounded by the densest bush and grass imaginable. Call it a deep gully. I ran down the one slope as fast as I could and got about halfway up the other side before I had to slog it. I made the top, and saw a man coming along the other side and asked him: 'Say, have you seen a man with a rifle?'

"'No, *patrão,* but I did hear some shots just around here.'

"'Where exactly was it?'

"'Ah, close. It was just a little while ago.'

"So, I started shouting, and finally got an answer from Luis. Well, thank God he wasn't dead. He came running up after a few minutes and I asked, 'Luis, what the hell's going on here?'

"'Baas, where on earth have you come from?'

"'From the camp! Where else? What the bloody hell's going on, Luis?'

"Luis answered: 'These women won't talk to outsiders. I told them to tell you that I had wounded a buffalo. He's hiding right down at the bottom of this little river bed you crossed. Come here and I'll show you.'"

And there it was, a wounded bull buffalo back at the river bed Wally had run through. It was standing in the dense foliage not a foot from the track. Wally killed it with a single shot from his .375. The wounded buff, apparently, had been so astonished to see a man flash by so quickly—remember, Wally was running flat out to get up the other side—that it never occurred to it to charge!

Wally got past the hidden wounded buffalo through sheer surprise and luck. No thanks to the women at the river who could have warned him. But far worse was to come that day. . . .

After Wally had killed the buffalo, he ordered the rest of the men who had followed him from camp at the sound of shots to butcher the animal for rations.

The sun, a molten bronze orb, was slipping lower and the call of the emerald-spotted tree dove washed through the bush as the men set to with their knives, taking the hind legs and the filets for Wally's table, carrying the heavy legs on stout poles between them. Wally was walking in third place, behind the first two carriers, when horror literally struck.

"We were only about a hundred yards from camp when all of a sudden the man ahead of me took a jump and the next second I felt something on my leg. It felt as if I'd hit into a thornbush. I looked down and saw a snake as thick as my calf with its fangs embedded in my left leg, just above the ankle. I gave a reflex kick and the thing went flying. I screamed to Luis and the other men to kill it.

"'Quick,' I yelled. 'What kind of snake is that?'

"They clubbed it to death with sticks and Luis came to me and said, '*Patrão,* I'm sorry. It's the same snake you had last year. You are a dead man!'"

"Merda! I'll live." *Wally, possibly rather foolishly, ran for the camp, which was only some hundred yards away, to get to the antivenin kit, the darkness flowing into the long grass like a rising tide. The shadows were lapping over his back and the sweetness of the new grass was still strangely strong in his nostrils.*

"'Cook! Quick! *Depressa!* Bring me the snake box!'

"I had tennis shoes on and it was a hell of a job getting the left one off by the time I got back into camp. I had forgotten my knife and the knot in the laces had become so tight I really wondered if I could get the goddamn thing off at all. It was already hurting beyond description. Eventually, I was able to remove the shoe, but the pain and the swelling were so terrific I could hardly stand it.

"After what was probably only a minute or less, I had the snakebite kit in my hands. Now I was really sick, the pain almost unbearable and the swelling absolutely alarming. Especially when everybody handy was happily assuring me that I was going to die there and then!

"Well, I saw that the snakebite outfit had a little booklet inside. I'd never had to use a kit before and didn't really know how to work the bloody thing. So, there I was, just to the left of nowhere, and I open the booklet, one of the tent guys having brought me my reading spectacles.

"It was a most interesting piece of literature, obviously written by somebody who had never been bitten by a deadly snake. The first eight or ten pages were all about how they'd made the serum, where it was made and all sorts of other stupidities, *except* what you were supposed to do with the goddamn stuff. I could feel myself dying by the second, but this goddamn booklet wouldn't tell me where or how to inject myself. Lord, but I thought they'd never say what to do!

"Finally, I got down to the chapter that said that there was a sharp lancet in the rig with which you were supposed to cut a gash in yourself, avoiding arteries, then fill the syringe with one of the four ampoules of antivenin, injecting it into the wound.

"The booklet said to put one of the ampoules into the wound you had made on the bite and another halfway up your leg, if that's where you were bitten. The other ampoule should be put by injection into your stomach. Wonderful, the miracles of science.

"So I looked at this lot to try to find the lancet or razor blade. Nothing. It had been stolen.

"'*Hatlisa*! Hurry!' I shouted in Shangaan. 'Who has a sharp knife? I have to cut myself.' Finally, a bush type turned up with half a rusty razor blade he carried in his hair and probably had for several years. It was a lot of things, but sterile wasn't one of them. He gave it to me and I made two deep gashes in an X over the fang marks. The leg was so swollen and painful by that time I was doubly horrified to learn, on inspecting the ampoules of antivenin, that two were out of date and, according to the manufacturers, of little value. Cheery news. . . .

"Blood was pouring out of these gashes and I got one man to suck on them, warning him to spit out the blood and venom. I'd still love to get my hands on the son of a bitch who wrote that pamphlet in the snakebite kit. . . .

"Actually, as this chap was sucking on the wound, I had a chance to continue through the booklet and inspect the ampoules themselves. As I said, two of the four in the kit were more than two years out of date; the remaining two had a month to go before they were, theoretically, ineffective. Well, one tries to make the best of things. . . .

"This was a polyvalent antivenin, good for just about anything except *boomslang,* the back-fanged tree snake. The pain was so terrible by then that I could hardly concentrate on the so-called literature. Yet I knew I would die then and there if I didn't do things properly.

"Well, I thought, what the hell do I do? I'd better take one of the good ones that had a month to go and put it right into the bite. I took the syringe, sucked up the antivenin and squeezed the whole thing in there. The pain in my leg was already so severe that I never even felt the jab. I thought now, well, I'd better take one of the old ones, out of date, and stick it in the calf of my leg, which I did. Then I took the last good one that had a month to go and I squeezed that into my thigh. I injected the last ampoule directly into my stomach, even though it was out of date. *That* one hurt.

"Now I was in terrific pain. I was in agony. So I said to Luis, 'Check the truck immediately and see that it has petrol. I must get to hospital as quickly as possible!'

"He refused, as I have already told you. 'No, Baas. I do not want to be with you when you die, which will be soon.'

"'I have no time to argue with you, *filho da puta! Traidor!*' I let him have it, calling him a treacherous son of a bitch and a lot of other things. 'Get me the cook, then,' I bellowed.

"'*E-e, tatana,*' said the cook in Shangaan. 'I can't go, Baas. They will blame me too when you die. They will say I killed you. *Ndzi rivalele, tatana.* I am sorry, Baas.'

"'Bring me a pencil and paper, quickly. I will write a letter to the authorities to tell them that, if I die, you are not responsible for my death. You can show them the letter with my signature, dig up my body and show them the cuts I made with the razor where the snake bit me. You have the skin to prove what kind of snake it was and that I had no chance. But I *must* have a man to go with me to try and reach the sawmill, where they will take me to hospital. Who is a real man here? Who of you is loyal? Or are you nothing but women?'

"I then wrote a brief note to my wife—I knew I was dying—advising her what to do for the future. I explained that I had been bitten by a Gaboon; I told her that none of my men was to blame if the authorities thought they had killed me for some reason. I said good-bye to her and to the kids, certain that it was the end. I told her what to do about the future. I was now sure I would not see them again and that the letter would be sufficient for the authorities if they suspected that the men had poisoned me or killed me. But I still had to try to reach the sawmill where I might get some help. I knew only one thing: If I stayed where I was, they would bury me the next day. Well, if they weren't too drunk. . . .

"Finally, a man stepped forward who said he would come with me. A real bush type, he had been hanging around camp, helping cut up meat. I really don't think he had ever been in a vehicle before. This guy had probably been shanghaied through threats, as he knew absolutely not the first thing about motorcars. Still, I got him to wrap me in a blanket and carry me to the car and lift me up onto the driver's seat where I got the Toyota going. Happily, he spoke Shangaan and fair Portuguese.

"One of the big problems with this particular vehicle, which had been to hell and back, was that it tended to develop a fuel blockage and would stall. When this happened, I always had to crawl underneath the engine with a wrench or spanner and loosen the petrol line, blowing it clear with my mouth. It happened so often that I carried the proper size wrench on the dashboard.

"We were about eight miles out of my camp when a blockage occurred. Can you imagine! I was vomiting black blood and was crazy with pain. I explained to this chap what had to be done but, hell, he'd never even seen a wrench and a fuel pipe. They were utterly alien to him. He just couldn't manage. Realizing the whole thing was centuries beyond him, I had the guy lift me out and carry me to the front of the car where I pulled myself underneath. I was in such pain by that time I didn't even notice the burns on my hands from the hot pipes and engine. In complete darkness, I found the connecting fuel-line nut by feel and I blew it clear. The engine started.

"The trouble really came a couple of miles later. I was so doped up from the snakebite medication that I couldn't drive more than about five miles per hour. This wore the battery down as flat as the Kalahari. I, of course, had the lights on by this time and they were a constant drain on the juice box, which finally quit. Dead. *Gasta*!

"My God, now I'd really had it. What possibly could have gone worse? Dear Jesus, so this was where I was going to die. Well, it'd been a long road. I tried the starter a few times but got nothing but the characteristic *zzzzzzz* of a dead battery. I was in such pain from my leg that I couldn't even smoke my pipe. I thought about sending the meatcutter back to camp—ten miles by now—for a fresh battery. Then I realized I didn't have one there. He wouldn't have gone anyway, for fear of lions. So I sat for perhaps ten minutes behind the wheel, the pain getting worse by the second. Then I figured, what the hell! I hit the starter and, to my amazement, the engine turned over and caught!

"There was just that tiny bit of spark left to give it a kick. I revved the hell out of it to recharge and we were off again, despite my agony, at a better pace because I knew I was truly a dead man if that bloody engine failed again. It didn't, and at last the lights of the sawmill peered like leopard's eyes in the distance.

"I remember nothing until the next morning, and pain as pure as if it had been distilled in hell itself. I woke up on a bed with a lot of these sawmill people around me, giving me whiskey to drink as I told them what had happened.

"'*Pôrra para isto,* Wally! Don't worry, that's not a poisonous snake, anyhow. You'll be fine by tomorrow. Here, have some more whiskey. . . .'

"So I said, 'For God's sake, get me to a hospital. [It was 120 miles away on terrible roads.] Listen, dammit. I was bitten by a Gaboon viper, one of the most poisonous snakes in Africa! I'm going to die!'

"Unfortunately, the German guy who was running the sawmill was away at the time or he would have sent me straight to hospital. So I pleaded and yelled for a long time in Portuguese until the bunch finally relented and sent me with a driver to hospital. I was just drinking water the whole way and vomiting black blood. We got there at two in the morning."

This part of Wally's ordeal reminds me of something I witnessed in the then British Honduras. I saw a man who had been bitten by the infamous fer-de-lance *of Central America. Known locally as the* barba amarilla, *or "yellow beard," it is also a viper with essentially hemotoxic venom. God save you the consequences if it nails you.*

I wrote a magazine article some twenty years ago about this incident, in which the victim vomited black blood and was in agony until a "snake doctor" was found through some kind of jungle telegraph. I photographed the entire proceedings, which entailed a collection of stuff you would hardly think could cure snakebite, especially from a fer-de-lance. *Named after its lance-shaped head and yellow throat, this deadly viper is also locally known as the "jumping tommygoff"—a breed of trouble you don't need.*

The snake doctor began by smearing very hot armadillo fat over the wound. There was no cutting or sucking of the wound at all. A poultice of tobacco leaves was bound over the bite and the man was fed a mixture of crushed peppercorns in warm water, which made him vomit up large quantities of more black blood.

He was back at work two days later, when most men would have been dead. Ask me not, brother, what that was all about or how it worked. I have no degree in herpetology or snakebite treatment, but work it did. I saw it with my own eyes. It appears to me, on a highly nonmedical basis, that hemotoxic viper bites seem to amalgamate the poison in the stomach. True? Damned if I know. I can just tell you that I was there.

Wally was still vomiting large amounts of black blood, which was considered a bad sign by the hospital staff. Finally, the doctor arrived and the first thing he gave Wally was a tetanus injection. Rather like giving an aspirin to a drowning man. But I hesitate to criticize the profession. They've done too much for me. Yet it still seems that a man dying from the bite of a Gaboon viper would not be terribly worried about lockjaw. Then the doctor topped up the antivenin and gave Wally a potent pain-killing injection to put the poor man out, as he was really suffering.

"I told the driver to get through to my wife, quickly, explain what had happened, and tell her that I was in the hospital. Then I went off to sleep and didn't wake up till nine or ten in the morning. I was still in great pain and was delirious when my wife arrived and said that she wanted to take me across the border to the Umtali Hospital in Rhodesia. This she did and I was admitted there. By that time, my whole side was going black; it was a lovely serge blue.

"My wife spoke with the doctors and they told her that there wasn't much hope for me. In any case, they did what they could, and I was delirious for three days. But, day by day, I was getting better, and as time went on, I knew that I was improving.

"I was there for several weeks, still in great pain. My left leg was twice as thick as my right, and it was so painful that I couldn't even bear to have anyone so much as look at it. I was getting on comparatively well, though, and the doctors said that I was out of danger. So, I figured, bugger this hospital business, and I went home with my wife, where I was laid up for about three months before I could hobble about on a cane.

"So far as I know or have been able to determine, there has been only one other person who has survived the full bite of a

Gaboon viper. I don't know who it was or when, but that person surely has my understanding. Lucky, weren't we?"

It was nearly a year before Wally could walk properly and hunt again. As I was to discover, it was truly strange how often snakes were a part of his career. He was never bitten again. Yet there were some odd incidents with African snakes that nearly made his heart stop.

"I was building a safari camp once, out of season. My wife was with me and we had no client. While this camp was going up, she and I slept on a large piece of canvas. I actually had a tent but never went to the trouble of putting it up. The magnificent Mozambique moon came up and the men were sleeping nearby. Sometime in the horrendous hours, my wife woke me and said, 'There's something in the bed. Between us.'

"'Well, it could be ants,' I mumbled. I felt around with my hand. 'Jesus! It's a bloody snake!'

"I couldn't tell in the dark what kind it was; may have been a bloody black mamba. There was only one thing to do: I grabbed the flashlight in my left hand and the snake's tail in my right. Not being restricted by a tent, I swung it around my head about five times and threw it into the bush, centrifugal force keeping it from turning back and biting me or my wife.

"My men were mad as hell, as they were sure that the damned thing would come back for them. They thought I should have killed it, but with what? All the men sat up most of the night, but, whatever it was, it didn't return. There were a lot of bleary eyes in the morning."

Wally had one set of particularly favorite safari clients, Gerry Knight and his wife (the same people who were later to save him from a buffalo).

"We were hunting in the Limpopo area, the border with South Africa, and had shot a zebra which we loaded onto the back of the vehicle. (No easy job if you've ever tried to lift a reasonably small horse.) From there, we headed back to camp to skin it, as we weren't far out.

"On the way back, we had to pass a small depression with a layer of water still in it, despite the dry season. All of a sudden a tremendous black mamba reared up from the grass! It was some yards off and I grabbed my shotgun as the snake finally lowered itself and went up a tree, where I gave it a charge of bird shot in the head.

"I asked Gerry if he'd like the skin and, although it was really tough to get a skinner to take the hide off a snake, we dumped it in the back of the truck, with my men hanging on to the pipe rollbars as if it were still alive.

"We had a slight problem. It was!

"We'd gone about twenty minutes when the trackers and gunbearers started screaming. I swung around in my seat but could not see properly. Gerry's wife turned around and made a literal head-first dive out of the open windscreen, straight over the front of the car and the hood, badly scraping and cutting her legs in her haste to get away from the black mamba that was standing behind her neck. She had been inches away from certain death. Thank heavens the windshield was down, as I'm sure she would have gone through it!

"Everybody—rather understandably, as we had no cab on—jumped out. But I was able to grab a machete or *panga* and, with a wild swing, cut the mamba's head off. How it had survived that shotgun blast I'll never know, but in the end, we all laughed at ourselves. Really, there was positively nothing to laugh about. Mamba bites are no joke. It is locally called the 'three-step snake'— that's about as far as you can expect to go after being bitten. We were all goddamn lucky."

Obviously, after half a century in truly primeval bush, one is bound to run into a few snakes. One strange instance Wally experienced concerned a python and two American clients in Mozambique.

"It was a big bastard, and when I saw it I jumped out and grabbed it behind the head. The bloody thing then surprised me by throwing several coils around my body. I talked my men, who loathed snakes to a degree no white person could ever possibly understand, into peeling it off me. They were nearly overcome with fear and revulsion.

"After the clients had taken the pictures they wanted—and it was one hell of a big python—I threw it into the bush at the side of the road and started walking back to the car. All of a sudden, the men started shouting at me: '*Olha, olha!* Look, look!' I turned around and asked them what the hell was the matter.

"'*Todo fudido, patrão!*' they yelled in unmentionable Portuguese as they wildly explained that the python had gone under the car!"

Wally got down on his hands and knees but couldn't spot it. He checked the tracks to see that the snake hadn't simply passed under the chassis, but there was no spoor on the other side. No, it's true, it wasn't a poisonous snake, but who wanted to share accommodation with a fifteen-foot python? They also bite, as I can guarantee you. And their teeth can break off, which creates hell's own fun digging them out of one's own meat.

At last, after a long search, Wally found the snake wrapped around the left front brake drum. "Ah, hell," he figured, "if I go for a hundred or so yards, the thing has to be thrown free." So he hit the accelerator and then stopped some distance down the road.

No go. The snake was somehow still there, and apparently had all intentions of filing for permanent residence. Wally decided to speed up, and when he pulled into camp, he handed the vehicle over to the staff mechanic. He had stopped earlier and seen that the python was no longer wrapped around the brake drum; it was completely entwined around most of the engine.

The mechanic came running and asked what should be done to the car. "I think there's something wrong with the engine; maybe the clutch," Wally told the mechanic, practical joker that he was.

"'Don't worry, *patrão*. I'll fix that.' He then opened the hood and pandemonium broke loose, as the mechanic gesticulated wildly at the car and screeched in Shangaan, '*Nyoka, nyoka, nyoka*! Snake!'"

The clients were also afraid of the python, since it was enormous, but by the next morning it had gone off into the bush on its own.

This snake story of Wally's reminded me of an odd experience I once had when I was a professional hunter in Botswana. It concerned a leguaan, *or monitor lizard, a creature that can well exceed seven feet in length, and which has the bite of a bulldog. I was with two American clients when one of these relics of the dinosaur age dashed out in front of the Toyota. I hit the brakes rather hard, and as the local Africans have as much regard for lizards as they do for snakes, I knew that it would be up to me to see what had happened. (My crew told me that the* leguaan *had, by tradition, brought the message from* Modimo, God, *that man must die, whereas the chameleon, slower by far, had been entrusted with the divine message that man would never die. As the tale has it, the* leguaan *got there first; hence my crew's fear and loathing of the creature.)*

Well, the leguaan *surely had not been hit by the wheels, or I would have felt it through the steering shaft. But where was he? No tracks out the back, front, or side. That left one place.* Pagati. *Inside. Somewhere in the body works but, for the life of me, I could not spot it. The crew stood back. Nothing was getting them to go poking around for the creature.*

I couldn't imagine how on earth that bloody thing could live. It was well over 100 *degrees* Fahrenheit *outside, so imagine what it must have registered under the hood! How he wasn't burned to a crisp, I don't know. Maybe there's a lot more to the term "cold-blooded" than we think. The rascal was hiding somewhere in the chassis and was probably fairly well scorched, but he didn't jump out. We did not see him again, but the next morning his spoor led out of the engine housing.*

Ah, well, I suppose it's damned tough thumbing a ride in the Okavango.

Wally recalls another snake incident from the old days in Mozambique when he was out with the well-known professional hunter Baron Werner von Alvensleben. I had met the Baron in New York years previously and remember his Heidelberg student dueling scars and his great reputation as a spearman on pigs and, I believe, Cape buffalo, using packs of dogs.

Werner was practically neurotic about poachers, and when he and Wally found a hunting car in the bush, they immediately suspected a sophisticated operation. They sat down and waited for the return of the owner to find out what was going on. It wasn't until dawn that the man came back. Werner was sitting on a hessian sack on the hood of the car. He was comfortable.

A white man appeared at dawn, and Werner and Wally asked him what in hell he was doing there.

"Catching snakes. My business. And you, sir, are sitting on one of them. They're very delicate, you know. Kindly get off that sack."

Von Alvensleben did a maneuver that would have won him a gold medal in any Olympic competition, the Baron bailing off the hood like a demented dervish. There, in the sack on which he had been sitting and sleeping, was a banded water cobra, Boulengeria annulata. *Why it had not bitten him through the rough cloth is anybody's guess. Maybe just luck.*

There is no known antivenin.

The stranger opened the bag and poured out the snake, which really put on a performance. In a second bag, he also had a black mamba, which he teased with a stick, somewhat to the discomfort of Wally and Werner. Finally, he put the snakes back in the bags, thanked the men for keeping an eye on his car, and went on what I hope was his merry way.

Wally did not come across too many snakes in that particular area, but then, snakes are never obvious. He does recall an interesting bet between two German clients. They had arrived at camp in the morning, and after lunch, Wally suggested they just have a drive around to become acquainted with things on safari. "We can start serious hunting tomorrow."

At lunch, one man asked, "But what about snakes?"

Wally said that there were hardly any around and that they were most certainly not a problem.

"Meine Herren," *said Wally, "I haven't seen a snake for months."*

"There you are," said the other client in English to his partner.

"Ja, *but there must be snakes here. This is Africa!"*

"Yes," said Wally, "but you never see them."

"Well," said the doubtful German, "you may be right, but I'll bet you a case of whiskey that we see a snake on this safari."

The second client accepted with the comment that he would most certainly enjoy the whiskey. "I'm damned sure we won't see one. . . ."

The next day they went out hunting and were standing with binoculars looking at some impala. Wally suddenly yelled, "Look out!" as a monster of a black mamba came down the path right at them. "I thought you said there were no snakes here," said the first client.

"No, there aren't, but you'll enjoy your whiskey." He then killed it with his .375 H & H Magnum.

Let's flash back now to the early days, when Wally arrived in Lourenço Marques as a youngster. He had no idea that his destiny would be anything but that of a shipping clerk, confined to a desk in an office. The dangers, thrills, and high risks of big-game hunting and life in the bush were far removed from the teenager's mind as he set off for his first job in Mozambique.

2

INITIATION

Wally's youth was not much more than you'd expect from the average boy, except for one thing: He had the African bush, which he learned to love so well, and which was to govern his life for more than half a century.

Wally left school at 14 in 1926 and journeyed to Lourenço Marques, the capital of Mozambique, where he joined his brother-in-law, August Wood, as a clerk in a shipping company. The city, now called Maputo, lies at the southern end of the country.

This was the same year that Wally killed his first animal on a hunt: a duiker, which is a smallish antelope. He was using a .22 and had teamed up with a couple of kids who were also keen on hunting. They would spend every spare moment in a place called Catembe, south of Lourenço Marques, where the surroundings were wild and exciting.

Wally's brother-in-law managed to pick up a battered .303 British Lee-Metford with one hundred cartridges from a Scandinavian sea captain for the handsome sum of two pounds. (The captain used to shoot sharks with it.) The .303, a good standard British service caliber, very quickly replaced the slingshots and such with which Wally and his pals had been shooting lizards.

With the magical possession of a gun, he and his friends now started hunting an area around Moamba, a 120-mile round trip by train northwest of Lourenço Marques, which they would make every weekend just for an afternoon's hunting. Even today, Wally's eyes glisten and sparkle in the reflected campfire as he recalls those days.

A friend of August Wood's was running a cotton scheme that wasn't working out well and was about to close down. It seemed that this man had a Model T Ford which Wally dearly coveted. He was, after all, now sixteen, and he felt he should have a car. So he set off with August and a mechanic for the cotton farm at about nine at night, intent on buying the car. It was to be the first time he had really been in the black bush. Of course, they couldn't see except for August's headlamps, but they found a camping site as the farm was still some distance away. August had warned Wally: "Stay in the car, kid, and don't move." The two men built a fire and spread out a canvas tarpaulin.

Wally didn't give a damn if something ate him. He was going into the Africa he loved, the Africa of unknown night. He was plenty scared but lay down on the canvas. August said nothing. The youngster had not lain there five minutes, watching the fire between the V of his feet when a hyena, close by, began his symphony.

"I was still scared as hell," said Wally to me on the Mupamadzi, "but that bloody hyena welded my soul to Africa."

Still nervous, he decided to sleep on the outside of the two men but couldn't nod off in his excitement. He heard soft padding in the bush nearby and "accidentally" rolled into August to wake him up. He didn't sleep an hour and kept poor August up the whole night.

The next day the men needed meat, so they decided to take a wildebeest from a herd they had come across.

"You seem to handle that .303 pretty well, Wally. Why don't you shoot us some dinner?"

One shot. One wildebeest bull.

"He who shoots him butchers him," said August. Wally, under expert guidance, set to for most of the afternoon, pleased as a pig in the proverbial, which was exactly the substance in which he was up to his elbows.

Later, the two men shot a couple of impala. One must bear in mind that hunting in those days in Mozambique was rather like going to the supermarket today, if you were prepared to take your chances.

No laws, no restrictions. People there lived *on game, and there was no difference in shooting an eland or buying a side of beef.*

At last they reached the cotton farm and Wally made a deal to buy the coveted Model *T at the extraordinary price of five pounds. In those days that was a lot of money, the rough equivalent of* $25.00, *which wasn't peanuts when you consider that a cowpuncher in the United States earned an average of* $14 *a month for a 16-hour day.*

The car was a half-ton model, and when they got back to L.M. *(as* Lourenço Marques *was always referred to), August Wood and the mechanic were kind enough to spend a weekend teaching Wally how engines worked. They removed the engine, replaced the rings, pistons, and bearings, and went right through the car, teaching Wally until two or three each morning. Wally had a natural aptitude for mechanics, which was to save his life many times, and make him secure in the bush during all the years he hunted some of the most remote areas in Africa.*

He was too young for a driver's license, but that didn't bother him one whit. He would take the Ford out every weekend on hunting trips with friends, and it worked grandly. Of course, a better or more reliable machine for the money was never built. No offense, Maseratti or Ferrari. . . .

When Wally was finally old enough, he obtained Mozambique license number 59. Naturally—if you can imagine a place as remote as the bush of Mozambique in the 1920s, and the conditions of the "roads," you can readily understand why Wally always carried a handful of extra bearings as well as four extra pistons and connecting rods. He became so deft at changing pistons and rods that he could complete the job in half an hour.

One of the interesting facets of the Ford was its oil consumption. It went through the stuff like a beachboy—about one hundred miles to the gallon and, on steep hills, Wally had to drive the car up backward! But, with its integrity and Wally's knowledge, the Ford always got him into the bush and back. It was the finest experience for the young man who would later perform mechanical miracles in the bush to survive.

Although he owned about a dozen different vehicles before he was twenty, Wally kept the Model T for years. It became friend, companion, and lifesaver to him.

Wally's wife of so many years of loneliness and loyalty was one Lilly Lena Louise Isselbacher, a German lady whom Wally met and fell in love with in the 1920s in Mozambique. She had come out to the Portuguese territory as a nurse/companion. Wally and she had two children, Walter, Jr., and Erika, both of whom now live in California. They have given Wally four grandchildren, and a great-grandchild has arrived. Lilly died in Germany in 1968 while on a visit to her relatives. She must have been a strong and adventurous soul, enduring great hardships with Wally, who became a member of that most unpredictable profession, ivory hunting.

Mozambique, being a Portuguese possession, was neutral during World War II.

Lilly was pro-Allied forces, and she encouraged Wally to join up. She was still a German national, however, and Wally was turned down in Southern Rhodesia, then a British colony. He was suspect in some people's books and rejected as a volunteer. Wally battled to have the decision reversed, but the answer was an unswerving no. The war effort missed a good man in Walter Johnson, but such was the paranoia concerning fifth columns, spies, and the usual lot.

So Wally finally shrugged his shoulders and spent the rest of the war hunting elephant. A reopening of elephant hunting in Mozambique on an unrestricted basis had taken place around 1937, because of the horrendous damage the animals were causing to native crops and the great death toll among the tribesmen who tried to protect their property and food supplies.

A great deal happened to Wally in the intervening years and he came close to death on many occasions, particularly when lions were involved. In the late 1930s, Wally was asked by the authorities to take out a notoriously successful man-eating lion which had been ingesting large numbers of the indigenous folk with no prejudice whatever. In Wally's words:

"I met a very nice guy by the name of Jack Liversedge one day, who asked me if we could go out hunting together sometime in the near future. I said, 'Sure, why not? Always glad of the company.'

"I had to shoot some elephants anyway, and we always had a helluva good time together so we set out for the Vila Gouveia area, northwest of Beira, and at a certain stage, we had to go on foot as the rivers were too swollen to cross with vehicles.

"On the way, we came to a very small native settlement of huts and fields under cultivation, where a tremendous dance was on. So, we said, that's great. We stopped for something to eat and some men brought the drums out. We sat there for hours, just watching. I had five men with me as well as Liversedge, an old pal Bob Squires, and a little chap called Bellino, an Italian who became a great friend.

"'So,' I said to Luis, my head Shangaan gunbearer, 'where do we sleep?'

"'*Patrão,* right here. Here's an open place. Let's put down the canvas here.'

"But the chief of the village insisted that we sleep under an open-sided hut, so we rolled up the tarp and got under this thing. The singing was still going on; I don't know what time they must have stopped, maybe around two in the morning. But I was woken up at four A.M. by one of my men, screaming.

"'What the hell's the matter?' I asked, still half asleep.

"'A lion has taken one of the men out of the hut, just here. Now!'

"I quickly grabbed my flashlight and my .375 H & H, and this guy showed me, not fifty yards away, where a lion had broken into the hut and nailed this poor chap. The lion had pushed all the wooden poles apart, made a hole and dragged the man, screaming, out to eat him.

"It dragged the man across the ground, the snags of the hut wall having torn off some of his clothing. There was blood on the cloth and on the ground. We listened, and could actually hear the lion eating the poor bastard. And not far away. I fired a few shots with my rifle in the hope that maybe the lion hadn't yet killed him, but it was most definitely in vain.

"I figured I'd better go after the man-eater, so I switched the flashlight on and started into the bush, but Luis said, 'No, for God's sake, *patrão,* don't go after this thing. It'll kill you!'

"Well, getting killed by man-eating lions or anything else

was never one of my life plans. The odds were bad enough anyway.

"'Please, Baas, don't go now,' Luis continued. 'In a few hours it will be daylight and we can see what we are doing. We can't see now.' [Good advice.]

"He suggested that we all go and have some coffee, which we did, all wondering about this lion business. As soon as it was light, we went over and had a look. It was clear enough for a blind Boy Scout.

"Right next to the hut there was a *kraal* full of goats. The fence was only about three feet high and the lion had passed it. It could have easily taken one of the goats, but it passed them up and came to the entrance of this hut, which had no door. It came to the opening, saw three of my men lying inside this *kaia,* one on one side of the small fire and two on the other side.

"Oddly, it didn't go in the front but went around the side of the hut. For some crazy reason, despite there being an open doorway, the lion went to the trouble of tearing a hole, which he passed through.

"Now why, with an open doorway, would it bother to break through the side of the hut?"

After many years of experience with man-eaters, Wally and I agreed that the lion's behavior proved that it ate people for a living. It was unused to open doors and suspected a trap, thus going to the trouble of ripping a hole in the side of the hut rather than simply walking in and grabbing somebody. Typical man-eater performance. As Wally went on to say,

"Funny how man-eaters choose their victims. It actually stepped over two men and grabbed the man on the other side of the fire. He gave a short scream as the tremendous fangs sank into his brain, and that was it. . . .

"When dawn arrived, we saw exactly what had happened and decided to follow the drag marks of the body. We followed the spoor and came across the nauseating sight of two legs, bitten off clean at the knee joints—as neatly as a sword might have done.

"Oh my God, I thought. We started following the spoor where the lion had continued carrying the man. And as we went along, one of my men pointed and whispered, 'Look! There!'

"I felt my bile rise as I saw half of the man, largely eaten by the lion, lying under a bush. As you will see by the photograph I took, it was a gruesome sight.

"Actually, it was just his rib cage; he had no entrails or heart left but, somewhat surprisingly, both his arms and his head were intact. His eyes were open, and I have since had nightmares when I thought he was looking at me.

"Suddenly, we heard a noise in front of us in the bush, and one of my men said, 'There he goes!'

"It was a big open plain and I told them that we'd get him. It was all open grass and we could follow the tracks easily in the morning dew. But every time we came close to the animal, it would keep running, the grass rustling ahead. This happened two or three times, until Luis said, 'Come on, Baas. Let's sit down and talk this over.'

"We then had a real conference of war. Three of my men came over and gave their opinions. Luis was the first to speak.

"'Look, *patrão,* we'll never get the bastard this way. It just won't work.'

"'What do you suggest?' I asked.

"'Well, we'll take the body of the dead man, build a tree platform, and tie the remains of the body to the tree below. When the lion comes, we'll kill it.'

'Damned good idea. Yes. We'll try it,' replied Wally. But when the men went back to where they had last seen the body, the damned thing was gone. The lion had doubled back, grabbed what was left of the body, and run off again. "All we heard was a roar," said Wally.

"We spoored very carefully and actually found the body where the lion had dragged it. It gave one growl and was off. I said to my men, 'Come on! Let's take what's left back up to the tree near the village and we'll sit over it.'

"Well, they wouldn't touch the corpse. Black magic. Never touch a dead man."

* * *

This attitude, incidentally, nearly cost the life of America's greatest pioneering taxidermist, Carl Akeley, when he was badly mauled by an elephant. He lay bleeding to death in the icy rain high up in the Aberdare Range of Kenya, his men refusing to touch him. Much later, his wife came across him, unconscious, presumed dead, and saved his life.

"So," continued Wally, "I picked up the body myself by one hand, which was as stiff as wood. I remember how cold that hand felt. . . . But I pulled him along easily as, after all, it was only part of a body, and we took him to the tree we had decided on. Then we went to the *kraal* where we had our blankets and all our stuff.

"We figured we'd get some men to go and build a platform, like the *machan* in India. But just then, we heard a car coming. It had six black policemen in it, dressed to the nines. They were carrying guns and the whole lot, so I said to them, 'What is it you guys want?'

"'We heard that a lion killed someone last night, and the Administrator has sent us to kill the lion,' said the police sergeant.

"I said, 'Go back and tell the Administrator not to worry, because I'm here. He knows me, because I've been to his place a few times and I'll get the lion. So you guys bugger off.'

"'But where is the body?' asked the sergeant.

"'It's underneath a tree just up here. But we want to get the lion first.'

"They said, 'All right.' I told them that the last time we had seen the lion was down on this open plain, running away from us. I said I'd be most happy to leave it to them if they could figure out a way to get it. I told them to go ahead.

"They rounded up a whole lot of native women and kids and had them bring anything that could make a racket or noise, and they beat the grass, spreading out in a long line and coming together to push toward the end of the plain, where all the policemen were now up trees. When the lion came sauntering by, they planned to shoot it.

"Well, this whole crowd got together and was told what to do. But hell, all I saw was a line of old men walking single file down this plain instead of being lined up abreast. So it was simple for this lion. All the lion did was circle around and go back away from the beaters and the guns.

"Anyway, the bunch told me that they couldn't get the lion, so now they wanted to bury the body. I said, 'Hell, no! Don't bury him. We need him. I need him because the lion's going to finish him tonight when he comes back. Then I'll get the lion.'

"'Impossivel, Senhor Johnson,' said the sergeant. Orders had to be followed. I argued:

"'No, man. You go back to the Administrator and tell him that I'll get the lion. It's the only way I'm going to be able to kill the bastard.'

"'Sir, we have strict orders from the Administrator of this area. He says bury the man, we bury the man. *Ordens são ordens.* Orders are orders.'

"'Well, I guess that if you have to do it, you have to do it,' said Wally. The policemen started digging a hole. The only problem was that their hearts were not exactly in it. The hole was four feet long and only about six inches deep. It wouldn't have taken a couple of lamb chops, let alone a man's body, legs or no legs.

"They made this hole and were whacking away with a pick and shovel, one or two of the men just standing there. I asked what they were going to do now. 'We'll just put him in.'

"I said, 'No! You've got to dig a deep hole. That's not deep enough. The hyenas will have him tonight.' But they weren't too keen, as it was a hot day. They eventually went down about another three inches, but when they put the body into the grave, it stuck right out of the ground."

Wally turned on the men. "Listen! I told you it's not deep enough. You must make it deeper." But they didn't want to dig too deep, as they were tired or something. They just refused and dropped the body into the shallow trench.

* * *

"But one of the arms, stiff as a crowbar, was sticking out. I battled to convince the guys to dig deeper. I mean, his bloody arm was sticking out! One of the policemen pushed the corpse down into the grave as the others were putting in the sand. They just didn't want to know about hyenas or lions. In fact, you know what the sergeant said? 'Oh, hell, senhor, the lions and hyenas will get us all, anyway. What's the difference? *Sorte, Senhor, sorte.*' Fate! There he's talking about bloody fate instead of cooperating in getting the lion! Africa! I could have kicked the bugger!"

But the whole lot got a huge scare moments later when, all of a sudden, this dead man's arm poked straight through the heap of sand. Wally laughed at the panicked men and said, "You see, he's calling you to join him!"

That did it. "Man," said Wally, "you've never seen such digging. They made a proper grave and buried the poor chap adequately. I told the sergeant to tell the Administrator that I witnessed that the men had done a good job.

"We went back to camp. After talking about it, we decided to take a goat and tie it up near the grave, build a tree platform, and shoot the lion when it came to get the goat or to attempt to dig up the corpse.

"All of a sudden we heard a noise and we saw Bob Squires, my good friend, come running. He and Jack Liversedge, both armed with rifles, were still out in the bush, close to camp. Bob crashed in, shouting over and over: 'Oh, my god!' I asked what the hell was the matter.

"'Jesus,' Bob said, 'I was walking along with Jack and all of a sudden, I fell down a game trap. I nearly broke my legs.'

"The blacks there made a lot of traps; they'd dig a deep hole (about six feet deep) and they'd taper it at the bottom. Any animal that falls in is jammed by its own legs. The tribesmen would cover the hole most cleverly with leaves and sticks, scattering some dung on top. Any animal falling into this thing is nailed. The men then come along and spear the trapped animal to death. Bob was just goddamn lucky, because these holes are often filled with big, poisoned spikes. There are usually indications to other tribesmen that the trap is there, such as a blaze on a tree or a bent bush. But Bob didn't know what to look for and, in the half light, he probably wouldn't have recognized it anyway."

"'Come on,' he said, 'I'll show you where the damned thing is.'

"And, as we went along, Bob fell down another trap. Again, he was lucky there were no poisoned spikes and that he didn't break any bones. He suddenly thought the whole thing very funny. I didn't see the humor.

"In any case we had something to eat. I called Luis over and told him to take a goat and tie it up close to the grave. They found an old man, about seventy years of age, and told him to go and get a goat and tie it up at the tree overlooking the grave.

"The old chap got the goat from the *kraal,* and as he was walking along toward the tree, he spotted the lion. It had been caught in one of those traps Bob Squires kept falling into. The old guy came running into camp, shouting in Shangaan that the lion was in a hole and that we'd better come quick.

"We rushed out, hoping to plug the devil. I crept up to the trap, getting closer and closer. But when I looked, the animal had vanished. Somehow it had managed to get out. . . .

"We decided to build two tree platforms instead of only one. The idea was more firepower, so I put Luis and Bob on one and Jack and another guy on the other. We waited for hours, the goat bleating, but no lion showed. God, our bums were sore. We were stiff all over, the goat just calling continually. Nothing. Half frozen, we were so thankful for morning.

"Jack and Bob had to return to Umtali in Rhodesia, so I had to forget about the man-eater for a while and take them back, as I had to go there anyway. I then returned since there were a lot of elephant on Gorongosa Mountain and I needed the money from the ivory. Unlimited elephant hunting was now open, and I had to make a livelihood, man-eaters or not.

"On my way back, I passed through several villages on a high, imposing mountain. Nobody about. No activity. I thought, hell, that's damned strange. Where are all the girls who usually do the hoeing, and the men around the *kraals*? I didn't see anybody at all. Well, the reason was that there was nobody there."

"'*Patrão,*' said Luis, 'there's something very wrong.'

"I got him to shout. At last, one man put his head out of his hut. Then the whole lot came running out. I asked what on earth had been going on during my brief absence.

"'The lion has eaten another five people since you left. He's even attacking in the daytime now! Even the women and the children in the fields. We had a woman killed yesterday, along with her baby. The lion ate them both. He has been killing almost every day. You must help us!'

"'Well, where was the last place he killed somebody?' I asked.

"'About three or four miles from here.'

"I asked how I was supposed to know exactly where to find the beast. I told them all I had to go elephant hunting anyway. It was a question of survival for me, not spare time. I said we were all wasting our time until the lion could be located.

"Just then, a man came rushing in, saying that there was a buffalo in his crops and would I please come and shoot it as nobody had had any meat for the past week or more.

"'Baas,' he said, 'the people are hungry. They are afraid to go out because of the lion and they are hungry. We cannot work in our fields. Please come and kill the buffalo.'

"I had my .375 H & H Magnum and I stuck in five shots, which I figured was enough."

Large error. The Cape buffalo is the most resilient animal on the African continent.

"I walked with the man to his fields, but the buff had gone. I was ready to go back, but he insisted: 'No, no, let's go and follow it a little bit. It won't be far.' We followed it and I ran into five other buffalo. They were five big bulls, all together. I picked out the biggest one, shot it and dropped it. Then the other four started coming straight at us! They were probably trying to get away from us as they didn't know where the shot had come from, but they were headed right down my throat. I quickly took a shot at the first of the four. It was dead, or so I thought. As I went by, the damned thing got up!"

A man with Wally's experience should have known, and most certainly did know, the value of an insurance shot. Far be it from me to be critical, but have a look at how close he came to dying then and there. . . .

"I put another shot into it at a few feet and was damned lucky to finish it off. I heard the other buff I'd wounded bawling not far away. The man with me then said, 'Baas, it's dying!'

"What had actually happened was this: As I gave the killing shot to the second buffalo, which we could all hear bellowing, I suddenly saw our lion, which had jumped on top of the buffalo. The cat had it by the throat, which is why the buff was carrying on so.

"I snapped off a quick shot, and as the lion turned and came directly for us at full speed, I closed the action on an empty chamber. What the hell happened to that fifth shot, I'll never know, but I had four hundred pounds of lion just about on me—moving at something like five seconds over one hundred yards from a cold start. One terrific roar and he was straight at me. And I found I was alone, the rest of the guys having buggered off into the trees—high up into the trees.

"There was no possible way I could reload a bolt action in such a short time. I felt I was going to be mauled to death right then. I threw my rifle down and noticed that there was a small, and I do mean small, mopane tree next to me, so I figured that if this goddamn lion was trying to take me, I might either be able to get up the tree or at least keep it between us and save my life.

"I got one foot up and I was about three feet from the ground, hanging on to this stem of the sapling. The lion ran up and started to crouch and I can so clearly remember thinking, well, this is the end.

"He crouched almost on top of my gun and I only had this tree in front of me; no protection at all, not even a knife. No ammo. Nothing. What the hell, I remember thinking, it's been a damn good life.

"My God! All of a sudden, he just staggered around, rolling over and breathing in a rasping sort of way. I watched this business for a while, as he wasn't dead and was still quite capable of subdividing me. I climbed the tree a little higher, but it was really a waste of effort because that lion could easily have reached up fourteen feet or more.

"There I clung, up this pathetic small tree, just watching the lion, as were the blacks from the adjoining trees.

"I figured, well, he's lying down, he's not actively eating me, so I guess that bullet has taken effect. But I was still scared that he might revive yet and come for me again. I heard the men start shouting at me, asking if the lion was dead.

"I noticed that the breathing had stopped, so I called back that the lion was apparently dead, although I wasn't one hundred percent certain. I waited for them to come within sight of me. They saw me up this tree and asked, 'Where's the lion? Where's the lion?'

"I said: 'Well, he's down here, dead.'

"They said, 'Well, why don't you get down the effing tree, Baas? Why are you still up the tree if the lion is dead?'

"I had to do something to save face, so I came down the tree. Believe me, I maintained quite a distance between me and the lion in case the damned thing revived. Later, when we were pretty sure it was finished, one of the men threw a spear at it, taking it in the chest. Not a twitch.

"It was a beautiful lion with a super mane, one any client would have been proud of. I took a close look at it and saw where it had a wire snare around its neck, having been caught by poachers in a cable noose, the great curse of Africa. When I opened its mouth to have a closer look, it had no bottom teeth. They were all broken off at the roots, which couldn't have been too pleasant for the lion. It was clearly the man-eater which had killed so many of the tribesmen.

"'Come and look here,' I called to the men. 'Here is what you get from your poaching and your snares. How many of your people have died? How many of you have lost wives, who are expensive, and children, who are valuable? (I was putting the message into their terms, of course.) You, not the lion, are to blame for all these deaths. You remember the first man he took? Well, this is the same lion. Remember how there were fang holes in one side of his head, while the other side had only scratches?'"

All demurred as Wally told them a few truths.

"We then quickly went back to the chief's village, and hell, everybody was happy about this great event. All the villages around were advised that the lion was done for. Then a great gang of warriors appeared and picked up the lion over their heads, about ten of them, and ran to the Administrator to prove to him that the lion had been killed. Actually, they ran to my car, which was well over a mile away and over a river, so I drove the lion and some of the men to the Vila Gouveia Administrator, who had a look at it. He was ecstatic."

Wally was presented with a glowing letter of commendation and all the trimmings, including a truly extraordinary lunch. The Administrator, as it turned out, was something of an opera buff who knew the libretti and scores of many of the old war-horses of Italian opera. He had trained his chef/manservant to respond in a bright tenor voice to all his baritone requests, boomed over the lunch table. Imagine snatches of Verdi as the soup is ordered, the chef singing back that it was on its way, to be followed by the traditional cozido português, *hot pot, and almond flan, not forgetting the wines! As Wally recalls, there was a kind of crazy hilarity that day, the sort of reaction that sets in after a dangerous, fear-ridden situation has been survived.*

It was as well that Wally had many an occasion to laugh and relax, because what you are now about to read is anything but funny. It is a tragedy, a mystery that Wally cannot fathom to this day. It haunts him and always will.

3

THE MYSTERY OF FLORINDA

Both Wally and I have had many weird experiences in Africa. We both, for example, experienced the anguish of having staff members simply vanish from camp—and stay vanished.

I still remember the confusion and anxiety that prevailed over my camp once when a tracker came running to the cocktail area where the clients and I were relaxing after a successful lion hunt in Botswana. He called me urgently, saying that the chief skinner, a Bushman of great skill, had walked off the job, leaving the lion half-skinned.

We all went to the skinning shed and another skinner quickly completed the job before the hair slipped, which would have ruined the trophy. Two trackers set off, trying to locate the Bushman. His tracks led off into surrounding bush, where they were soon lost. He never returned. His few possessions were never collected, and nobody was ever able to tell me why he just disappeared; pay day was just around the corner, the tobacco supplies were good, and he enjoyed status in his job.

But Wally's experience of safari staff simply disappearing had far more serious implications. He was actually accused of murder. Read on.

* * *

"A terrible thing happened to me sometime during 1955.

"I had started mining gold and had quite a staff, all of whom would consume prodigious amounts of meat when they could get it. One morning, my headman came to me and asked if I would shoot a buffalo for the men. Realizing that they had been on straight cornmeal for quite a while, I agreed. Several other mines near ours at Vila de Manica were short of meat, so I advised them that I would take a buff or two for their people as well.

"I took Luis, my tracker and head gunbearer, a couple of other men, and a guy named Florinda. Florinda was also a Shangaan, and was very keen on hunting. We took off at dawn for an area near Gorongosa Mountain. When we got there, we pitched a very meager camp indeed and were onto buff at half past twelve in the afternoon of the next day. Luis was leading, followed by Florinda, then me with the guys who would cut up the meat.

"At this time, I had an extra 9.3mm Mauser rifle, which I lent to Florinda as he was one of the few Africans who could shoot quite well. I figured he might be able to kill one buff while I shot the other.

"It was quite thick cover, but we soon found a small group of buff in a relatively open space. We were crawling along, getting ready for a shot, coming nearer and nearer, when I felt Florinda tap me on the shoulder. Not twenty yards away was a group of buff we hadn't seen, some lying down, some standing, and I noticed that there was one very big bull off to one side. I was watching it when Florinda tapped me again.

"I whispered in his ear, 'Wait a minute, they haven't got our scent.'

"I took careful aim with the .375 and dropped him dead with a spine shot. The others went off in a boil of dust as Luis reached the dead buff. It was a real beauty, huge in body and horn. I looked him over and said to Luis, 'Where's Florinda?'

"'Ah, he's probably gone behind a bush to go to the toilet. He'll be along soon, *patrão.* Maybe he saw a chance for another shot and is going up to those buffalo.'

"We waited ten minutes and I said, 'Hey, Luis, where the hell is this guy?'

"'He's coming, Baas,' said Luis as he rolled a black shag cigarette."

But Florinda didn't show.

"'What the hell is this?' I asked. 'Where's he gone? It's getting late.'"

Wally wanted to send Luis back to where they'd last seen Florinda when they shot the bull, but at that moment, they heard a shot in the distance.

"My God, what's happening now? Then I realized that Florinda had that spare rifle. As I hadn't followed up the rest of the herd, he must have taken it on his own to shoot a second buffalo and had run after them. Luis agreed that we just hadn't seen him take off, what with all the dust and noise.

"So we kept waiting but he never came, and we started to walk down to the area where we had heard the shot. We shouted, whistled, and yelled. No answer.

"I really couldn't figure this damned thing out. We carried on a bit farther and I decided to fire into the air to let him know we were there. But there was nothing as the crash of the Magnum died away. Again. Again nothing. I asked Luis what he thought the shot we heard was all about.

"'It has to be that he shot a buffalo, Baas. He had five shots. Perhaps he wounded it and it has killed him.'

"We followed the herd, which had gone in the same direction as that where we had heard the shot. But there were no vultures circling or dropping on what might have been a buffalo or a corpse.

"'Look, Baas, he must have shot a buffalo, covered it over with bush, and headed back to camp as he could not find us. He'll show up later. *Não faz mal, patrão. Êle volta.*'

"Here's Luis telling me not to worry, that the guy would come back! I just knew something was very wrong. We walked back to the dead buff and brought up the vehicle, loading the meat. The rest of the men all asked Luis where Florinda was and they too agreed that it was very strange. But we all agreed that he would turn up in the morning, if not that evening."

Wrong. Nothing. No Florinda.

When Wally got back to camp and found that Florinda was still missing, he fired several more shots to help him locate the camp. No answering shots.

"At first light, we returned and started to track him and we discovered that he had been following the buffalo herd. Then we found blood but whether it was human or buffalo was impossible to tell. The trouble was that the dust of the herd had completely covered the tracks of Florinda.

"Luis said, 'Don't worry about it, Baas. He'll likely be in camp when we get back. He probably slept up a tree last night and made his way back this morning through the bush. There are a lot of lions around here, so he'll be back in camp for sure.'

"We went back to camp with that hope. Un-uh. No sign of him. The next day we got back on his spoor and spread out with all of my men to comb the bush. I began to wonder if he'd wounded a buffalo which had subsequently caught him on his horns and had perhaps carried him a long way before tossing him clear. But there was no more blood or sign of any kind. No vultures either.

"We combed that bush back and forth as thoroughly as with a hairbrush. No results. I shot up most of my ammo, all the men constantly shouting and whistling. But we still couldn't find the slightest sign of Florinda. We searched a huge area for four days without the remotest clue until I realized it was useless. There was nothing to do but go back to my home at Vila de Manica, on the Rhodesian border, and see the local Administrator to tell him what had happened.

"The thing that nagged me was that borrowed rifle. If Florinda had been eaten, what the hell had happened to it? Even lions and hyenas don't eat rifles, and with a team of crack trackers, we would have found it. Where had it gone and how?

And what about smaller stuff like his belt buckle and knife? Not especially digestible.

"As I hopped off the vehicle after a long hot and bloody worrying journey home, my wife gave me a kiss and mentioned that Florinda's father was there, come from his village. I told him and my wife the whole story and that I was on my way to see the Administrator. It went this way, all mixed up in Shangaan and Portuguese:

"'*Kwini n'wana wa mina?* Where's my son?'"

Wally asked him if Luis hadn't explained what had happened.

"Yes," said the father. "He said he didn't come back with you. And I know what happened."

"Well, what happened?"

"You killed him. Musungi! Musungi! *Murderer!"*

Wally started to laugh.

"What the blazes are you talking about, mukhulu?*" addressing the old man by the deferential term.*

"No, you killed him and stuffed his body down an ant-bear hole."

"You're off your bloody nut, man," Wally said. "I told you what happened, the same as my men, who were also there, told you." But the father was determined.

"Listen," said Wally, "I really don't know what happened to your son, but I certainly had no reason to kill him. If you want, I'll take you down to that area personally, and if you want to spend a month looking for him, it's certainly okay with me. I do understand how you must feel. I am a father too, mukhulu."

The father thought about it for a while and answered,

"Well, no. But if you give me sixty pounds I won't tell anybody about this murder. I won't tell the authorities what really happened."

Wally exploded.

"You swine! I'm going right now to the Administrator to tell him all about it and what you have just said. You bloody snake!" And Wally was off.

The Administrator, sort of the Portuguese equivalent of a District Commissioner under the old British colonial system, told Wally not to worry about it, that Florinda would show up sooner or later. "Just too bad if he doesn't. You did all you could."

But Wally wasn't taking that. The Administrator thought for a moment and suggested that he head off to the Chefe de Poste, his underling, to get some police for a search party.

"I told the Chefe *the story of Florinda's father accusing me, then I went back to see the father."*

The old man hadn't budged. He was squatting under a tree, waiting with that inimitable African patience. Or was it cunning?

"Right," said Wally. "Get some clothes, blankets, food, and all you'll need for as long as you want to stay. Ask Luis. You are going with me. First to the Chefe de Poste and then to look down every goddamn ant-bear hole you find, you bastard! I'm even getting some policemen to protect you. Now move! Hatlisa!"

The father arrived with his father and a brother of Florinda. They and Wally then went off to the authorities, who gave them two policemen to help look for Florinda, on condition that they be sent back as soon as possible. Wally agreed with thanks and the six shoved off in Wally's vehicle, arriving in the area at night.

Wally explained the terrain and the circumstances. The father then asked, "What are you going to do now?"

"Do??? Absolutely nothing! You are going to stay here now. Take your food, take all your stuff off the car, and you bastards can all go and look for Florinda. You say I put him down an ant-bear hole. Try to find some. Look down them and see if you can find Florinda."

As they were talking, a pride of lions started roaring quite close by. The father, grandfather, and brother took fright.

"Look," said the father, "we're not staying here!"

"The hell you're not. You're going to look for your 'murdered' son. You accused me of killing him. So, go and find the body. Then go to the authorities. If you are right, they will put a rope around my neck and a black hood over my face, so you will not have the pleasure of seeing my tongue go black and stick out. Go and find your son, bastard. He was worth much more than the sixty pounds you placed on his life. But just remember what will happen to you when the authorities find out you are making false accusations."

"That did it. They began to plead with Wally: "Baas, we don't want to stay here, there are too many lions."

Florinda's father began to cry and plead again to go back, but Wally stood firm. He was not going to be shoved around.

"Why?" asked Wally, "Are not the lion skins worth the sixty pounds you ask for your son? Why don't you go and spear them, you liar and coward?"

"Patrão," *said the father, "I believe you now that you did not kill my son. But it came to me in the night."*

Wally knew he was lying. Had he given the old man the £60 just to shut him up, that would have been a tacit admission of guilt, and who knew where that would have led.

"Please forgive me, patrão, *for such an accusation. You are a good man. All your men tell me so. I regret this. Please, can we go back now?"*

"I forgive you, but if you ever place your sandal upon my ground again, I shall be guilty of that of which you accused me. Only, it will not be the body of my friend but of his father. Get your things and get into the car!"

"Hau!" exclaimed the policemen, impressed with Wally's oration.

"So I put the lot of them back into the vehicle and took this man back to his village. I heard no more about it. But for many years I would lie awake, watching the sequined Mozambique sky or the rising full moon of that marvelous place, haunted by Florinda's disappearance. It still bothers me.

"Right at the beginning, I just couldn't rest properly—my conscience was getting the better of me—so I decided to go and have one last good look to try to determine his fate. I went down hunting ivory at the same time, taking Luis and five other old hands. Before I started hunting, we searched for an entire week, spreading out and checking under just about every bush or tuft of grass for some clue. Nothing. Always nothing.

"I just can't figure out what happened to him. He was armed but only fired one shot. Yes, there was blood—but whose? Whatever actually happened has remained a mystery that troubles me to this day.

"Did he just walk away to join some clandestine political organization? Not at all likely, he was alone. Was he kidnapped? If so, where was the spoor of the snatchers?"

Whatever happened to Florinda was never discovered. One second he was next to Wally, the next he had evaporated like ectoplasm. He just plainly and simply disappeared.

Wally hunted ivory in that exact area for some years after the incident and he always alerted his people to keep a sharp eye for a 9.3mm cartridge case as well as for Florinda's boots, skeleton, and especially his rifle. Nothing ever turned up.

How just like Africa that a man can seemingly disappear, just vanish. But then, the African bush is a strange place. Wally has one consolation—his clear conscience. He tried. Hard. Rest well, Florinda, wherever you lie.

4

GOING BANANAS

It's funny, the influences that play a role in directing our lives. Wally told me up on the Mupamadzi in 1985 of a book he'd read which directly resulted in his falling victim to that oldest of illnesses—gold fever.

He had already started his professional ivory hunting before succumbing to the gold bug in 1939. This was as a result of reading a book by Dr. Karl Peters, at one time Governor of the Protectorate of German East Africa, which subsequently became Tanganyika under the British after World War I, before becoming the United Republic of Tanzania in 1964 (when Zanzibar was included, following independence in 1961).

Wally was young. He'd met and married his wife in 1935, when he was twenty-three years old. His daughter, Erika, was born in 1937, and his son, Walter, Jr., in 1940. (A vintage year. That's the same year the author was born.)

Let him tell you something of his African gold adventures.

"That year, I bought a mine from a Spaniard in Mozambique. It broke me, but I paid nine hundred pounds for it, not realizing in my inexperience that the only gold left was in the columns that supported the roof! I clearly remember crushing some of the ore and panning it. It was as rich as hell, but it never came to my mind while I was deciding to purchase the mine that if I took the central pillars out, the whole bloody thing would come down on my head.

"In the meantime, I had acquired another mine called the *Cantão,* which gave up about one ounce per ton, which isn't bad. I eventually found one of the mines mentioned by old Karl Peters. It was called the *Windhagel,* meaning a dust devil, but the damned mine kept falling down, as it was truly ancient. This happened twice, so I abandoned it despite a good yield of gold.

"In the years that followed, I owned many mines, and must say I made a decent living out of them over the years. I also tested the riverbanks in the Maconde country to the north. When I was hunting at a place called Masinga, I met the Maconde people for the first time. This tribe is famous for its wood carving. That they all had tremendous, eaglelike noses seemed to prove that this was one of the places where the Arabs of old had come to buy and trade for gold. The Maconde are also largely Muslim.

"One interesting thing, among others, was that their women all had a two-inch nail sticking through the lower lip. Whether this was to make the women so ugly that they would not be worth taking as slaves by the Arabs—as was the case with the Ubangi people of central Africa—I don't know. But the Macondes' method of gold-gathering in rivers was most interesting.

"They would take a big rock in a wooden basket to act as ballast and then they would jump in, dumping the rock before filling the basket with river silt, which they would pan. The gold dust would be stored in vulture quills and used to pay their taxes to the Portuguese.

"Before being bitten by the gold bug, I had left the employ of August, my brother-in-law, after several years. I managed to get hold of the Mozambique franchise for Goodyear Tire and Rubber. As I had hardly any capital, the first year was a disaster. This was just before World War II. Yet I managed to get some retreading machinery by hook or crook, maybe mostly crook, and after the second year, I never looked back. I was actually, genuinely, most definitely rich!

"Although Portugal and her possessions were neutral, there was still a tremendous shortage of tires, and a double fortune to be made in retreading, which I did. What saved my tailbone was that I found several dozen bales of raw rubber washed up onto the beach just outside Lourenço Marques. Talk about manna from heaven! That stuff lasted me nearly through the war, as I'd learned how to vulcanize it."

But life wasn't always like that. To give you some idea of what kind of person Wally is and, indeed, the kind of person his late wife, Lilly, was, let me tell you about Christmas Eve 1942.

Wally and Lilly were hyena-hungry broke. People owed them money for their work but were not paying promptly. The Johnsons had always given an extra monthly check for Christmas to their employees, but that Christmas there was no question of bonuses. Wally spent the whole of Christmas Eve trying to collect money from his debtors but was turned down time and again with one excuse or another. It looked like a barren Christmas for their loyal employees, and Wally had a quarter of an hour left on that day before having to tell his staff that the coffers were bare.

Then the telephone went with its traditional British double ring. It was the railways, advising him that they were ordering tires for their fleet of trucks and had a check made out to him for several thousand pounds. If it wasn't too much trouble, could Wally come over and collect it?

It wasn't too much trouble.

That story always touched Wally's life, and he knew that if one did good to another, it would come back in some way. He had been good to his employees and this last-second reprieve seemed to prove what he believed about treating all people decently.

Well, Wally had made plenty of money from the tire business when he was approached by a pal of his.

"Over a snort or two, this guy talked me into going into banana farming. Hell, he had all kinds of convincing arguments, and I decided to take his advice. I was now twenty-eight years old, and when I looked into the details of this proposal, although I was no farmer, it seemed I couldn't lose even if most of the competition came from the industrious Chinese and Indian communities.

"There was a tract of two thousand hectares available, roughly the equivalent of five thousand acres, a sizable chunk of land even for Mozambique. It was eighty miles from Lourenço Marques on the Incomáti River (the Portuguese spelling). The river flowed like a sluggish worm right through the middle of the property, ideal for banana planting. It was reputed to come down in flood every fifteen years or so, pretty well on schedule. Since there had been a whopper of a flood two years previously, I figured that I had about twelve years to go before another one hit.

"First mistake. Africa doesn't do things by half-measures.

"I bought eighty thousand banana trees and two big Caterpillar tractors and employed everybody who would work for me. Things went beautifully. I was praying for the soul of the chap who'd talked me into the idea in the first place, wondering if I could get him canonized.

"We spent the whole season well and the banana trees were eight feet high. That was exactly eighteen inches above the top of the flood water that hit us. . . .

"When God turns on the Incomáti, he's not fooling around. It took the six and a half feet of water three months to subside. The entire crop, along with most of my equivalent half-million dollar investment, was a total loss. All my friends told me that the flood was just the greatest of freaks. Expensive one at that, my dear pals."

"Yes, sir. May I help you?

"Ummmm. I'd like eighty thousand banana trees, please."

These plants also got to about eight feet when, well, I can't bear to tell you. Two years in a row!

Hell and dammit! I've got so much in this lot that I can't just walk away now! thought Wally. As usual, everybody was quick to urge him to give it one more try. It wasn't their money.

* * *

"I now had £150,000 into the scheme, which was one hell of a lot of boodle. There was £150,000 into the equipment and labor, plants and such, as well as another £150,000 in the land. At five dollars to the pound at the time, imagine how much that little venture cost!

"Yes, as they say, third time lucky."

Came the third year.

And the third flood.

Yes, we have no bananas.

Wally was broke and possibly asking alternative arrangements for the soul of the pal who had suggested this idea in the first place.

Before this disaster, Wally had met a young man who had a geologist brother. The geologist said he'd been around Mozambique and had found many signs of gold, diamonds, and other precious stones and minerals. Wally was encouraged to give him £15,000 to go north, ostensibly in partnership with Wally, to prospect and report back.

A year passed before Wally could get away from the farming venture and go up to see what progress had been made. He sent a letter which the geologist claimed had never arrived, but when Wally asked why there was fresh thatch on his hut, he couldn't answer.

The man had been living in great style with Wally's money all that time, sure as hell not prospecting or digging for gold. He'd only started work about four days before he got Wally's letter, which must have scared the hell out of him. There was a reasonable amount of gold on the mercury table (which element sticks to gold), but certainly no more than a few days' work. Wally was surprised to find the geologist's brother there.

"Hell, I'd been paying these bastards' wages for more than a year when the younger brother said to me, 'Look, Wally, it just doesn't pay.'

"'So now you tell me, fifteen thousand pounds later? Get out of here before I kill you all!'

"With all this and the floods, I'd lost every cent. I was ruined. Now what?

"Having sold my tire business in L.M., I only had this little gold mine in Mozambique, north of the Save River, where I was to spend so much time hunting and mining. This small mine was all I could save after my financial disasters with the goddamn bananas and the gold schemes, but I thought I could make a living out of it and ivory. I put up some tents, and Lilly, bless her, stayed alone for months at a time as I rooted around and shot ivory so we could keep our navels from our spines. The idea of a house, to someone who until recently had been a very wealthy man, was out of the question.

"Gradually, our lot improved and I had a man making bricks so I could build a one-room home. While I was out after ivory, Lilly would work the mine and keep things together. The rest of the staff was working the mine under her supervision. This mine, most unfortunately, was the one held up by only the pillars of gold ore.

"We had to abandon the entire works at Vila Gouveia, but I soon found a very promising site at Vila de Manica, just across the border from the then Southern Rhodesia. Up came the tents again, and Lilly, without a word of complaint, set about making a home for us.

"This was the Wednesday Mine. We put up a mill, with a waterfall from a mountain stream supplying all the power for the crushing of the ore and even free electric power for the house we hoped to be able to build—both rooms of it. Lilly still lived in a tent while I was off hunting ivory. I had to do this in order to get the money to build a toilet and a kitchen. It took me two years of ivory hunting to afford these facilities.

"My wife knew about as much as I did concerning the washing of gold free from the ore, although I was more familiar with the underground works. The kids were at school across the border in Umtali, so we could at least see them often, as it was only about eighteen miles by road.

"While Lilly was overseeing the milling of the ore, I had to go ivory hunting. The first such season provided the money to buy roofing and a door, and the next gave the money for window frames and glass. I was gone from one to three months at a time, so you can appreciate how stalwart Lilly was during my absences."

Many of Wally's friends from Umtali would ask to come along with him when he went out for ivory, but he couldn't always take them because of the weight they would displace, limiting what might be taken up by tusks. Ivory hunting wasn't a holiday for Wally. It was his livelihood. Yet quite a few of his pals accompanied him, as he hated being alone.

One of the places Wally especially liked to hunt was near a spot called Panzila, the name given by an old man who had spent ten years in Lourenço Marques. Wally bought him a couple of tots one night and the old boy told him of some South Africans who used to come up to that area years before, find pieces of "shiny glass," and take them home with them.

He asked if Wally had ever been to the Massengena area of Panzila. Wally hadn't.

"Well, said the old man, "if you ever get up there, you may find it worth your while. There are some old diggings up that way which might be worth your trouble. Aguardente, *please."*

Wally filed this in the back of his skull, and when next he was in the Save River area, he asked some locals if they knew anything about such proceedings. Yes, they seemed to remember something like that in their fathers' time.

"A long time ago," a gray-head told Wally, "white men came from the south with picks and shovels and they took the 'frosty glass.'"

"Was there any special place they used to dig?" asked Wally.

"Oh, yes," said the old man. "They even left a wheelbarrow and a pick. It was near a hut where I once lived as a boy, but the hut is not there anymore."

"Where was it?" asked Wally.

"I don't recall. I am getting old and my children's children have children. They have no respect for their elders, he added idly."

Wally looked for days but could find no old mining implements. It was raining like Doomsday and Wally was out with a young man who had the first Land Rover in Mozambique. Two of Wally's men were in the back. Their hats were cocked against the sluicing down-

pour and Wally was staring at his feet to keep the water off his face. He had no coat.

"As I was staring down, I saw some shiny crystals and picked them up. Hell, I thought, maybe these were the diamonds the old men had been talking about!

"I showed them to the young guy after the rain stopped two hours later. I had quite a few crystals, some clear, some red, and some with other colors. So I took them back to camp and put them into my tobacco bag, knowing that when I got back I could ask a trusted pal if they were diamonds or what.

"When I got back to Umtali, I took the stones to this chap who knew something about precious stones.

"He said, 'Well, I can't be certain they're diamonds, but when you go back that way again, bring me a sack of soil where you found them and we'll analyze it. In the meantime, count and describe them and I'll dig up somebody who knows a lot more about these stones than I do. We'll see what the story is.'

"It was a year before I got back. Yes, some were diamonds. But a hardtop road had been built over the site, and goddamn if Luis and I could ever find the place again. Perhaps it was just not meant to be. . . ."

In the meantime, when Wally got back to Vila de Manica, his wife reported a dramatic falloff in the production of gold on the mercury collecting plate. Was the mine playing out? Or was it time to play detective? Wally decided upon the latter.

His men had gotten smart, smarter than one of Wally's African names, Xigwili, Rich Man. But not for long. Xigwili was going to catch them out.

What made Wally smell a large predatory rodent or a colony thereof was the fact that after taking samples of the vein and crushing them, then panning the powder, he found that the gold content was quite exceptional.

So where was the gold going? Only one place.

Of course it was being stolen by the mine laborers, especially by those working where the crushed ore came through to be picked up by the mercury. You can't say much for their honesty, but they were indeed clever and enterprising.

"The old Rhodesian penny had a hole in the center, and the men would coat the pennies with mercury and suspend them on a wire just above the collection table. Soon they were coated with gold dust, which was easily removed and the trap reset by those bastards. They would then take the gold dust from the pennies and rub it deeply into their brilliantined hair. When they got home, a quick wash provided a month's wages. Clever swine they were. I have no idea how much they cost me, but most of the gold was caught by the coated pennies before it reached the table.

"There was a major change in personnel after that. Most small miners couldn't make a living because of this and other tricks. Most went broke and went home, wherever that was.

"I do have one pleasure in retrospect. I rather think that the majority of the thieves died early of mercury poisoning. Under the circumstances, that was a fair trade: gold for mercury, a deadly heavy-metal poison, especially when repeatedly rubbed into the hair. I mourn them not, although I am not a hard man. When I think of the years of privation they caused me, I don't feel overwhelmingly regretful."

So ended Wally's major foray into El Dorado, but he was to have other strange experiences in prospecting, one of which still taunts him today.

"I came across some black sands in a place called Guro, south of Tete."

How strange! That happens to be the area of the farm belonging to the Serras Pires family who, like Wally, eventually had everything they owned snatched from them in the name of "freedom." Adelino Serras Pires, the eldest son, my good friend, and a renowned hunter, was abducted in 1984 by the Tanzanians. He was flown to Mozambique, imprisoned, tortured, and accused of being everything from an agent of the CIA to a clandestine Girl Scout selling cotton candy without a license. Through world pressure from the international hunting community, he was finally released.

In any case, Wally came across some heavy black sand. It intrigued him and he filled his tobacco pouch with the stuff. Then he promptly forgot about it.

Some months later, he befriended a man named Miller, a mining engineer from East London, South Africa. Miller had been working on the beach there, extracting titanium from the sand where it had washed up. He had quite sophisticated machinery to separate the stuff from the sand.

Wally said to the engineer, "Well, that's damned odd. I saw some black sand on my way up here and put it in this little tobacco bag of mine. Wonder what the hell it is. Take a look."

They poured the black sand onto a piece of newspaper. Miller looked at it and said, "Well, could be columbite, tantalite, or any of the heavy metals. Look, I've got an assayer down in East London who'll take a look at it. Maybe you can mine it. . . ."

Wally thanked the engineer and two weeks passed before he received the following telegram: WALLY GO BACK TO PLACE WHERE YOU FOUND THIS STOP TWO DIAMONDS IN SAMPLE MILLER.

Wally was quite excited despite a following letter, which explained that the diamonds were not gem quality and that they were small. He wrote back to Miller, telling him that he was returning to the area, as there might be some "really good stuff." He took Luis along, who assured him he could find the place again. "Sure, Baas, I know just where it is."

But after two weeks of searching for the isolated spot they had seen quite some time back, Wally gave up. The bush changes and, if you are a prospector, usually for the worse, since you often cannot recognize one spot from another.

Four years later, Wally was talking with a man who had staked a claim next to his at Vila de Manica. The other miner said, "Are you mad? You should have looked harder for those diamonds. Come on, man. Tomorrow morning I'll go with you. Do you more or less know where it is? We ought to be able to find those sands again."

Wally called Luis over. "Do you think we still have a chance of finding those diamonds, Luis? It's been years and we couldn't find them the last time."

"I think so, patrão. *It comes to me where they were. We were in the wrong place."*

"That's for bloody sure," muttered Wally.

They left for the spot Luis had in mind and they panned in a wide area for days. Then they all decided to hell with it.

Those diamonds are still there.

Back to ivory hunting for Wally. The prospecting bug would continue to bite on and off through the years. Like malaria, the fever would return upon occasion, but it wasn't Wally's destiny to stray too far from the arduous life of hunting big game. Far more amazing experiences awaited him.

5

MAKING DO

This book is really a tri-pronged eel spear, in which I want you to be exposed not only to the personality of Wally Johnson as a man—and a damned brave one at that—but also to his tribulations in hunting dangerous game, and his general life-style, which saw incredible political turmoil during the revolution that overthrew Portugal and her African possessions in 1974–75. Wally was a very wealthy man at an astonishingly young age, but in that struggle he lost all he had.

In order to understand what it meant to hunt elephant in the primeval bush of a place like Mozambique in the 1930s, and to better grasp the way of life—and often death—let Wally begin. As one of the finest ivory hunters who has ever lived, he learned one lesson very quickly: self-sufficiency and ingenuity, often under pretty terrible circumstances.

"Sometimes you'd go three days without spoor. Not a track. Often there was no water, and you'd drink out of the most unbelievably filthy pools and old elephant footprints in the rainy season, the elephants having urinated into them. It was that or die.

"You'd freeze to death by night and broil by day, starving to death and dying of thirst the rest. But hell, you'd just carry on as best you could. No choice. You had to, or you'd be finished."

* * *

Before Wally describes his actual adventures as an African ivory hunter, some background as to "working conditions" should be given here so that you can better understand what he was up against.

If you weren't good, there were no second chances. If you got into a jam a thousand miles from northeast nowhere, it was you and your ingenuity that got you out. Or your bones stayed. They wouldn't even have the dignity of being "sun-bleached." The hyenas would take them the second night, if not the first.

After the lions were finished with your meat. . . .

Professional ivory hunting was not a sport. It was a business conducted under the toughest circumstances. Many are the graves I have found in my own professional hunting that were not even marked with the hunter's name. I remember one grave in particular along the track between Chitangulu and my old camp at Nyampala in Zambia. It ran something like KILLED BY AN ELEPHANT.

So the most important aspect of staying alive as a pro was that of mobility, of being able to get around and get home. Wally was a past master at this, as the following stories will illustrate.

A good example of garden-variety survival happened in the dry season of 1933, when Wally's six-cylinder broke down eighty miles from Lourenço Marques. The connecting rod had come loose and had smashed through the side of the crankcase like a steel javelin. He blew out the piston, another nicety, and had a completely pierced crankcase.

Wally needed some gaskets. One was feeding about four hundred yards away—a waterbuck bull! It was the only "gasket" around, so he took his .375 and killed it after a careful stalk, and took the skin. While it was still wet, Wally drilled a few holes through the engine block and then closed the two valves to the exhaust block as well as the ingress valve.

He then flattened a tin and sealed it securely as a gasket with the fresh waterbuck rawhide under it. Although he got home, he noticed with his usual astuteness that he had made it on five cylinders and that with the tappet closed, the car ran much better.

Wally had a small trailer which he often used when on safari. Most unhappily, it had a nasty habit of shearing axles in soft ground.

One evening, he broke the damned thing again. Luis was with Wally, and both men were short of ammo since the war was on and supplies were difficult to obtain.

As blackness fell like a sack of charcoal, Luis said, "Baas, I don't like this at all!"

Wally recounted, "I looked up and couldn't tell you how many lions were surrounding our campfire. And close."

The lions were apparently quite used to gunfire, as they hardly moved when Wally dropped one on general principles with one of his few remaining rounds.

"These were bad chaps," said Wally to me on the Mupamadzi. "Surely man-eaters. We threw firebrands at them and actually hit them, but they'd just snarl and move back a bit, only to return. They simply sat, watching Luis and me. I figured I'd killed quite a few, even though I didn't even have a flashlight. But in the morning, there was no sign of blood. Maybe the others had licked it up but we didn't stick around to see."

Eventually, Wally abandoned the idea of putting in a new axle, so they crossed the river and just towed the trailer, broken axle and all, from the far side. They came home on one axle, though Wally always carried two.

He then found an old one-ton Ford truck, which he bought from an Indian.

"It was a decent piece of machinery and I used it to take Walter, Junior, out elephant hunting. I had a problem, though. . . .

"At that time, I had a .375 H & H Magnum, a 9.3mm Mauser, and a .318 with fifty rounds, but the barrel was rusted on the .318. When I fired it, it would expand the brass case into the craters in the breech and when I tried to eject the empty case, the extractor would tear it in half. It wasn't too healthy for shooting elephant, as I only had one or two shots, but the caliber certainly did the job with solids and gave the penetration. Now and again, I'd find some .375 fodder, but it was rare. I used to have to pay the equivalent of six to seven dollars per shot, which wasn't exactly cheap. Then a funny thing happened. . . .

"I heard of a fire in a gun shop at Umtali where most of the goods had been destroyed. I drove over, looking for a new barrel for the .318 or a .375. You see, I had had some very close calls with the .318 and I knew my luck would eventually run out.

"What I had had to do with the .318 was take nail polish and coat the erosion holes full before the pressure blocked them again. This was not an especially pleasant basis for elephant hunting, but at least I could get off three or four shots as something big and gray came down on me in earnest. Sometimes I'd get as many as four shots off before the extractor started tearing the empties in half. Now and then I could get ahold of a few cartridges for the .375, but not very often. I just had to make do.

"Well, I went to Umtali and looked through the debris of the fire at the gun shop. Lo and behold, all ye! What lurked but a 9.3mm barrel—with the stock burned off, of course. I picked it up and asked the owner what he wanted for it.

"'Give me a couple of pounds for it, mate,' he said, so I took it. I was really looking for a new .375 H & H barrel, but this piece of Mauser steel seemed not to have lost its temper and I suspect it had been a new gun when I picked it up.

"Six months later, elephant hunting, I took a day off, as I was really beat. Somehow, I picked up this 9.3 and, over a hot beer, started wondering if the barrel might not just fit into the action of that bloody .318. Tell me there isn't a Deity somewhere. The finest dating service in the world coudn't have made a better match! Of course the solder of the front sight had melted off, as had the sights, but I found them.

"The only problem was that the screw length was half a turn either short or long, so the spot where the sights went was on the bottom of the barrel. I heated a soldering iron in the fire and reattached them as best I could. This could be a lot of work but I was determined to spend the day on it, as I had a fair amount of 9.3mm ammo.

"Son of a bitch! First time! The sights were dead on and it was a mamba of a rifle. I tied it to a tree and fired three shots to be sure the temper hadn't been destroyed by the fire. It stood up like the walls of Troy.

"Although I preferred the .375 as a caliber, I was damned happy to have this alternative, as I knew one day I would get killed with the .318 as it had been. The 9.3mm Mauser didn't have quite the oomph of the .375, but it was a very popular European caliber and compared favorably with the Holland. Anyway, I had ammo for it and didn't have to blush anymore in Umtali when I went in to buy nail polish and was asked what shade I would prefer.

"I still consider and always will consider the .375 Holland & Holland Magnum as 'the only gun.' In fact, I shot many hundreds of buffalo with the 9.3mm Mauser to save .375 ammo. I had no problems, but I would have preferred the .375 if I could have spared the ammo."

A great example of the stupidity of some professional hunters—and I don't indict even a fraction as incompetent—was well illustrated once by a pal of Wally's. At the time, Wally was in the Panzila Forest, where the elephant would come out at dusk near the Save River. It was the rainy season, and generally pouring, but it was the best time to hunt ivory.

Wally had a load and had broken camp, heading for home when, some thirty to forty miles from his base, he saw an odd vehicle mired in the swamps. He recognized it as an American Jeep. A man jumped out and said: "Wally! What in hell are you doing here?" It was another ivory hunter named George, whom Wally knew from the Lourenço Marques area. "The question is, what in hell are you *doing here?"*

Wally remembered George from those days three or four years back and knew that he had never owned a car. George told him that he'd bought a Jeep cheap a couple of years after the war. George used to hunt in the Lourenço Marques area and Wally hadn't *forgotten him. He proceeded to tell Wally about the Jeep.*

"They were a good price and were supposed to be a good vehicle, but it's taken me two weeks to come from L.M. I really don't know

why these things are supposed to go everywhere. Mine sure doesn't. Capute, pá. *It won't budge, chum."*

"Is the engine okay?" asked Wally.

"Oh, yeah."

"Well, let's have a look."

Wally wanted to laugh. "I instantly looked down and saw the poor bugger didn't have the four-wheel drive toggle engaged. After two weeks of being mired, the car immediately started moving!"

"What the hell did you do there?" George asked.

"You didn't have it in four-wheel drive."

"Isn't it always?"

"As you've spent two weeks finding out, no."

Wally showed him the lever and explained how it worked. "Imagine buying a car like that without knowing how to engage its main feature! We sat up late, speaking of old hunting experiences and we both left early the next morning.

"Once, I was out with the young chap who had the first Land Rover in Mozambique. We had just come up to the Save River, my favorite hunting area. The only problem was that the river was very fast and deep, as there had been a lot of rain in Rhodesia that year, and I realized that it was visibly rising. This guy had to get back to his job across the border in Umtali, but there was no way across the river. The bloody river was now half a mile wide and it was rising! I can still see Luis, squatting in that bush African way, quite prepared to sit out the flooded river for the next few months, saying, '*Patrão, não pode pasar. O rio está cheio.*'

"Of course, a blind man could see the bloody river was 'full.' We were stuck! But I knew a place all the way down on the coast of the Indian Ocean where we could cross. Then we figured that if we went all the way down to that pontoon—which might not be operating with the high water—we wouldn't have enough petrol to get back in any case. Somehow, we would have to get that Land Rover across the half-mile river.

"We went to the local village and tried to buy, rent, or purloin six or seven dugouts which we could lash together. The answer was no. Nobody was parting with any *xikwekwetsu,* as the dugouts were known. The only craft available was a single dugout which, at full fare, would carry three people. Maybe. The damn thing was leaking in any case.

"I decided to seek an enterprising soul among that tribe in the hope that he could make something in a hurry that would get the vehicle, even if in disassembled chunks, across the Save. Lo and behold, if a man didn't come forward, saying he could do the job if my pal and I could take the Land Rover to pieces, small pieces.

"This man found a very big *marula* tree, which grows the fruit upon which the elephant get so drunk. He took off a slab of bark with the skill of a brain surgeon, using pegs to wedge the strip of bark, which measured fifteen feet in length and about seven feet in width. After the bark was off, it really did look as if a passable boat could be made from it.

"The man squeezed the ends together to make bow and stern, and thumped in wooden pegs where there had been knots and a few branches. Then he got a certain wild onion, which grows along the river, and pounded a heap of them into a waterproof glue. We had a goddamn boat!

"We had a slight problem, though—the evisceration of the Land Rover.

"We began to take the car to pieces, realizing that any part lost would mean a month's walk. First the front and rear differentials, then the body, leaving the gearbox and the engine. Off came the wheels.

"Now the crossing. Because of the ferocious current, each trip would take the local boatman, paddling alone, a half-mile downstream. He lost another half-mile crossing back over to our side, so we realized we'd have to tow him back to reload. Although it was a real bitch to tow the thing back up, we came to the realization that we'd be there forever if we didn't. Against that current, it was some job.

"Next, we removed the axles, then the body, then the gearbox and engine, which nearly swamped the boat. On that crossing, there was half an inch of freeboard, and if we'd lost that load, we'd still be walking.

"Finally, we loaded the chassis. It was unbelievably heavy,

but with the help of a bunch of villagers, we got it balanced. With a grand bribe, we got hold of the other small boat—they could now see our fix and could have held us up for anything—and we lashed the two boats together for support and stability. Hell, if a hippo had come by, he'd have thrown enough of a wave to have sunk us.

"Having gotten all the components across without loss, we now had to return for our personal goods and then reassemble the car. It took *five and a half days*, but we got the bastard back together and running. We made it home. And I would have said that it couldn't be done. It would never have been done without the skill and strength of that lone tribal boatman."

I can assure you that there's a lot of "making do" in professional safari work. I've done a bit myself, but let Wally intrigue you with another of his stories.

He was with an Italian friend named Bellino who used to help out on the mine as well as come along on safaris. In this instance, they had Bellino's Ford truck and a small trailer. They came to a big hill called Panda, which was about 160 miles from Wally's home at Vila de Manica. The two men hunted there for a couple of weeks until the drive shaft suddenly snapped. No minor problem. And it happened in a river bed, at least eighty miles from the nearest store or road. The shaft was broken right in half.

Wally sat down and thought about it. The broken piece was about nine inches long. After he fooled around for an hour or so, Wally discovered that the exhaust pipe fitted over the broken piece exactly.

He cut off the broken bit with a hacksaw, as well as one and a half feet of exhaust pipe. He, however, had to drill some holes for bolts to make the connection. Trouble was, he didn't have a drill. Or maybe he did. . . .

Wally figured that the only way it would fly would be for him to shoot the connecting holes through. So they put the drive shaft on the ground, placing the muzzle of Wally's .318 against the shaft, and sent a solid whining though. A caliber noted for its penetration, it left a hell of a big jagged hole on the far side where it came out.

"Oh, hell, what do we do now?" Wally asked Bellino.

"Try the .22. It won't do as much damage."

"No, I reckon I'll just put some sand in the tubes; that way there won't be so much damage."

This is a logic I have never followed, as the sand would not only expand from the impact of the slug but deform it to make an even more ragged hole. Yet Wally is in a class of his own as a mechanic, Gunga Din, and I shall not say him nay.

In any case, the Italian talked him out of it and they tried the .22 Long Rifle. The first shot from the .22 Long Rifle just splashed lead back, lacerating Bellino's legs, making him bleed all over hell. Happily, he was not really hurt and had a sense of humor, thinking it pretty funny as the gore drained over his shins.

"Cretino!" *he told himself in his native Italian as Wally laughed after the scare was over.*

"Listen," said Wally, "let's try the .30-'06 and this hole will be much neater."

They did, and it was. The two men put in some bolts and unhooked the trailer. By local manpower, they got the truck to the top of the ridge.

"Hell, I rehooked the trailer," Wally said, "and the bloody thing didn't go five hundred yards before it broke down again! I found that the exhaust pipe was too thin to stand the strain of the torsion. What to do?

"I found a steel-hard piece of mopane and decided to try that. Not to tell you more of mopane than the proverbial penguins, but it is a resinous hardwood, often knocked down and stripped by elephants, which hardens tremendously during the wetness of the rainy season. Despite what you'd expect, it becomes as tough as steel and will dull an ax into a Buick bumper with a few swipes. When the seasonal fires come along in the dry season, elephant-damaged mopane will burn to the tips of its roots because of its natural resins and even though they are underground, leaving a perfectly fine white ash, smoother than talcum powder. Yet it is an incredibly hard wood when not burned. Even termites usually get heartburn fooling around with mopane."

Wally put in the mopane to reinforce the connection, but he only got another mile before it, too, snapped.

The Italian said, "Hey, give me a rifle and I'll walk to Vila Gouveia with the drive shaft and get it welded."

"The sun is very hot, my friend. Better put your hat on. Vila Gouveia is eighty bloody miles away, and it would take you six days. Also, for your kind information, there are no welding facilities there. Anyway, it's all through the bush. There are no roads."

Yet the Italian insisted. Wally's parting words were: "Maybe I'll be there before you are."

"Per l'amore di Dio, come? *How on earth do you think you will do that?"*

"Don't you worry, chum. I'll figure out some way to get this whore rolling. I'll hoot as I pass."

Bellino didn't believe it, though, and went off with Luis despite Wally's advice. They took food, water, blankets, and a rifle, saying they would be back in a week to ten days.

Wally was on his lonely, but he was not idle. He found, among his stuff, a pair of shackles. He then rounded up a dead-straight mopane tree of some four inches in thickness, shot some holes with the .22 through the mopane, and attached the wood to the end of the gearbox, hacksawed to size. He had to block up the back axle so it wouldn't move, as any movement upward or downward would either break the wood or pull it out of alignment. He then tied up this Rube Goldberg *attachment with baling wire, and, by* God, *it went perfectly!*

After six hours, however, the green sapling Wally had cut had started to warp and the whole car was really shivering. He was getting ready to cut a new shaft, but after so many hours of bush-busting, he knew he was near a road. At last, Wally broke from the bundu *near a bridge. Unbelievably, it had a sign that had* not *yet been stolen for spearheads. It read:* DANGER.

Oh, ho, ho! Metal! *Wally cut the post off, went through the whole drill of shooting new holes, and fitted the new shaft. But wouldn't you know it: not a hundred yards down the road he met Bellino and Luis—who had a new drive shaft! They had cut the road, gotten a ride to Rhodesia, and were on their way back.*

Oh, well, sometimes so goes the bush. . . .

Wally has a bushelful of "making do" tales, but I have chosen only a few that especially caught my fancy. One, in particular, put him years ahead of fuel-research experts.

He was out hunting ivory and ran out of gas because of a fuel leak. There was no gas station handy and he was about one hundred miles from the edge of anything. In a tribal village he found some kerosene, locally called paraffin. Now he knew that a gasoline or petrol engine surely wouldn't run on this stuff, but he had the smarts to distill it into a fuel that would run his car. He made it home.

In another instance, Wally did the same thing with palm wine, the potent vucema *of the Shangaans. He had to distill it five times, but it ran his car's engine and there was no shortage of the stuff. Imagine what a belt of that does for your constitution. . . .*

But as the following chapter will demonstrate, the guys with the white hats don't always come up smelling like lilacs. . . .

6

THIRST

One evening, as we sat around the fire on the high banks of the Mupamadzi River, the lions roaring not a hundred yards away, a leopard sawing not much farther on, and hippos honking in the river close enough to be hit by an easily lobbed rock, Wally spoke of an experience that brought back all the horrors I had known in Ethiopia in December 1968, when I myself came close to dying of thirst.

"This is how it sometimes goes wrong," Wally told me. "You try to always do it right, but that's not how it comes out sometimes. I'd been hunting in Botswana with your good pal, Daryll Dandridge, with whom I know you did a lot of safaris in the Okavango of Botswana.

"Daryll and I were sharing a camp in 1981, the one called SPLASH you built with him. He had an Italian client and I a Texan. I don't know which of us had the bigger language problem. In any case, I had an old man with me; he was a Masarwa, the black-and-Bushman mix, and a real expert on sable. He could find sable when sable couldn't find sable.

"Daryll went off up to the Selinda Spillway to hunt elephant, but after he'd left, the old man put us onto a sable that was a real beauty. It was standing near a thick clump of cover, and I told the Texan to stalk it for about two hundred yards and take his best shot. He did—but he only wounded the sable.

"I don't know what the hell I was thinking of besides that lovely animal as I jumped off the Toyota with just my rifle to finish it off. No water, food, nothing. Trouble was, I was so sure we'd get it straightaway that I even left the engine running. So the old man, my gunbearer Benai, and I took off after this Texan and quickly caught up with him. It was now eight A.M., and at three that afternoon, I decided the client had just nicked the animal and that it wasn't worth following up any longer. Not down. Not out.

"But *we* were.

"As it was, we were all half-dying of thirst; it was a poker-hot day without a cloud in the sky. I never dreamed we would have to follow so far, and as we were all whipped—especially the client, about whom I was getting worried in terms of heat collapse—we decided to give it up and go back to the vehicle. Grant you, he was tough as rawhide, but a man can go only so far without water.

"On the way, we got mixed up in the middle of about two hundred elephant, and for a while I thought I was going to have to shoot our way out. I even changed to solids for the .375.

"To add to the charm of the moment, the client suddenly collapsed. Christ, I was close to it myself.

"'Where's the bloody car, *madala?*' I asked the old man.

"'*Duze, Morena,*' he answered. 'Close, sir.'

"I didn't know if he really knew, but then, it was uncanny how these guys could find their way around. After ten minutes, I got the Texan on his feet and he made what was really a valiant effort to go on, but it was clear that he would just die if I pushed him too hard.

"I figured that the best thing would be to send Benai for the car, as he could drive. But, of course, since it had been running from eight that morning, we'd be lucky if there was any fuel left. Anyway, it was starting to get bloody dark.

"We waited for quite a few hours, dry as dice, until I tried to encourage the client to continue. He collapsed twice but was certainly game. Thank God! Frogs! We found a pool of water and made a big fire so Benai would see it, if there was any fuel left in the car.

"Hell, I walked a few yards and found we were right on a road! I was unarmed but collected a bunch of firewood. I had the client fire a shot and Benai responded with my rifle, not more than twenty minutes' walk away! Another hour's wait and I had the client fire again. The return was crisp and close. It sounded just down the road. It was darker than your tonsils but nothing happened. Where the bloody hell was Benai?

"About ten P.M. it started to rain, or, should I say, pour. We were freezing, as we had nothing. A couple of days' rain in Botswana in July is not that unusual, although the fact that it was out of season was hardly comforting. I figured at four A.M., when the rain let up, the hell with it. I took the client's rifle, leaving the poor bugger unarmed.

"'Look,' I said, 'if lions come, just get up the highest tree you can find. I suggest that one over there. I'm going to get us out of here.'

"'No, don't worry,' the client said. I felt like hell leaving him, but I knew the poor man would die of exposure if I didn't get help."

It was starting to get light as Wally moved off, figuring on a twenty-minute walk to the car. He took the old man with him and they found Benai's tracks, but going in the opposite direction!

"I followed Benai's tracks from 4:40 A.M. until 5:30 that afternoon through deep sand, again with no water. Then I lost the track. I was dying of thirst.

"'Jesus, man,' I asked the old man in Fanagalo. 'Where's the car?' [Bear in mind that through this ordeal, Wally was in his seventieth year!]

"'Oh, *Morena,* it's just a little farther on.'

"'It can't be! We didn't walk so far yesterday,' I said. I was flat beat, so I told the old man that if he was so sure, would he please fetch me some beer off the back of the Toyota. He left, and suddenly it was dark again. No sign of the old man. All of us split up. The client unarmed and alone. God, what a nightmare!"

Then, like the glowing gates of heaven, Wally saw a pair of headlights coming down the road. As they approached, he realized that this wasn't his car.

It was Daryll Dandridge with his client and Wally's.

What had happened was that Daryll happened to take a shortcut and was astonished to see the Texan by the side of the sand track.

"What the hell are you doing here?" asked Daryll.

"Waiting for Wally," said the Texan.

"What? When did he leave?"

"Early this morning. About four-thirty. I'm damned worried about him."

The Italian client was furious, but Daryll, bless his soul, insisted on tracking Wally. When they finally found him, the Italian wouldn't even look at him. Wally was in a bad way, but that didn't move the client, who let off a stream of ripe Italian swearwords.

"Mannaggia la miseria! Che casino! Che coglioneria! Ladri! *You son of a bitch, you cost me four hundred dollars today looking for you! You take my hunting time for your stupidity.* Bastardi! Ma va fa un culo! Figli di puttana, tutti. *I want to go home right now, back to Italy. This safari is rubbish."*

There was no stopping the man in his foul rantings and total lack of reason. Wally, now with some moisture in him, ignored the boor and thanked Daryll for all his trouble and patience. "Not many bloody hunters would have taken the time and trouble to track and find me. You have saved our lives, Daryll."

The Italian then went completely berserk, jumping out of Daryll's car, grabbing his .458 Winchester Magnum and, in black-faced fury, he opened up on Wally's car, firing a shot through the back of it. After all the strain, Wally broke into uncontrollable peals of laughter. The Italian just looked at Wally like a guilty small boy in bewilderment.

When Wally got himself under control, he asked the Italian, "What in hell are you doing?" The bullet had happily passed through the tailgate and had hit a spare spring lying in the back, doing no real damage, although a 500-grain .458 might have done plenty.

"Do you know what this has cost me, spending the whole day trying to find you?"

"Well," replied Wally, still suppressing a chuckle, "if you had been lost, dying of thirst, I'd have gone and tried to help you. Now, seeing that you have shot my car, you can take it back to Italy and put it on the wall as a trophy. Daryll, do you want to finish it off? I think it's only wounded. On second thought, I can think of another place, signore, *where you might stick it. I'd even help put it in place."*

The Italian client was even more furious when he saw that Wally wasn't remotely annoyed. Eventually, however, even he broke into laughter as the tension shattered. He left with Daryll—and with great admiration for Wally.

7

IVORY

The years Wally spent as an elephant hunter were among the toughest of his life and perhaps form the colorful core of his story. As he has described, they were a horror of thirst, hunger, and fatigue which, when you see him today, pushing seventy-seven years of age, makes you wonder how a man could live that way for so long and make it. Well, you don't know Wally. A tougher piece of biltong never came along.

It was, as he said, 1937, when the Portuguese Government opened elephant hunting on an unlimited basis in Mozambique. Wally was then twenty-five years old. He conducted his last safari when he was about seventy-two. That's a solid forty-seven years of pro hunting, plus another eleven years of buffalo hunting for crew rations. He was tough, fit, and highly able. He killed something like thirteen hundred bull elephants over those years, as well as another sixty or so cows taken in self-defense.

That places him above Karamojo Bell and many of the better-publicized hunters. But then, who would ever have heard of Bell, had he not written?

Before getting into Wally's experiences, let me have the privilege of describing some of his dictums.

Whereas Arthur Neumann, highly praised as a collector of big teeth north of Wally's hunting grounds and much earlier, was criticized for using a rifle as "light" as a .577 double (not a Nitro, thanks to Howard French), Wally was essentially a heart-shot man with the various higher-power .30 calibers. We have spoken of the 9.3mm Mauser with the upside-down barrel and the .318. He took few brain shots in comparison with some of the greater published luminaries of the art in which he deserves a place of honor.

I questioned Wally at great length on his ivory career and shall give it to you pretty well as it came.

"When ivory hunting opened in '37, the first thing I heard of was the death of a chap called De Waal. He had shot an elephant, perhaps on purpose, in the leg, and went up close with his camera to take a picture. His men later said that he approached the elephant from the front and, for some insane reason, tried to touch the tip of the bull's trunk with his rifle muzzle. This he actually did, probably in the belief that the elephant was *hors de combat.*

"Well, it wasn't, much to the fatal distress of Mr. De Waal. The elephant lunged forward, De Waal falling over a convenient log, and the elephant stamped him into chunky-style peanut butter and jelly.

"There was another young man I heard of who thought he saw his fortune in ivory. He was with his father, Juan Domingues, when they spotted two bulls at a water hole. The father had the son back off and went in with his .470 Nitro double rifle. He saw that he couldn't get a shot unless the elephant turned around, as he had only the arse end of the second bull in view.

"The elephant instantly slewed around. Domingues fired one barrel for the brain. He never fired the other.

"There was no effect, and nobody ever found out why he hadn't fired the second shot—as the rifle was in order. He was tusked through the head, a most final end.

"The body was carried to camp, called Kanisadu, to which the son had been ordered to return. Portuguese kids don't disobey their fathers. . . .

"The man was buried there. I remember it well, so many years ago."

* * *

Wally called for a cold beer and we went on with his forty-seven years with elephants.

Wally recalled another tragedy which occurred soon after the opening of elephant hunting. There was a German whom Wally knew well and who was running a sisal plantation. Sisal looks like vegetable bayonets, but elephants love to eat the interior pulp, despite their terrible sharp points. The plants are mostly used to make cord, and if I'm not mistaken, are members of the agave family.

This man went after elephant one day. Wally said that when he saw the corpse, it was obvious that the man caught up with the elephant or, rather, it caught up with him. The poor man had been absolutely smashed. Even his own workers couldn't recognize him. He had been literally torn to pieces.

Many other people were killed over the years by elephant in Mozambique. As Wally says, "It's not a very easy business. You've got to goddamn well know what you're doing, and you must have your wits about you.

"I used to take Walter, Jr., out elephant hunting, and he'd killed a few, starting at age eight. At one stage I had a young friend with me who was dying to take an elephant. Well, I decided to take him to an area near the Save River. We started going to native villages to find out where elephant had been raiding crops.

"I must explain to those who didn't know Mozambique in 1937 and who probably have a very different perception today of the problem that people were *dying* by the hundreds because of the depredations of the elephants. It was absolutely pathetic. I was there to see it. Elephants had been protected and had grown so in numbers that they actually started taking over whole areas of black cultivation. People were literally starving to death because the elephants had eaten their fields before they could harvest them. It was truly a catastrophe.

"That is why, in 1937, the authorities recognized the problem and opened elephant hunting on an unlimited basis.

"It was elephants or people. Period.

"I'll tell you some tales of local tribesmen in a bit which will demonstrate how they treat their own kids but, for now, elephants.

"The young man I had with me got his chance to go elephant hunting on his 22nd birthday.

"I walked him up to a very good bull at fifteen yards and the guy killed it with one shot in the brain. We moved on toward the Save River, the rains having just started. We quickly realized that we couldn't make it with the petrol we had so, as I had done with the kerosene or parrafin some years before, I found a local village, bought up their entire supply of palm wine, distilled it five times and, by God, we made it home.

"The stuff was better than gasoline. I well remember the name of that little place. It was Machaze.

"I then heard of a German who was running a sawmill reasonably nearby. He had a bunch of his countrymen selecting trees and cutting them. I saw one good bull among a bunch of thirty to forty jumbos in that same area and was preparing to select one. What I didn't realize was that part of the herd had gotten behind me and I was 'sandwiched' between them, some forty yards either way.

"I heard a noise, turned and saw a big cow coming straight for me. The German, who had joined the party, took a shot and hit her hard, but she didn't fall. The German took both tusks right through the back and was pummelled to mush, dying instantly. He was pinned to the ground like a butterfly under glass. I was really sorry; he was a good man.

"I knew many men killed by elephant. After this terrible incident, I carried on anyway."

"On every hunt toward the Save, I would ask the tribesmen if they had seen any elephant around. One said he had, and the next day, we found seven bulls. Luis stayed with them while the man came back to advise me.

"It was one of those steaming-hot Mozambican days, around noon, when I came up to the elephant. Looked like there might be some goodies. I could only see the tusks of a couple of quite moderate bulls, about forty pounds a side. That didn't mean there weren't better.

"They were standing dead-still, flapping their ears to cool the big veins as I tried to figure out what to do. Finally, I saw two good bulls and shot one dead. There was another huge bull there that had had its tusks broken off short, so I left it. Jesus! But there were elephants all around me! Then I spotted a sixty-pounder and took him. Unfortunately, it ran around the big one with the broken tusks, and although I'd hit it very hard, it went off with the big chap with the broken tusks.

"But I'd had a good look and wasn't fooled. I followed the smaller feet, as I knew it to be the better tusker. I thought maybe it'd dropped from the chest shot, but five minutes of walking showed that they had separated.

"I came into fairly open country and there, some distance in front, was one of the bulls, badly hit and walking slowly. I ran as fast as I could to cut it off before it could reach the forest ahead, but I was whipped and it was a long run. I walked fifty yards behind the bastard, getting more tired with every step, but I kept to fifty yards behind it. The elephant was obviously badly hit so I stayed behind, hoping the animal would drop. But I saw it was gaining on me, so I had to start running again.

"I got to within thirty yards, waiting for it to turn its head and look back so I could take a side brain shot. Hell, it swung its head from side to side but just wouldn't give me the angle for the brain.

"Well, I looked at this thing and I knew its bum intimately after so many miles. All of a sudden, it seemed to be getting bigger! Ridiculous, I told myself. But it *was.*

"The damned thing was charging *backward!*

"That son of a bitch got to within ten yards and I was all lined up on his spine when he swung around on a penny, leaving you seven cents change.

"I dropped him with a frontal brain shot.

"Of course this bastard knew I was right behind him all the time and just figured when I was close enough for him to run to the rear. It's fascinating how intelligent elephant are and how they look after themselves.

"On another occasion, I was hunting at a place called Chinzine and stopped off at the *Chefe de Poste,* as I happened to know him. The custom, and perhaps the law, was to check in before entering an area. One had to let the *Chefe* know that a stranger was there, as, sooner or later, his men would advise him that it was a gunrunner or a poacher or some other form of dubious character. So, you'd drop by for *chá* and advise him you were now in his area."

The official was very pleased to see Wally. "I'd like you to do me a favor, if you could," said the Chefe.

"Surely. How can I be of help?"

"Well, there are two bull elephants that have been around for about three weeks. Every night they raid one or another village. They may hit this one tonight or tomorrow. Maybe they're ten miles away. The locals are terrified. Only a couple of days ago, not later than half past seven at night, a woman tried to drive them off with a big tin, beating it with a stick. The elephant turned around, knocked her down, and killed her most thoroughly, believe me. I saw the body. Close to here. She was really dead. I have three men out, two with Martini-Henry .450 rifles and one with a .30-'06, but the bloody bush is so thick that they just lie up in the day and only come out to raid after dusk.

"Could you shoot these bulls, amigo, *as we both know they'll kill more people if somebody doesn't take care of them? The locals are afraid to go into cover after them. Please do me the great favor and get them."*

Wally answered, "Well, if I'm going to sleep at one of the villages here, how in hell am I supposed to know which one they'll come to? I'd like to help you, but I'm not a goddamn clairvoyant."

"Right. There are two water holes nearby and they have *to go to one or the other. Usually in the early morning or late evening, after raiding the farms and before heading back to the forest. On one of these pans we've had a tree platform built and two of these men have spent three nights up on it. They've heard the elephants drinking but can't get a shot as they only have a small flashlight and can't see them. Actually, they took a few shots, but the visibility was so poor they don't think they hit them.*

"One of my men saw, before he could get off a shot in daylight, that one of these elephants had a couple of arrows sticking into it, probably poisoned. This couldn't have helped its temperament."

Wally, who had Walter, Jr., with him during this episode, finally agreed. "Okay, we'll go down and sleep at this tree platform to see if they'll come. You say they weren't there last night?"

"Apparently not," replied the Chefe de Poste.

Wally continued, "That ruddy platform was made from bubble gum and baling wire, so we decided to sleep at the bottom of the tree, rather than on the platform. I hadn't used a night-light before and figured I'd be better off on the ground with elephants.

"We put our blankets down not far from the water and we were lying there in the evening, around seven, looking up at the stars, waiting, waiting. But it wasn't long before we heard movement.

"Right in front of us, not fifteen yards away, we heard the water splashing. I whispered to Walter, 'Hell, boy, that's got to be an elephant there. I'll get my gun ready and when I whisper to you to put on the light, do it!'

"When I thought everything was right, I nudged Walter to put on the flashlight. Hell, here were these two bulls, close enough to kick! I could actually see the water dripping from the trunk of one of them.

"I killed this bull with a side-brain shot and the other started to run. So I put a shot into that one; I don't know where I hit it but I was pretty sure it was in the heart, although the light was very faint.

"After a few seconds I heard a crash, so I was pretty sure I had dropped him. But something bothered me. When Walter put out the light, I said, 'Hey! I saw something very funny on the ground right in front of us. Did you see what it was?'

"'No, Dad, I didn't.'

"'Well, turn the bloody thing on again!'

"My God, when he turned the light back on, there was a humming noise that I'd never heard before. The whole ground a yard from our blankets was actually alive with a carpet of insects.

"We went a bit closer to look and, by heaven, there were literally millions of scorpions! I don't mean a couple of hundred thousand but actually *millions* of these scorpions. Hell, I don't know what they were up to, maybe migrating or something. I don't know where they were going or if they knew themselves. Christ, if we'd waited another minute or two, these scorpions would have been on our blankets and that would have been that. A real horror movie. . . .

"It was really weird the way they were humming and were literally a sea of pink pincers and stinging tails. We grabbed our blankets and ran around the other side of the lake where we had to sleep. I was damned glad to get there!

"We went back to the elephant I had shot first and there was indeed an arrow in him, confirming the comments of the *Chefe de Poste.*

"We went back to the Chefe and reported that we'd killed the one with the arrow in it but that we hadn't been able to find the other wounded elephant. We were pretty sure it was dead, though. I simply had to leave the day after, but we spent the whole day following the other bull. Hell, I hated to leave the ivory.

"On the way back I happened to pass this Portuguese and he told me that the other one had never come back, so if it died or just left the area, I don't know."

"It was after this that I went on safari with a client. It had been raining for a few days, a beautiful morning came, and we went out hunting. The client had just shot a kudu. I was about to get off the vehicle to walk over to where he had taken aim and dropped the animal when I got a huge scare. Same thing as years earlier. Millions of the little pink bastards swarming at my feet! We simply couldn't get out of the car to get the client, who was a couple of hundred yards away. We just had to drive off and around to pick him up. The scorpions were so numerous that we couldn't even get near the kudu itself for hours. Where the hell they all went in their millions, nobody has ever been able to tell me. Maybe down holes?

"An incident like that sure takes your mind off jumbo for a while. . . ."

"When I first started off ivory hunting, I thought the best plan would be to shoot at night, but I quickly learned that

A charging cow elephant taken at close quarters with Harry Manners's No. 2 Brownie box camera, circa 1943.

Wally (second from right) with one of his first vehicles in the Mozambique bush.

Wally (far right) returning from an ivory safari in 1938.

Wally, in 1939, with a whacking big jumbo.

Wally with the buffalo that he ran past at one yard.

Wally fooling around. His hands cover the joint of one greater kudu horn attached to another. No fake intended as some have done.

Walter, Jr., with 135-per-side elephant tusks his father Wally had taken in 1948. Walter, Jr., also a professional hunter, is now retired.

These are the four elephants shot in one day in 1943 that supposedly caused the incredible dry-season rain as predicted by his men.

Victim of the man-eater Wally shot in 1952. Note that the leg and foot above the man's head were bitten completely through. A not-very-appetizing reality of Africa.

Photo of Wally with the man-eating lion he killed after it had killed several tribesmen. A fine specimen with a coveted black mane.

Fred Bear, fourth from left, along with camera crew, Wally in the middle and Walter, Jr., on the far right with one of Fred's excellent buffalo. One arrow, brother!

Fred Bear, president of the Bear Archery Company of Grayling, Michigan, and Wally with a huge lion, taken with a bow and arrow. The lion weighed 456 pounds!

Robert Ruark with three extraordinary warthogs, which he so dearly loved to hunt. The middle one is the trophy he prized above all others, and you can see why! A complete curl! I must say that the other two ain't bad either!

Robert Ruark, Wally, and his wife, Lilly, at Wally's mine in Vila de Manica.

Ruark fooling with a python; a copy of his book is prominently displayed. Big python, hey?

there just wasn't enough light and that follow-ups would be pretty impossible. So I hunted daytime, under terrible conditions, but managed to take forty-three elephants in one month, which represented a fair amount of money then. I remember from that episode that the biggest elephant I shot was eighty-five pounds a side, but I once saw one that went an easy hundred pounds a side.

"Trouble was I couldn't get a clear shot.

"I particularly remember a lot of big elephant at a place near Zumbo, where I killed at least thirty in one hunting trip alone. The ivory yield was exceptionally good. Now, we never wasted the meat from such hunts but would dry it in the dry season, when it was a bonus for the men working for me. It was a form of currency. 'Meat for meat,' as the Africans put it.

"But the men I had were often craftier than the elephants. One day, coming back from an extended hunt such as the Zumbo one, we had a whole load of ivory as well as a great deal of dried meat, tied into bundles like kindling. I happened to be looking out of the rearview mirror when I saw one of these bundles of dried meat fly out!

"Obviously, these guys were stealing meat as they came close to home so they could come back later and pick it up. Just like the gold-in-the-hair and copper-penny routine.

"I stopped the truck and said, 'Hey, *xana u tirha yini kwalaho?*' I asked the man nearest me what he was up to. In Shangaan. No explanation for the meat flying by.

"'Oh no, *patrão.* You are mistaken. It must have fallen out and nobody noticed.'

"'When has elephant meat grown wings?' I asked. 'I thought they were too heavy to fly!'

"I had to keep a sharp lookout for such incidents because you can't maintain the respect of your work force if they hoodwink you. And I don't care what country you're talking about. Human nature is the same everywhere."

"When elephant hunting opened, I quickly got the hang of the game. I had previously concentrated on meat-hunting for buffalo and on other kinds of animals. Little did I realize how much I had to learn and how fast I would have to learn it.

"And I hadn't a clue about the perils of elephant hunting.

"My accountant at the time was Harry Manners, author of *Kambaku* and an elephant hunter of some distinction. He now lives in the Kruger National Park of South Africa at Skukuza Camp, where he runs a curio shop and is a real drawcard.

"Over the years, Harry and I enjoyed a grand relationship, having spent, as we did, literally thousands of days together after ivory. He is a fine hunter and a grand gentleman whose friendship I treasure. Harry is renowned for his 185-pounder, which will stand as one of the truly great elephant trophies.

"In my years pursuing ivory, I shot and lost a couple of elephant in the same category as Harry's incredible jumbo. I lost them because I was not as lucky or—quite possibly—as good as Harry. Oh, for sure, I took my very big ivory—stuff that will stand with the best—but one always thinks of the one or two absolutely exceptional elephant that just got away, despite all the precautions, all the hard work, all the exhaustion.

"When I started shooting elephants, I did the same thing that Karamojo Bell did, which was to saw the skull in half to find precisely where the brain lay. The elephant I lost made me anxious to find out just where the vital spots were.

"Well, at this point, I had a .30-'06, not much of an elephant gun, and I think Harry was carrying an even lighter caliber, perhaps a .256 Mannlicher. We went off into the bush with dreams of riches, but as I said, same as Bell, who commented that he 'let a lot of rain in' as he first tried the brain shot before he figured out where it was by sawing the skull in half, we, too, had our disasters. The angle between the eye and ear didn't always pan out. Often I lost bulls with that shot."

As someone who has cropped and hunted some eight hundred elephant, I must say that I find this quite surprising, as I never lost a jumbo with that angle. I found it completely deadly. One simply lined up the location of the ear holes and took the relative angle. Far be it for me to tell Wally Johnson how to hunt elephant, but that was my *experience.*

Still, Wally preferred the heart shot as being more sure. So, you like catsup or you don't. If you're selling hamburgers for a living, that's your business. No offense to Wally, merely a personal observation.

Noon on the Save River. It was as hot as a new horseshoe, and Wally was on an elephant hunt.

"I had asked the locals if there were any elephant, and one of them told me there were. Luis and this fellow left early the next morning. We eventually located seven jumbos, and it looked like there were some good ones. I could only see the tusks of two, about forty-pounders. The others were impossible to see as they were standing dead-still in the shade. They were just flapping their ears to keep cool. I stood for twenty minutes but didn't know how to handle the situation.

"What was I to do? The goddamn wind threatened to change and then the elephant would take off and I wouldn't get any at all. What now?

"I finally saw a sixty-pounder and dropped it with an ear shot. There were two big bulls, both with tusks broken off short. I saw another good one and he went off with one of the chaps with the broken tusks. I stopped for a moment to have a look at the one I'd killed and found him a disappointing forty-five pounds a side. I killed three more out of that bunch after a long run, but it was well worth the effort. They averaged about fifty-five pounds.

"I carried on with my hunting plans and a particular chief delegated some men to conduct me down to a mountain where he had a notion there would be quite a few elephant. I heard them and went up, finding twenty-odd bulls. The best ran about fifty pounds a side, quite respectable.

"I killed two and the rest ran around the hill, with me hot on their heels. In total, I shot eight bulls, the smallest being about thirty-five pounds. I was so pleased with my luck that I decided to delay my return home. I then arranged to have the ivory chopped out in exchange for the meat, which was a literal mountain. I then left the ivory with the chief, who I knew would safeguard it until my return, as he would want more meat. I figured the ivory was as safe with the chief as it would have been at home. You couldn't do that today, I don't think.

"Anyway, I made a hundred-mile circuit with my men in search of more elephant, but with no luck, so we went back to collect the tusks, which had been perfectly held for me."

"A couple of years later, I had a very interesting confrontation with a local tribe while hunting elephant.

"I had killed four good bulls and asked the chief if, in exchange for the meat of two—I wanted two for my own men to take back when dried—he would have his people chop out the ivory.

"'Certainly,' he answered, but when it came down to it, this fellow figured he could have all four carcasses if he refused to have his people chop out the ivory, which is the age-old arrangement.

"'No,' he said to me in Shangaan, 'my people will not take out the teeth. It is beneath their dignity. You must just give them the meat.'

"'Right,' I answered, 'I hope they like it very well done.'

"'What do you mean by that?'

"'You son of a bitch!' I said in Portuguese. '*Filho da puta*! I shall burn this meat to charcoal, after removing the teeth, if your people do not help me.'

"He thought about that a bit while Luis, covered by me with a rifle, came up with two large tins of kerosene.

"'Do you have a match?' I asked the chief.

"'*Está bem, senhor,* I see your point. My people will cut out all eight tusks in exchange for the meat of two carcasses.'

"'You are a wise and perceptive man,' I said in Shangaan.

"'Yes, sir. Wisdom is one of the reasons I am a great man.'

"'And wise you are. Now get the hell to work.'"

"The best elephant I ever shot was 160 pounds a side, but I know I once got one better than 200 per side that we just couldn't finish off. It disappeared. Now that was a lot of ivory, if you can imagine what it would be worth today to a trophy collector without scruples. I have every reason to believe that

that elephant crossed into the adjoining Kruger National Park, where it died. We couldn't pursue a wounded elephant into a park like that. All hell would have erupted. Yet no hunter forgets something like that. You curse yourself for ever afterward.

"One of the big problems was selling the ivory, although it was quite legal, because of the machinations of the Indian traders who were the middlemen in Mozambique. The following story illustrates this.

"When my son was only seven, I took him elephant hunting and I winged a huge elephant. I told Walter to stay back while I crawled up to it. But apparently the old bull could either hear or smell me. Christ, it was thick. . . . I could hear the animal, but not see it. This changed. Suddenly I looked up and saw more elephant that I ever want to see again. All I could see was elephant in front of me! Then it just turned its head as part of its demonstration charge and I got a chance at the ear, which I immediately took. It dropped.

"Dear God, what an elephant! I had no idea it was so big! The damned thing went 135 pounds a side. I was elated, as I didn't think it that big.

"Although I had killed bigger bulls, I was so delighted that I immediately took the teeth to Lourenço Marques to sell them. It was there that I started finding out about the economics of selling ivory.

"The local Indian ivory dealers knew they had a captive market and they exploited it. The going rate was one pound sterling per pound, but not in L.M. There, three Indian ivory dealers were in cahoots and worked together. Man, most successfully, as I was to learn. You'd go to the first one, who would offer one shilling and three pence a pound. He would say, 'Mr Johnson, you've been in the bush so long, hunting elephant, that you haven't heard the news. The price of ivory has dropped drastically. I lost money on my last transaction, so you'd better take the tusks to somebody else.'

"The next trader would say, 'Oh, I've lost so much on ivory, you must take it to somebody else.'

"The third one would offer a couple of pennies more, and you were forced to take it, as it was so weighty and expensive to transport. They were smart bastards, all in telephonic communication with one another as I went from one dealer to the next; they, in the meantime, figuring, quite literally, what to offer me. They got stinking rich. After ten months' hunting, I started to believe that the price had indeed plummeted."

Finally, Wally discovered that even though he was by then an old Africa hand, he'd been rooked for years for thousands of pounds. But there was no recourse to the perfidy. Wally simply had to swallow it. . . .

On the subject of the ivory dealers in L.M., Wally recalled another incident. He'd run into some South Africans who had wounded a huge bull. They lost it, but Wally saw what were undoubtedly the tusks of this jumbo a couple of weeks later at the store of one of the Indian dealers, a man known to have a constant crew of natives out with rifles he had issued to them. The ivory was tremendous, over ten feet long and very heavy. Wally took a photo of the pair, but, along with practically everything else he owned in Mozambique, it was lost during the Marxist takeover.

From the description, it was surely the huge bull the South Africans had shot and lost, the spoor perhaps having also been conveniently lost by the storekeeper's employees.

"Man, I've seen a lot of ivory. It was my business for nearly half a century, and if those tusks weren't over two hundred pounds a side, I'd eat them! Well, what the hell could I say?

"In general, we didn't make much out of ivory hunting, but not having any money [after the three years of banana disasters], I still made a go of it. I bought an old International truck for ten pounds, fixed it all up over a period of three to four months, and went out, even though I only had a .30-'06 rifle. Guns were hard to get and I was really broke. Later, I was able to buy a Brenneke 11.2 × 72mm rifle, along with fifty cartridges. But it was such a weird caliber for Mozambique, although a good one, that when I was out of ammo I was out of business.

"As I said before, elephant hunting is one of the hardest jobs in the world. You walk all day, finally come up to an elephant, the bastard gets your scent, and it's off. Way off! Sometimes you follow two or three days; no food, no water. Too heavy to carry. So you drink any goddamn thing you can find in the bush. Then you get up to the herd and again the buggers get your scent. Forget it.

"It's two dry days back to camp. Why the hell ivory cue balls aren't more expensive than they are, I would love to know. . . . You get back to camp and are soon repeating the same performance.

"Elephants are damned smart, and here's how they operated. They'd raid the native villages of corn, or, as it is known in Africa, maize, and anything else they could eat. Then they'd go like hell for ten to twelve miles. We'd follow until they stopped at about midday, sleeping in the shade in the blast-furnace heat. I was always looking for a big tusker, naturally, but at about half past five, we'd all stop and wait. That's when they would all make for the local native villages.

"My technique was to scream at them. The whole lot would swing around to see what kind of idiot was on their tail. I could then see if there was a good bull or two among them and I'd take it out. Often the ivory was lousy, but then, the big bulls don't tend to mix with the herd cows. The old boys were well aware of the hunters' tactics and were immensely aggressive and intelligent.

"This got a bit risky when there was a herd of thirty or forty, as they'd sure as hell come for you. Females were always trouble, just as in some other species. But if I saw a big track mixed in with those of cows, I'd follow.

"Early in my career, having shot only five or six elephants, I came upon two bulls standing facing each other, about forty yards away. I crept up, chose the one with the better tusks, and took aim. It dropped. The other one screamed and tried to lift the dead one. I didn't know it then but was about to find out that I was among quite a bunch of elephant.

"I suddenly had a funny sensation of my rifle being lighter. I looked down and saw that the floor plate of the magazine had recoiled open, the cartridges spilled out. I was unarmed.

"Thank God the rest of the herd came to the dead one and

tried to get it up, wedging with tusks and using their trunks. It was a sight that made me very sad, but at the time I was frightened as bejesus and not interested at all in the social customs of *Loxodonta africana.*

"I ran like crazy but saw that the females, five per side, had actually lifted the near-dead bull. He must have had some sexual reputation. In any matter, off the lot went, knocking a path fifteen feet wide, thumping down trees like wheat chaff. It took me fifteen minutes to pluck up the courage to go back, but I eventually did.

"I found the bull dead and the rest of the herd gone. It was curious. I felt like a *voyeur* as I discovered that the other elephants had all urinated on the dead bull."

I have seen the same thing, including the urination, as well as the phenomenon mentioned in an earlier work of a cow elephant wandering around with an elephant leg bone in its mouth.

"I was truly touched by their intelligence and their social structure, but at the time, we had to thin out the herds. People were starving to death. Children didn't stand a chance in some communities. You can watch all the fund-raising Ethiopian documentaries you wish to, but until you've actually seen a human being starve to death when you could have done something to prevent it by providing meat and getting rid of the marauding herds, you're whistling in the dark. The level of life, and of humanity, in Mozambique was appalling, and I have good grounds to believe it is worse now—much worse.

"Anyway, the various *Chefes de Postes* began to issue rifles to the locals, so severe did the elephant problem become during that period. That seemed to be the only alternative to the wholesale destruction and subsequent starvation. Of course, because of sheer incompetence, the countryside was alive with wounded elephants. Naturally, there were as many—if not more—people killed. A great deal of this had to do with the greed of the *Chefes.* After all, where did the ivory go that was acquired by the lent rifles? Obvious.

"Dried meat was also a highly lucrative business. There were hundreds, perhaps thousands, of untrained armed tribesmen wandering about the bush with Martini-Henry .450s. But somebody had to do the job, no matter what the motive. The life of a child is a lot more important than that of an elephant who ate his or her food.

"I remember once going up to an area called Panda with my old International truck. There were no four-wheel-drive vehicles in those days, and we'd normally leave the vehicle and walk sixty to seventy miles in two days. I recall that two hundred miles was nothing for a trip after elephant."

(If you doubt this, check Karamojo Bell, who quite accurately decided that he'd walked sixty thousand miles in his pursuit of ivory, and he'd hunted not nearly so long as has Wally Johnson.)

"I camped near a big lagoon and asked the locals about the elephants. Hell, they told me that there were many many elephants raiding their crops. I was the first white they'd seen in years, and they were delighted when I told them I'd come to shoot elephant. I saw tremendous crop damage and the tribesmen promised to show me the next morning just where the jumbos were. These chaps were living entirely on fish and were starved of meat. The idea of an elephant carcass or two put them into paroxysms of ecstasy.

"Came the raw, bleeding dawn and, sure enough, they put Luis and me onto a double pair of tracks that I reckoned would go some eighty pounds a side each. They were *big* tracks. The elephant had passed during the night but seemed simply to be moving, hardly stopping to feed at all. We left at six in the morning, first light, but couldn't catch up. The men said that in the direction they were going, there was no water at all and that they'd be back. There was a *pan* nearby, which was the only possible place where they could drink.

"Hell, I hit it smack-on. We found them on their way back, waylaid them and shot them. The tusks turned out to be an average of eighty pounds per side. Fine ivory.

"In that area, ivory really wasn't so good, but the people were starving. Elephant raiding on the villagers' crops had assumed incredible proportions, but one couldn't shoot them all and solve the problem permanently. A good average for tusks was forty to fifty pounds. Just a couple of years later, a hunter was damned lucky to take a sixty-pounder. As we went from village to village, Luis, privy to bush gossip, explained that the elephant depredation had been terrible. Everybody was bone-thin and the children were dying. Many had died already, and those who had survived were digging in the bush for roots and were eating them on the spot so somebody stronger didn't snatch away this 'food.' It was pathetic. I had seen enough of this and stopped hunting to go and see the *Chefe de Poste* and ask what the hell was going on with his district that the people were dying in wholesale lots.

"'What the hell's happening with your people that they're dying like poisoned locusts?' I asked him. 'Why the bloody hell can't you get some meal up here from Lourenço Marques and at least feed these people?' I didn't care for the niceties of manners that day. And he was a lethargic nobody. A backwater civil servant. Hell, I was angry. He said,

"'Oh, I know they're all dying. I've already written letters down to Lourenço Marques to the administration, but they haven't sent any maize up yet.'

"Well, the *Chefe* promised to send another letter, but I don't know if he ever succeeded in getting emergency aid to those villagers or even if he gave a damn."

Wally did the best he could, and then some. He shot a few elephants for meat, but this wasn't enough. Typical of the people, their diet had to have cornmeal too.

"I did what I could and dished up the two bags of mealiemeal I had with me and gave them meat. But there were hundreds of these wretched souls just in one little area, and two 50-kilogram bags wouldn't go very far. That's a total of about 220 pounds.

"I gave the worst cases the most meal, but it just broke my heart to see these people dying of hunger in front of my very eyes. All the while, these elephants were kicking up hell, ruining the fields, so there was no hope of these people feeding themselves. I started hunting again and killed nine jumbos, but by that time most of the villagers were so weak they couldn't farm in any case. Finally, I went upriver and killed another nine elephant.

"These people were really in bad shape. But the eighteen elephant provided meat that must have helped. I then drove two hundred miles—not American miles over blacktop—back home, and got the last eight bags of mealiemeal I had in my stores. It took eight days to make the round trip, and petrol wasn't cheap, but I know I saved lives."

Bloody good man, Wally . . .

"In those early days, there were a few of us who were real professionals. We too were issued with old rifles by the government. I remember George Derek, Charlie White, and others. We would go for bulls only, and yes, we dried and sold meat, too, in the better times. Why waste it in a protein-starved land? Seeing as those elephants had to be done anyway, we didn't feel so bad, although any hunter worth his salt feels compassion. . . ."

Wally's remark here reminded me of how distressing elephant cropping can be when whole family units have to be wiped out in an effort to preserve habitat. My Luangwa days were not all joy, I can promise you.

Wally, like all the pro ivory hunters, had his share of bad scares while dealing with elephants. One involved a man who was a keen photographer and who was anxious to get shots of elephants or whatever was on the plat du jour.

"Actually, he was a friend of mine, and, just as it was coming on dusk one day, we hit a very big elephant track and followed it. It was nearly dark when I saw a small piece of elephant arse and made out something looming in the bush a dozen steps away. I noted that the elephant's ears were back, but there was a small clearing between me, the photographer, whom I was covering with my rifle, and the jumbo. The elephant was facing away and I couldn't see if it had tusks worth taking. This guy filmed for quite a few minutes and I had the idea that I could shoot it if it was decent.

"Jesus, all of a sudden, it spun about and came for us at eight feet! I was damned lucky to brain it at that range. That goddamn thing *knew* we were there and was just waiting for its chance. I'm pretty sure it had heard the camera and had 'surprise-charged.'

"It had a big hole under its eye that was full of pus. It had obviously been fighting with another jumbo, which had jabbed its tusk right into its head. This explained why the elephant was so cheeky and came for us.

"On many more instances than you can imagine, I have had elephant come at me for no apparent reason. Usually they were wounded in one way or another, sometimes by the issued .450s and sometimes through other causes. You never knew, but you had to keep constantly alert. At that time, elephant was open game throughout Mozambique except for two areas: the Pafuri, next to the South African Kruger National Park, and the Maputo Game Reserve in the far south of the country.

"I bought an airplane, learned to fly, and used to take Walter, Jr., flying over the Maputo area. We saw immense herds of elephant many times out on the plains, and one day, at about noon, we saw a tremendous bull right out in the open. He was a monster.

"I remember that we swooped down practically on top of him for a good look. He would easily have gone 150 pounds a side!

"I don't know what happened to that bull, but I know what almost happened to us. I cut the engine and swooped down for a closer look and the bastard wouldn't restart! It gave me a hell of a scare, as I thought I'd crash with Walter right into this small bunch of elephant. At the last instant, the goddamn motor caught, but it scared the bloody hell out of both of us."

Wally killed another 160-pound per side bull in the Massengena area of the Save River, but sadly the region was soon shot out. He remembers one hunting expedition when he shot thirty-five bulls in three weeks, the average tusk weight being around sixty pounds per side, a very respectable total. But what with the storekeepers supplying arms to the locals, it was a chunk of luck to get a forty-pounder a couple of years later.

"The rainy season," says Wally, "was the best time to hunt elephant. The spoor was easier to follow, they were used to wandering out of the forest, and, with the soft foliage, it was easy to get up to them. There was also somewhere a hunter could drink, as the dry-season conditions made hunting so *very* hard.

"After that heart-breaking starvation episode in the Panda area, I eventually got all the ivory home and returned at once to a very good area on the Save River. In fact, I came to a village where the elephant had been so active that they had killed a young man just three days before my arrival.

"So many of these idiots would go out in the pure blackness to save the crops in the *shambas,* and they couldn't see the elephants in the dark. They'd walk right up on them and you can imagine the consequences. I doubt a forensic surgeon could have reassembled the pieces.

"A local told me he'd seen elephants right in the same area, so I engaged him, along with Luis, to follow them up. Sure as blazes, there was a herd right out in the open. It had been a sweaty two-hour walk, but there were two decent bulls, bold as the Ruins of Zimbabwe.

"As I knocked the two off, another bull I hadn't seen ran past the two dead ones. I ran for half a mile but never caught him. I don't think it was that good anyway. Well, I returned to the two dead ones but there was nobody home! They had both been stunned with brain shots and had cleared out when they woke up! One must have gotten up against the other and, clearly, by the spoor, they had supported each other away with what must have been monumental headaches.

"I was *positive* they were both dead, but it's a damned good thing I didn't prop my rifle against one and have a pipe. It might have been my last. Thank heavens for that third bull. . . . I tried for days with Luis to find those two but they just vanished. This merely shows you that you can never relax as a hunter. You can never take anything for granted because something will surprise you when your guard is down. And that usually means severe injury or death.

"On that same trip I came upon another bunch of elephant. There was a good bull in the middle, of course, offering no chance of a clear shot. I had no idea how hairy this episode would turn out to be but was shortly to discover that I should have stayed home.

"I had Walter, Jr., with me, and after waiting half an hour to see the ivory, I decided to shoot at the big cow covering him. I had three cartridges for the .375 and eight for the .318, which I gave to Walter. The cow immediately charged and Walter killed her with one shot in a frontal angle. But as he did so, another cow came like lightning and I still couldn't see the damned bull. Walter covered me and killed the second cow, only to find it replaced by a third! Walter dropped this one too, but when we saw the bull, we saw it was a *tondo,* a male with no visible tusks. That son of a bitch was bloody *huge.*

"Now the herd had the scent. Ours. I shot another cow and was now out of ammo for the .375 H & H, as I had to give it two shots. When the *tondo* was coming right at us, I had had to use the first round to floor it, but the cow Walter had shot wasn't down and the rest of the mob were on us like a swarm of bees. The wounded cow started for us, screaming.

"'*Run*! For Chrissake, *run*!'

"Oh, it was a wonderful African afternoon. I grabbed the .318 from Walter, the one I had to line with nail polish, and when I fired at this bloody thing bearing down on us, the chamber jammed and only ejected half the empty cartridge. I tried as if my life depended on it—and it most surely did—to get a new round in, but it was hopelessly jammed.

"I ran as hard as I could, seeing Walter flash through the bush a hundred yards ahead. I knew I was a goner; I could actually feel the earth move under my feet as this goddamn thing thundered down on me.

"Suddenly, there was no sound behind me! Like the lion of years previously, it had just fallen down and died. God, but was it close! The trunk couldn't have been three feet behind me when it fell.

"Whew! I was lucky to get away from that one. I said some things that I don't believe the manufacturers of that .318 Nitro would either have appreciated or used in their advertising. I never used that rifle again. I would sooner have thrown rocks."

Interesting to note that Karamojo Bell's only really close call was also with a .318. At least his was in working condition.

"I continued on the Save River and killed twelve bulls, all good ones, in two weeks. One of the problems in that particular area was that elephant were especially savage because of their being caught in cable snares that were set by the locals for other game but which inevitably got the odd jumbo.

"Elephant didn't stay caught for long, though. Hell, it was gruesome. Some had their trunks severed and starved to death while others had their legs nearly cut through by wire snares. These snares are still the great curse of Africa."

Wally had some interesting experiences with aberrant elephant, killing one with a single tusk on one side and three on the other. Another had five tusks on one side, not big ivory, but certainly rather unusual. There is one in the Explorers Club in New York and I swear I can't recall how many tusks it has; maybe five. It's on the top floor in the corner, should you happen by.

There are plenty of theories as to this phenomenon, most seeming to center around lightning striking the tusk. But all such tusks I've ever seen have had an undamaged individual nerve, which, at least to my way of thinking, would tend to dispel this theory. I suspect it is just a genetic aberration.

Lightning kills elephants dead as golfers, and there have been well-recorded cases of as many as five bulls, which were touching one another, slain, as the term used to run, "all stark," by the will and mighty hand of Allah.

"I was out hunting in a remote area called the Simbiri Forest which I didn't know very well. I had a pal with me, and together we killed four jumbos, pretty good ones. The bush was so thick I couldn't figure how a bull elephant could possibly get through it. You'd think that just the trees would block its tusks. But, of course, that's why they loved it.

"When we came across two sets of tracks, we would split up. Hell, I hadn't gotten ten bloody yards into the bush when my man gave the sign for jumbo. But it was so thick I just couldn't make out the outline of the body. It was just a couple of feet away and I made out another elephant standing next to it. Luis thought I'd gone crazy. He bolted, very wisely, not wanting any part of this picnic.

"I quietly checked my rifle and the trees started breaking under a double and simultaneous charge. I shot the nearest elephant three times, starting from six paces, and had the presence of mind to jump behind a small tree. Hell, it was better than a sharp umbrella.

"It turned its head to catch me with its trunk as it loomed over me. I gave it another .375 solid 300-grain slug. It was so close that I literally shot it under the chin, between the jaw V, through the tongue and up into the brain. That's close!

"At that moment, I heard screaming behind me and saw that the other bull had somehow passed me and was chasing Luis. I swung around and saw that it almost had him. Then the elephant blocked my vision by kneeling and I figured he had Luis for sure. Elephants usually kneel on their victims before they get around to the jollies of stamping and tusking, so I started thinking of employment agencies I knew as I shot it in an attempt to break the hip.

"The elephant got up quite slowly and I was relieved to see Luis running away to beat hell. My rifle was now empty and I had to reload as the elephant started to run off.

"Great God, I'd had no idea what an enormous tusker it was! I didn't have time to fill the magazine but got one in. I didn't dare take the precious seconds when I might lose him. I was using a British brand of ammo that used to come in little five-packs. I ripped open the packet with my teeth and quickly stuck in one round which I promptly deposited in the elephant's rear in another attempt at the spine or hip. It fell on its rear legs and I had to get out another cartridge and drop it again the same way when it got up. I had to do this a bloody third time!

"Altogether, I put five solids in him. He was well over a hundred pounds per side. I followed the animal onto a big flood plain with lots of high grass. Hell, I even climbed trees to see if I could spot it. I told Luis to keep following.

"I thought maybe it had dropped dead in the grass. Then I saw a small but shady tree on the plain and told Luis, 'Look, that elephant will be under that tree.'

"'No, Baas, the elephant will not be underneath. Look at the spoor. The tracks are going to the right.'"

Even though Wally figured that the jumbo was under that tree, he was talked out of it by Luis. Sure enough, the tracks were later discovered to have fish-hooked back to the tree, where the bull stood most of the afternoon. Wally cursed himself for not following his instinct as an ivory hunter.

Darkness was falling like a black mantle now and the two men had made it back to camp. The chap with Wally had also killed an elephant, quite a respectable tusker, although not in the league of the one Wally had killed and lost. Wally told him the story and the man had what I consider the gall to ask,

"Please let me take him. I've never gotten a really big one like that."

Wally was hesitant but the man was most convincing.

"Okay, you take over from here and I'll tell you what to do. My man will take you onto the tracks. Take a helluva lot of water and food because although he's got a lot of holes in him I don't know when he'll die."

This man was immensely pleased at Wally's gesture. Wally went off the next morning, killed an elephant and was back in camp by ten.

The other man was there too.

"Congratulations!" said Wally. "You got him!"

"Well, not exactly. . . ."

"What the hell happened and what are you doing here then?"

"There was an acre or so of trees smashed up, it was so wild, so I

figured I'd come back tomorrow. I'll take some more food and stuff and return and get him."

Wally said, "Hell, you're a fool, man! You should never have left the spoor. You'll never find him now. And for this I gave up one of the best elephants of my life?" Obviously the guy had come across the elephant and it had scared him to death. He went to his tent when he saw Wally in such a rage.

"No. I'll get him tomorrow," he said over his shoulder.

"Forget it, dope," said Wally. "He's long, long gone."

"It was just bad luck and bad judgment," said Wally. "I killed the 'askari' or guard bull, rather than the big chap. Most of the really big ones have younger bulls which stick with them, as they hear and see better when danger is around. In this case, I killed the askari as I couldn't see the big bull. I really don't know what happened to the big one. My guess is that it died and somebody picked up those fantastic tusks.

"A few days later, I was at a water hole and there were two bull elephants in it. It was a very big *pan,* so I decided against a shot. Too far to be sure. I just sat and watched them. Then I heard a noise in the bush behind me and up came another two big bulls. I crept around the side of the *pan,* since the bulls were fighting in the water. They got my scent as I reached the other side and decamped in one hell of a hurry, but not before I could kill a seventy-pounder.

"Amazing. They were gone like ghosts. I followed them throughout that day at a trot and none of us ever stopped, elephant or human. I knew I had to get back to the one I'd killed to get the ivory, which I did.

"A curious but humorous thing happened the next day. I had been following the spoor of a big bull and I knew I wasn't fifty yards behind. I remember that it was unbelievably hot. Suddenly, the front tracker gave a bloodcurdling shriek. The elephant had passed a tree with a big beehive and had either hit it or shaken the tree. We never saw that tusker. The bees saved him. Hell, everybody was stung half to death, and if you think that what you hear of the savagery of African bees is balderdash, come out and try them sometime.

"I recall being out once hunting elephant and we came on a big herd but there was a strange whistling noise that kept wafting over this bunch. Damned if I could figure out what it was. When I came up to the elephant, I found that the noise was coming from the herd itself. I watched them for some time and Luis whispered to me, 'Look! There's one with no trunk!'"

It had been completely cut off by a wire snare. Wally managed to put it out of its misery. It was already weak from starvation.

"I recall another occasion when I was following a very big elephant. I could see that it, too, was in very poor condition and I wondered why. After I killed it, I found that it had a heavy spear in the back of its skull from a drop trap and I guessed it had been suffering for over a year. The blade had just missed its neck vertibrae where it was meant to fall. From the amount of pus and rot, that animal had been in agony for a long time.

"Africa is often a cruel, unforgiving experience."

After Wally had been hunting elephants for decades, things began to change from unrestricted hunting to the point where he started taking out clients on license.

Oh, yes . . . the clients.

8

CLIENTS

After he wrote such political indiscretions as Something of Value, Uhuru, *and* The Honey Badger, *Robert Ruark became* persona non grata *in East Africa. But the only place I have ever seen a complete set of his books for sale was at the airport in Nairobi, Kenya!*

Business as usual.

It is rumored that Ruark was forced to flee from Kenya at night, but I cannot vouch for this. He certainly, however, did pitch up in Mozambique, where he developed a fine friendship with Wally Johnson, which lasted through five extended safaris until his death in 1965 at age forty-nine. An American, he was to become something of a legend in his lifetime, a controversial, engaging man with whom I enjoyed interesting talks over the inevitable pink gins. Ruark loved African safari life, and his talents as a writer shared this passion with the world.

On what I believe was Ruark's first safari in Mozambique with Wally, there occurred an interesting, if painful, incident for all concerned. . . .

Wally was working at the time for Baron Werner von Alvensleben, who was the principal of a company called Safariland (or, in Portuguese, Safarilandia*). The company had large government* *hunting concessions. One of their first camps was named Camp Ruark, as Bob had been the first client there. It was situated on the lush, reed-smothered banks of the Save River.*

Ruark was a highly individual and talented man, who had shot specimens of all the big stuff in East Africa (Kenya and Tanganyika) before rousing the ire of the late President Kenyatta. He now really wanted a place in Africa where he could write and relax—when he wasn't apart from his Spanish villa or New York penthouse. He also had one more abiding passion besides gin: wart hogs!

"Hell, I never saw anybody so fond of hunting those bloody wart hogs than Bob," said Wally. "In those days they were almost vermin and Ruark had a ball. Yet, at that point, he wouldn't walk across the street, had there been any to walk across, to shoot the biggest lion in the book! He wanted to relax, and Africa was in his blood as much as malaria.

"Pretty much throughout the time we were hunting together, Bob was doing a syndicated column for a New York newspaper, as well as one for an American outdoor magazine. He was also working on books. He had highly unusual work habits, often starting his writing in the middle of the night. He always claimed that he did his best work at two in the morning. Obviously, Bob was very easy to have on safari, compared with most clients, especially first-timers, who wanted 'everything' in the first two days. Sometimes we'd dash for the Rhodesian border to personally post off his stuff to America. Crazy bugger, but we got on grandly.

"Anyway, we were out one day, looking for wart hog, when we came upon a tremendous baobab tree (which the locals said *Xikwembu,* God, had planted when He was drunk, as it had been put in the wrong way up). Now the baobab is host to all manner of wildlife, from bushbabies *Galago senegalensis,* to hornbills.

"Also bees.

"This last was to prove the case that day. There was a huge comb some twenty feet up a smooth stem, the gray bark covering pithy wood into which the locals usually pounded hardwood stakes to reach the hive.

"The tree was too big to climb and there was no hardwood handy. We'd been out for a couple of weeks and really craved some of that honey. Well, before anybody could stop him, Ruark said, 'I'll get that goddamn honey down for you,' and he grabbed his shotgun and *fired* at it!"

Oh, brother!

"We were instantly swarmed. Ruark was so badly nailed his eyes were swollen to the point he couldn't open them, and two of the trackers were so hammered that they looked like bloated assault victims.

"I had Walter, Jr., with me, who most bravely went back to save his dog, a Doberman, which happened to be along and had tried to take refuge under the car but wasn't having much joy. Walter yelled, 'Christ, they'll kill him!' and grabbed the gunbearers, one of whom had long pants and the other a greatcoat.

"I've never been able to figure, after all these years, how these guys could wear those old woolen British Army greatcoats in temperatures of over 100 degrees Fahrenheit and never break out into a bead of sweat. In any case, Walter snatched the clothing and ran to get the dog, which was in real agony. Thank God nobody happened to be allergic to bee stings or we would have had some corpses for sure.

"Of course, Walter took a hell of a punishment, but he got the dog from under the car. He was constantly being stung as he tried to move the car but was afraid he'd run over the dog. Finally, he was able to grab the dog and rescue the vehicle.

"After that little lot, the camp decided it could manage without sweets for a while. . . .

"But we got the wart hog later on, after first having found the spoor of an elephant right *on* the platform of the railway station in a small town in the concession!"

You'll see Wally's photo in this book of the rare wart hog with circular tusks that Bob killed. I never saw one quite like it. The tusks almost form a circle, a most spectacular trophy. Perhaps it had some problem with the alignment of the tushes so they didn't whet properly against one another and wear each other down as is normally the case. Maybe the fool thing was a hermaphrodite.

"The second odd item about this episode was that Bob shot the wart hog through the heart with that .244 Holland and it ran in a death sprint for about forty yards. In doing so, it ran into or grazed a tree. It was going so damned fast that it actually knocked one of those magnificent tusks completely out of its head. When we came up to it after it fell, Ruark said, 'Hell of a nice tusk, Wally, but why didn't you tell me it only had one?'

"'What?' I said. It sure as hell had two when I looked at it in the glasses. I then called the men over and had them backtrack the pig to the spot where Bob had shot it. Bingo! We found the missing tusk. Somehow undamaged. I gave a sigh of relief.

"Ruark treasured that wart hog above all others, even though he had killed a few with much more impressive ivory by record-book standards. In at least one of his novels, he mentions the fact that the only place for a wart hog shoulder mount is on the interior of a bathroom door. This is the one he especially refers to. I was his guest—all expenses paid—at his Spanish villa, or, better said, castle, and there, in the guest bathroom, hung that wart hog. When one took the customary position, there was a grand panoramic vista of wart hog and little else. Great sense of humor, Robert.

"Just before Fred Bear, the famous archer, came over on safari with me, Ruark returned for what I think was his fourth trip. He always shot, as I did, a 375 H & H Magnum as well as a .244 H & H.

"His camp on the Save River was beautiful, but it was a huge area and the locals were poaching it heavily. They had actually built a fence of sorts which was about six and a half miles long. They had left openings every ten yards or so around the only available water, each opening having a deadly wire snare covering it. I don't know how many animals Bob and I had to have killed a day that we found suffering in these wire snares, but there were certainly hundreds. My men had to spear them as humanely as possible as the cost of ammo was atrocious.

"We knew we had to stop this and we wrecked the fence,

taking the wire. It was one hell of a big control job, but we were eventually sucessful.

"On another safari, Bob returned with a *National Geographic Magazine* crew. Everybody but I thought it a merry idea to go to a pool where the hippos and crocs had not been shot at and the idea was tossed around that it would really be macho for Ruark to get out into a dugout and show the hair on his chest.

"I knew he didn't like the idea very much, but he figured that for his image he'd better do the deed. I didn't especially embrace the concept either, as I was supposed to cover him from a second but off-camera dugout.

"Ruark knew his Africa—perhaps barring bees—and he knew how bad hippos could be. Well, there he was, out in that flimsy dugout when a hippo charged, falsely, thank heavens, up to about one foot of his canoe. He yelled, 'Paddle for shore! Paddle for shore! Quick, dammit!' I don't blame him in the least. He very well might have been killed right there and then, with variable lenses covering the event in color.

"He was actually shaking with fright. If you had been in that canoe, you'd have been rattling some bicuspids, too. It was *close.* Bob finally managed a single comment, after a long and straight gin: 'Never again, you bastards.'

"Well put, Robert.

"His death, despite the fact we knew he was a sick man, still came as a terrible shock to us. The world lost a great character and a wonderful talent in Bob Ruark. I'll always remember his sense of humor, his practical jokes, and his kindness. A hell of a guy."

"I would never brook any nonsense from a client, but I once had a pal who drew a really bad one. This was in Botswana in the early 1970s. This client, one of those unfortunate, loud-mouthed braggarts who give hunting a bad name in some quarters, had wounded a lion and the pro insisted that they sit down for a bit, since this thing might die of its own accord, or at least stiffen up from the wound.

"'Oh, no,' said the client, preening his chest hairs. 'To hell with you! I'll go in myself if you're too afraid.'

"'You'd better not. That cover is thick, and the lion will get you. You have *no* idea what you're walking into.'

"'Aah, you're just yellow! I'm going to get my lion.'

Of course the lion charged from a couple of yards. The pro shot it off the client before it killed him. The man had to be flown out to hospital, and he landed up with a bill bigger than the cost of his entire safari. He was severely injured and learned too late that following up wounded big game is the exclusive preserve of a professional hunter, not a safari client, no matter how seasoned the client might be or how impressive his marksmanship. He doesn't live in the bush full-time and cannot possibly have the reflexes a pro must have to stay in business and be responsible for the safety of clients at all times and under all circumstances.

As Wally said, "I've had people like this before. The only thing to do is take them back to camp and pack their bags for them. Call in a charter, put them on it, and walk away. I never needed a client so badly that it would cost me my license. I always told them to go get another hunter if they wouldn't listen to me. 'We have your money and contract already, so it's quite up to you,' I'd say. Usually worked with the swollen-headed ones. Must say, I never had this from women. They were a delight on safari and listened. None of this wise-guy nonsense."

"No two clients are the same. I remember once having a tremendous north European out who bitched about everything—the pots, pans, beds, lamps, you name it. The prices, at least according to him, were astronomical, although they were a tenth of what they are today.

"One day, this slob wounded a wildebeest, and, as was usual, he made his wife, who was half his size, carry his rifle and ammo. We had gunbearers who were paid to do this, and who took pride in their work, but he would have none of it. I finally had to shoot the animal.

"That bastard used to rebook every year, but I managed to dump him off onto another pro who was unsuspecting. I had had enough of that boor.

"A screaming contrast to that man was Bob Squires, an Englishman whom I had met in Umtali, Rhodesia, and who became one of my most interesting and enjoyable clients in Mozambique. A mutual friend asked me if I was going on safari for a week or so and if I wouldn't mind having Bob along. He was dead-keen to get into the bush to do some filming and such.

"I wasn't doing professional safaris at that stage, but I was glad of good company. I met Squires, instantly liked him, and invited him along for a short trip.

"The guy nearly dampened his pants. 'Suits me down to the ground. I'll be there when and where you say.'

"I asked for no pay and decided to hunt around Vila Gouveia, where there was a lot of good ivory to be had, especially around a large mountain. We went with my old '29 International truck, Squires filming like Cecil B. De Mille the whole time.

"That night, in a mighty simple camp, I said to Squires, 'We'll head out at five tomorrow morning to see if any elephant have been raiding the local villages.'

"'Oh, fine. I'll be ready.'

"The mist hung in the hollows like something ethereal as we arrived at the first village at about six a.m. As we got there, a bunch of kids of between five and eight years old were huddled together, roasting what I knew were rats impaled on a stick. Bob asked me what they were doing.

"'They're making breakfast, man.'

"'What in hell are they cooking and eating?'

"'Rats, of course,' I answered deadpan.

"'Rats!'

"'Yes, rats as in r-a-t-s. Full of protein. Build strong teeth and bones. Here, have a look.'"

Wally picked up one of the sticks the kids had, with about six nicely sizzling away, the hair scorched off, the bodies ungutted, and he showed the lot to Squires.

"'You mean they *actually eat* these vermin?'

"'Of course,' I told him. 'It's meat. These kids catch them

around the village here every day. Look, Bob, you think nothing of eating rotting grouse and woodcock, which you so delicately call "high," and lots of people eat such revolting fare as haggis. Each to his own. You're in the Mozambican bush now. No time to get squeamish or draw cultural comparisons. We're the odd folk out here, not the kids.'

"'My great God,' said Bob. 'If I told this to the old people back home, they'd never believe me!'

"'Tell you what. Set up your camera and I'll have one of these little guys eat one or two.'

"'Helluva good idea! I'll set it up.'

"I told the kid with three to eat one; it still had a lot of hair on it but it was nice and fat, although likely quite rare. The first thing the kid did was to strip it off the stick and eat it head first with an impressive crunching sound that Bob's sound camera picked up with sickening accuracy. Bob kept filming until the boy squeezed it and the guts squirted out from between his fingers and dripped down his naked chest. Sucking his fingers, he reached for another."

"Talk about rats! I had borrowed a tent from a pal when I heard that Bob was coming along. I also got him a camp bed, a simple affair, but easier for a man not used to sleeping on the ground as I was. I always slept with my rifle next to my leg, outside the tent, and he would stay inside."

Wally had a lot of good times with Bob Squires. They used to sit around the fire at night after a day's hunting and filming, and Bob would listen to Wally's lion stories until his eyes were bigger than coasters.

"One night, I heard the most incredible screaming at about 3 A.M. I grabbed my rifle, wondering what in hell had gotten Bob.

"'*He's got me! He's got me!*' was all Wally could get out of the man.

"I was sure it was a lion or a leopard, but I couldn't find a flashlight. There was a fantastic commotion in the tent, but I just couldn't figure what had gotten my friend. Apparently he couldn't either.

"I was damned near ready to shoot when I realized that, except for Squires, the tent was empty. I poked the muzzle under the camp cot, expecting nothing less than a saber-toothed tiger, but the cupboard was bare. He was still carrying on, however, so I decided to jump on the cot and try to pull whatever the hell it was off Bob. Then I happened to stumble across the flashlight. I grabbed it and turned it on. He was now awake.

"'God, Wally. Awfully sorry!'

"'What happened? What bit you?'

"Bob was lying on the floor, wrestling with his own arm!

"'Hell, my arm went to sleep and flopped onto my chest when I rolled over and I thought it was a bloody snake! So I grabbed my wrist, not being able to feel it, and with no light, I still thought it was a snake trying to get me. Of course I couldn't feel it; it was numb.'"

Wally laughed like mad and never let Bob forget the night his own arm almost ate him. The next day, Johnson would break out into absolutely uncontrollable laughter.

Squires said, "Yeah, I know what you're laughing at, but I was really scared." Actually, the poor guy had had the fright of his life. Wally took him out on many subsequent safaris.

"After the closure of unlimited elephant hunting in Mozambique and upon my joining Werner von Alvensleben's safari company, I had many fascinating clients. This was also true of my experiences in Botswana where I hunted before, and especially after the Portuguese Revolution which led to Mozambique's independence in 1975. I am, in fact, a Botswana citizen—a prerequisite if one wishes to hold a full-time, professional hunter's license.

"In 1965 I had Fred Bear out as a client in Mozambique. He is the head of the Bear Archery Company of Grayling, Michigan, and is world-famous as an archer of truly formidable standing. ABC TV did a segment for *The American Sportsman* on our taking a Cape Buffalo with a bow and arrow, and a better sports program I don't think they have ever done.

"We also took a lion. With a bow.

"Fred was hosted at Camp Ruark, where there were plenty of buffalo. In fact, we used to call them 'garden buff,' as they would eat the local corn at night and then head back into the reeds at dawn. They were most difficult to get at, but Fred wanted a buffalo and a lion, so we decided to get stuck into the project, despite very thick conditions.

"Curiously, just as Fred arrived, a native came by and said he would show us a buff that habitually hung out in the same place. This in return for some of the buff's meat. The guy told us that it was eating his corn every night.

"I'd never taken a man out hunting with a bow and arrow before and didn't know exactly what to expect. So, like an idiot, I went into the thick reeds with Fred and Luis, two other trackers, and two photographers. Quite a safari. Looked like Teddy Roosevelt's bunch.

"The only place to walk in this crud was on elephant and buff trails, and you never knew what might be coming the other way. It was pretty tricky going, I can tell you. The visibility reached to nearly your toe cuticles, and every few minutes we'd hear buffalo crash through the reeds. Not a terribly comforting sound when the guy next to you is armed with a sharp slingshot.

"We carried on through the reeds until the local pointed out a sandy region that was not so thick as the reeds. It was here that the buff would be, he told me—as I suddenly realized that he was motherless on palm wine!

"I decided to bugger *this* lot—but I was on a narrow path with three locals ahead of me, Fred Bear right behind, followed by the two photographers in full cinematic regalia behind him. Why do cameramen have so much dangling stuff?

"I whispered to Bear that somebody was going to get killed in the extreme and that we should get the hell out of there. He took my word for it and we reversed order.

"In an instant, a buff bull came down the trail as if it were on fire! I saw the two trackers and the local throw themselves off the path. By the time I had knocked assorted personnel out of the way, the damned thing was five yards away!

"I shot it in the back of the neck and it dropped literally at my feet. I had a helluva fright, because if I hadn't been lucky enough to spine it, it would sure as hell have gored me and maybe Fred too. The photographers, having a second sense for this sort of thing, were some distance away and were quite astonished to see a buffalo bull lying where they had been standing moments earlier.

"We went out from then on and Bear killed kudu, impala, wart hog, waterbuck, and quite a few other species. As an archer, he was completely phenomenal. But he still wanted a buffalo, so we went back and hunted nothing but that species.

"One day, on an open plain, we found two good bulls, but as soon as they saw us they crossed into the thick bush on the other side of the plain. We ran like mad to cut them off, but they were determined to reach the heavy stuff. Finally, we headed back to the Jeep to catch them at the far side.

"Jesus! One lost his temper as we came together, and he smashed the rear of the car so hard he slewed it easily six feet to the side. I don't know why we didn't go over. One of the gunbearers holding some camera equipment was thrown out by the impact and right smack on top of that buff! I reversed as the buffalo was groggy from impact, and I got the man back into the vehicle.

"As I pulled this battered bugger back into the car, I heard Fred say, 'Well, I got him!'

"'Got what?' I asked.

"'The damned buffalo, of course!'

"'What??? You killed that buffalo?' Damn if Fred hadn't jumped out of a rolling car and arrowed that thing stone-dead with one shot! I couldn't believe it, but the body lay a hundred yards away, long past giving up the ghost. And this in the middle of a bloody charge!

"Later on, Fred Bear killed another buff with a single arrow. You may remember seeing the American television pictures of the arrow going through the air and leaving a vapor trail. Needless to say, Fred was most pleased."

Hell, he should have been. What a feat!

"The next item on Fred's agenda was a lion. That's not like ordering a cheeseburger or a plate of chili. Fred knew that he would be one of the first men in decades to take one with a bow, probably since Howard Hill or Pope and Young.

"I figured the best tack would be to build a blind and hang a wildebeest, which we did. Luis suddenly shouted, 'Hell, Baas, look at that snake!' I looked but before I could properly register that it was very long, maybe sixteen feet, Fred Bear up and hit it smack in the brain. One arrow. Thunk! Like lightning.

"We hung the snake on a tree and had just finished the blind when Luis said: '*Pôrra, olha, patrão!* God Almighty, look!'

"I looked up and, unbelievably, here came two huge male lions sauntering along with the assuredness of their great power. Afraid of nothing, they were at a full trot, their nostrils catching the waft of wildebeest supper. We all sat and waited for a few minutes and they were on the bait like they hadn't eaten in a month!

"They were both excellent, but Bear shot the better lion. It came for that blind like a shot. It probably didn't know *we* were there or it wouldn't have been there in the first place. Anyway, the bush tended to smother the sound of the bowstring as Fred let off. I figured the lion would just head for the thickest stuff it could find, and knowing how Fred could shoot that bloody machine, it'd just lie down and die of blood loss.

"It couldn't really have been more than a couple of yards away when it sheered off. I had it cold in the sights of the .375, but Fred had impressed on me many times the fact that an animal shot with a rifle rather than with *just* an arrow didn't count, so I held my fire until the last instant, when the lion swerved. Boy, I was *sure* I'd have to take that bastard. Its companion ran around the back of the blind, so I decided to wait and just see what would happen.

"There was no way to tell if the first one was dead but it seemed to be a spot-on arrow. Arrows kill by hemorrhage, of course, and that can take a bit of time.

"We waited until just dusk, the sun dropping like a fresh forging. The second lion, however, was getting mightily stroppy by this time, and was wandering around the blind a few feet away from us, roaring at the top of its lungs. He had *very* good lungs. It was now dark and we had no idea where the damned other lion was.

"So we just had to sit and wait. Then we heard the second lion eating. I said, 'Hell, Fred, I sure hope he isn't eating the one you killed.'

"'I hope not too, but if you think I'm going out into that ink to look, you're out of your mind. . . .'

"After some considerable time had passed and the second lion wouldn't leave, I fired a shot into the air to try and scare it off, but that must have sounded like a dinner bell. If anything, the bugger sounded more determined to break into the blind and get us. My God! What growls and carryings-on! Our trackers were scared to death; all of them suggested we climb trees but I gave them a severe warning that we had one very bad lion out there which would have us all before we could possibly make it to suitable trees, let alone up them, in the dark. I wasn't lying either.

"Totally dark, with constant roaring from mere feet away—that was the scene. Desperate, I then made a decision to dash for it in a group, all of us huddled close together. We made it, but I don't know how. The lion was no more than a few yards from us, with night on its side. I was terrified we'd be mauled *en masse,* or that—nightmare of all hunting pros—my distinguished client would die on me. And don't think such tragedies don't happen.

"Well, we came back in the morning and the first thing we saw was that the big python Fred had killed was what the second lion had been eating. We then followed the blood spoor of the arrow from the first one and found it a ways away, as cold as a tinned pilchard."

Wally always preferred American clients to others, as he explains here:

"Many Europeans were fantastic people and I certainly do not mean to slight them as safari clients, but, *very* generally speaking, Americans seemed to listen to you better, maybe because there wasn't the language barrier one often had with European clients. I also found that Americans are far less hidebound by traditions and are more adaptable in the field.

"To give you just a couple of examples of adaptability or the lack there of!

"On one particular occasion, I had a northern European out on safari and he asked me when we would be going out the next day.

"'Oh, seven or seven-thirty. Somewhere around there.'

"'What do you mean?' asked the man.

"'That's when we find it best at this time of year. Light and all that.'

"'But in my country, we *always* go at four A.M. sharp, so that's when we had better go.'

Wally stoked his pipe.

"'So what are we going to do for two hours before first light? There's game all around this camp. We don't have far to go.'"

Things started to turn nasty. A professional hunter is the equal of a duke on the hunter's turf and what he says goes. But this client reckoned he was a law unto himself and said, "Now look here, I'm paying *for this safari and we will hunt the way I want to hunt, the way I am* used *to hunting."*

Wally replied, "Okay, if you want to go at four A.M.*, I'll go."*

"'Very good. I'll wake you up and we're going to go.'"

Sure enough, the autocratic European shook Wally to sensibility. But Wally wasn't finished with this idiocy.

"We got all settled in the car in the dead blackness of that chill morning, this guy in full European hunting regalia, replete with a chamois beard in his *jäger* hat. He looked ridiculous. Off we went. I drove some three to four hundred yards from camp and stopped, shutting off the engine. I lay back for a snooze.

"'What are you doing?'" asked the client.

"'Ah, I'm just going to sleep a few more hours as I'm waiting for daylight,' said Wally. 'What's the point? We can't hunt at night, it's illegal and unethical. So, whatever you get up to in your country doesn't help here. This is Africa. Hang on until half past six and we'll start. What the hell, have a snooze.'

"That guy never again insisted on going out at four in the morning.

"I had another client from the same country who would also pull the same stunt, but by the time I had come to a stop just beyond camp, he'd be sound asleep. Even after daylight came, I would have to wake him when I spotted game. Hopeless."

Wally was exceedingly fortunate to have had very few accidents while he was a pro hunter, but nevertheless acts of God do happen.

One such example concerned an American and his wife at Camp Ruark. There was also another couple in the party, who were there as guests and to enjoy photographing wildlife. The party had been hunting four or five days when something crazy occurred.

One evening, just after dinner, everybody decided they were whipped and would go to bed. There were four tents, two big ones for the two pairs of clients, a small one for Wally, and another little tent for stores and equipment.

Not long after everybody had sacked, one hell of a storm came up, typical of the extremely violent cloudbursts one finds in the African bush. There was tremendous, deafening thunder, lightning like the Fourth of July, and scary gusts of a sword-edged wind.

Wally rolled out into the elements, instantly being soaked to the skin. So did the photographer husband when he heard Wally trying to save his tent, which the water had underwashed. Both were hanging on to it when there was a terrific crash, like a multiple freeway pile-up.

The tents were all under big trees for the shade, and a branch of a fig tree, weighing fully a ton, had ripped off in the wind, falling like a gigantic jagged javelin smack through the hunting clients' tent!

"My God," said Wally to the photographer, "they must be dead!" He shouted and got no reply, which seemed to confirm his dark suspicions.

He couldn't find the zipper of the tent in the dark, so he grabbed his knife and cut the tent open, expecting the worst.

Wally was astonished to find the couple in the wife's bed, both snoring like hippos. Two feet away, two thousand pounds of hardwood had driven itself through the canvas and exactly through the center of the husband's bed, and neither *of them had even noticed! "Hell," said Wally, "they didn't even know it was raining!"*

Actually, before he fell asleep, the husband had realized that it was *raining, as there was a tiny rent in the canvas just above his bed. That little hole saved his life. The odd drip came through and struck him in the face, so he simply moved to the double bed in which his wife was sleeping. His had been—definitely past tense—a single bed, but, half-asleep, he had swung himself out and had transferred.*

Well, when the bell tolls, it's not always a collect call for you, and the sheer luck of that incident seems to prove it.

"An interesting thing happened during another safari. The client wounded a magnificent buffalo and we lost it in the dusk. I said to this guy that we'd come back in the morning at first light and find the bastard.

"We were on the track as soon as dawn gave enough shadow to the hoof impressions for us to be able to see them. After half an hour, we bumped into a lion which looked as if it'd had a mighty hard night. Just ahead, we found an area that looked like ground zero at Hiroshima. All the bush was knocked down, with blood all over the place. Obviously, the lion had fought the buff and had tried to pull it down. We scouted around a bit and actually found another dead fully grown male lion which the buff had killed.

"Brother, but had it been killed. The hide was full of holes and cuts you could stick your leg into. It wasn't worth skinning out, as I was sure I could get the client a good lion later on in the safari. So we decided to keep on the spoor of the buff, which was like following a wine truck with a leak.

"After about an hour, one of the trackers—I think it was Luis—spotted a dark mass in the bush that looked like the buff.

"It was.

"At thirty yards, I told the client to shoot. He fired and it dropped. We found that it was the same buffalo but not exactly in the shape in which we'd left it the evening before. Man, was it a mess! It looked like it'd been through a reaping machine. Its hide was clawed to shreds and its neck badly bitten. But even with its bullet wound, those lions couldn't finish him. I suspect the battered lion we saw before discovering the buff quit early in the exercise but the other lion was more determined. Still, the horns were truly grand."

Wally's son, Walter, was once out with a client when they came across a pool of hippos. One does not fool around with hippos. They're exceedingly dangerous animals. But this man wanted some pictures, and he and Walter walked about sixty yards to get up close. The client got his photo all right!

As Wally says: "There was one big bull standing on the bank, and this man took photos for about fifteen minutes. He and my son then turned around to go back to the car when the beast instantly charged."

If you think a hippo isn't fast, you've never tried to beat one back to your rifle at the car. Wally described how the men ran like mad, Walter having to get around to the other side of the vehicle to grab his rifle. Before he could do so, the hippo actually took a bite that went right through the client's shirt!

"Fortunately, the doors of the car were open and Walter grabbed his .458 and actually shot the hippo *through* the cab! It fell at the client's feet.

"The really curious thing was that when the man went back to America, there was a photo of the inside of the hippo's mouth as well as part of the interior of the car's cab. The hippo had actually hit the camera's trip button and had taken its own picture at the moment Walter shot him."

That's taking self-portraiture a bit far.

So-called buck fever plays a large part in many safaris and accounts for a high percentage of missed chances. Wally tells a story of a grand elephant that was lost in the mid-1960s by a client he had. This man and his wife were with Wally on the Limpopo River, near the Kruger Park.

"I didn't think there were many tuskers over a hundred pounds a side left in that area, although it was an excellent concession for both buffalo and elephant. There was a lot of poaching there, but since it was good for buffalo too, I decided to give it a try. There was always the chance of a really big jumbo coming out of the park where we could take a legal crack at it.

"We had just killed a really fine buffalo and were on the way back to camp at about five-thirty P.M. About twenty miles from camp we took a bend in the bush track when I saw the back end of an elephant. It turned its head and showed dream ivory—way, way over a hundred pounds per side. I stopped the car and this brute started walking right up the track.

"We bailed out and got within twenty yards of this huge chap, the wife on top of the vehicle, taking pictures the whole time. As we came to ten yards, he turned left, heading into quite a lot of trees and grass. I grabbed the client as it stopped in an open spot, directly ahead, a perfect side-brain shot, broadside on. One of the best setups I'd seen in all my elephant days.

"'Okay,' I whispered, 'stick it in his ear hole.'

"This guy raises his rifle, safety off, round in the chamber. All set. Hell, it was a dream come true.

"But he wouldn't *fire!*

"'Shoot,' I hissed at him. 'Shoot, for Chrissakes! *Shoot!*'

"Nothing. I came close to killing the bastard I was so frustrated. This elephant was absolutely enormous. I just couldn't believe it. After ten times of telling him to fire but with no result, the elephant, for its own reasons, turned the *other* side to us, offering another perfect shot at ten yards.

"'Now! In that ear hole!' Christ! I'd walked tens of thousands of miles, elephant hunting, and I'd only seen a handful of elephants as good as that one. And this man just stood, staring at it!

"I then lost my temper: 'SHOOT!' I screamed. The old tusker was probably nearly deaf but it didn't miss that comment. It swapped ends and started batting away. So when does this fool decide to fire? Of course, at the arse at forty yards. I ran like bloody hell after it, his wife behind, still filming the whole thing.

"We followed for about three hundred yards, and, before all the saints in heaven, the bloody thing stopped. It not only stopped, it began *eating!* With a bullet up its butt! Having a wonderful time stripping branches, oblivious to us all!"

That's what is known as "hard-arsed" in the trade.

"Then this outstanding bull got our wind and was really off. I was sure the client had hit it, but now I started wondering. Although its behavior sure didn't show it, it had in fact been badly hit. Maybe it was just senile.

"I turned to this man, boiling. There's a limit to anybody's patience, and pro hunters are also human. 'Well,' I said. 'Do you understand what you've done, or what you should have done? It's getting dark now and we can't follow up anymore. At first light we'll be right back here, but I'll tell you now, I think you've blown it. Well and truly. And it was on a plate for you!'

"The drive back to camp was death. The atmosphere! And when we returned the next morning, at first light, we found that jumbo's spoor mixed in with a herd of about two hundred others. It was impossible to sort out the right set. We returned. I'll never forget that day. Neither will the client.

"I've never been able to figure out why he didn't fire when he had the chance of two lifetimes. Stage fright? Just dead scared? I'll never know. And there was no charge by the bull.

"But there's an interesting aftermath to this story. Two days later, a native came to my camp and told me of a man shooting a huge elephant. I got the details and found it was a Portuguese government official who had come up to that area hunting in a helicopter (damn his eyes, his soul, and may his unspeakables fall off into his soup) with a Portuguese 'professional.' They had spotted a tremendous and obviously wounded tusker in an open plain. So they downed the chopper, walked up to the elephant, and shot it. That kind of thing revolts me. I don't care if it's wolves being hounded by aircraft in Alaska or these butchers swooping down on wounded game in Africa—the revulsion is the same. I wish I hadn't been told the news.

"The elephant went 142 even per side.

"The client had the nerve to be all upset. I couldn't feel a thing for him and was glad when he left. To this day, the whole episode haunts me."

"I was in San Francisco some years ago and got a call from a young man who declared that he had but one aim in his hunting life and that was to kill a kudu. I asked him how much time he had and explained my fees. He said he could spare three or four days at the most.

"I tried to explain that the value of a decent kudu was directly related to the difficulty involved in collecting one and that that amount of time was cutting it pretty thin. Couldn't he give me a week? He might be out for that length of time and never even see a kudu, let alone a shootable one.

"'No,' he said, 'that's all I can manage.'

"'Well, if you insist, I'll take you, but don't be disappointed if you go home empty-handed.'

"'Hunting life?' Hell, when I got this chap into the concession I discovered to my total disbelief that he'd never fired a shot in his life! He knew absolutely nothing about firearms, so I not only had to get him a good kudu in four days, I also had to teach him how to shoot!

"The first day was literally shot as it took the whole time to get him to be able to hit a smallish cardboard box at fifty yards. Stalking would also be a nightmare. If he couldn't shoot, he wouldn't know anything about stalking, and to get within fifty yards of an old kudu is no easy trick.

"The second day we went out I was delighted to find a bunch of kudu and we got up to about sixty yards. He took a solid rest with one of my rifles and lined up an excellent bull. He missed him colder than last week's turkey.

"Over the next four days—he extended his trip to leave on

the morning of the sixth day—he fired at a total of twelve kudu bulls! Great God! They were practically hanging out of the trees! And never cut a hair.

"At lunch on the last hunting day, he asked me if I would shoot a kudu for him. I said, 'Hey, you said you've been dreaming of a kudu, right? If I shoot it and you hang it on your wall, every time you pass it you'll know who really killed it. It's no good. What value will it have for you? If you miss again, so you do, but you'll be an honest man. No. I won't do it.'

"We were now coming to the end of the last day, the grass splashed with gilt as bright as the empty cartridge cases he'd spent in three more tries. Nothing. We were on our way back to camp, not five hundred yards to go, when he missed the last kudu. I was certain he would have to do without his kudu. By God, a hundred yards from camp we spotted a very good bull with a bunch of cows."

"'Shoot it! Please!' said this chap.

"'No way. You will.'

"'I can't!'

"'The hell you can't. Now just calm down. Remember what I taught you. Don't jerk your finger. Just put your sights on the shoulder and squeeze slowly. Don't get excited. Now, go and kill him.'

"Hell, he was all nerves and knew it would be the last one he'd probably ever see. He squeezed off slowly and hit it dead-square. I heard the horns banging the ground as it tried to get up, but I knew it was down and out. 'Come on, man. Finish him off. He's *your* kudu.'

"'My God!' he said in awe, when we got up to a damned fine bull. 'My dream has been fulfilled at the last second!'

"'Pretty poetic, I must say, but how would you have felt if I'd shot it? See what I mean now?'

"Ah, well, he went away a very happy man. Some months later he wrote to me, saying that he was indeed pleased that I had refused to shoot his kudu for him, as it would never have the value it now had for him."

"Funny, some of the people who come out. I was starting up in Botswana, doing a few safaris there as well as in Mozambique in the late sixties. Little did I know at the time it would become my future home.

"I received a letter from an Austrian lady who said that she had already hunted South-West Africa and had taken a nice kudu and gemsbok. Now she wanted to take a lion and some other species. I referred the letter to the manager of Safari South—for whom I was working at the time—and, after a while this gal pitched up.

"I don't recall who was assigned to her as a pro, but the first stipulation she made was that in bagging her lion, it *had to be charging.*

"'It *must* be charging,' she told the professional and the manager.

"The pro heard this. So did his wife. . . ."

"'And how are we supposed to manage this?' he asked. 'It may not charge, and in any case, it's dangerous as hell.'

"'*Was macht das schon!* So what! That is the only way I will take a lion.'

"The pro and his wife talked it over and decided absolutely not. He wasn't going to take the chance of provoking a lion for the whim of some Austrian stranger with very odd ideas. The manager asked if I'd take the lady out, and as I was free, I agreed.

"One charging lion, please. Coming up.

"The first day out we'd made a small camp. Strangely enough, I looked up and there was a lion broadside on, not more than seventy yards away. The bastard was looking at us.

"'There's your lion!' I knew that with a chance like that, she'd kill it as I'd watched her zero in her rifle. She was good. She pegged the lion a good one. It jumped up into the air and was off.

"Oh me, oh my, thought I. My men were looking in one place as there was blood. I was looking in another and the client was looking at me. Suddenly, there was a terrific roar, right behind me. We had walked past it, within three yards!

"The bush was thicker than your mustache there. Thank God, the bloody thing ran away. It would certainly have had one of us from that range. I said, 'Okay, let's follow him.'

"We started on the blood again and saw that the lion was

losing quite a bit. This was bound to slow it up somewhat. But we tracked a long way, my tracker, Benai, leading, the client next, and me covering her.

"All of a sudden her rifle went off and the bullet hit the ground right in front of the trackers, who were not overly pleased with the incident.

"'I cannot understand zis!' said she. 'I had two zafety locks on!'

"'I suggest, madam, that you empty the chamber and load from the magazine if you get a shot. It takes less than one second.'

"She was white with apprehension as she obeyed. She was literally shaking with pure fright at what she'd almost done, but, as I said, she was quite a mean hand with a rifle and seemed to know what she was doing. But the pressure and concentration of stalking a wounded lion are tremendous.

"Despite the blood, we carried on until dusk, then having to give up for that day. We made a fly camp with no tents and slept on blankets on the spoor.

"At first light we picked up the trail again. Man, we saw a hell of a lot of the Okavango Swamps firsthand, often up to our waists. One hell of a job of tracking my men did to follow that lion through such deep water, too.

"The next day, the third since she'd wounded it, we found a small buffalo the lion had killed, so I reckoned it wasn't as badly wounded as I had hoped. It heard us and we heard it thrashing off. We couldn't see it but we could clearly hear it splashing through the water, but my men figured it had gotten onto a small island, one of the many abounding in the Swamps. The fourth day was a blank.

"The fifth day on the spoor was the jackpot. Four aces. I really must say how remarkable this woman was. We'd been out for five full days; no tent, no booze, no tinned bully beef. And heaven knows what would sting or bite your behind when you went back of a bush for a call or whatever, swamp water up to your waist half the time. But she kept up and some.

"She really wanted that lion. Charging.

"We were determined to get this bastard. Still, I had to keep in mind that it couldn't be badly wounded if it had killed a small buffalo and had carried on the way it had. We had seen at least a dozen other lions, nothing as good as this chap, but to spend five bloody days fly-camping on the spoor of a wounded lion really accentuates the true sense of responsibility of the genuine sport hunter. My client was going to have *that* lion or join a Bushman tribe.

"We were pushing through the scrub bush and one of the trackers just pointed off to the right. Not fifty yards away was that damned thing. Lying and looking at us. The client was right next to me, so I just whispered to her, 'Shoot! Just shoot!'

"She lifted her rifle and took aim. Nothing happened. Of course, since nearly bagging a tracker, she'd had an empty chamber and had forgotten to jack in a round. I thought the lion would charge, because when we heard that sickening *click* of the empty chamber, it jumped up but ran off and out of sight.

"I told you this was *some* lady. We spent another three whole days at this routine, neither of us being prepared to give up. The lion pulled us back to the camp, so we did get some fresh food and such. We could clearly hear it, as it seemingly mocked us at night, roaring close to camp. The client and I had both come to the point where getting that lion was a matter of personal honor. If that son of a bitch had died of old age, we would have beaten the hyenas to its body. We were going to get him. Period.

"One night it was especially close, close enough to have us be very worried. I told the client I was sure that that was our lion. I said that we'd head in the direction of the roars and see if we could find it the next morning, as it was less than a mile from camp.

"We weren't very far out of camp when my head tracker pointed into a bush. There, with a lioness right next to him, was a big male. The tracker said he thought it was the one we were after, but I just couldn't tell for sure and was afraid to tell the client to shoot in case it was the wrong one. We'd spent too much sweat for *that* mistake.

"We crawled up as close as we could until the lioness became startled. But the lion was still lying down. She knew there was something wrong but couldn't quite put her paw on it. I had a really good look at him and told the client that I was now positive the male was indeed her lion and that she'd better shoot it. She took a crack at it and all leonine hell broke out. It started roaring and generally going bonkers. Then, before the client could get another shot off, it ran away. We followed at a dead run until we almost ran past the big male.

"I grabbed her and said, 'Come quickly. The damned thing is only five yards from us.' It was struggling on the ground, eyeing us. I screamed to her to get ready as it was now going to charge!

"It got to its feet and launched its charge, almost on top of us as it was. Cool as ice, the client shot it through the brain, killing it instantly.

"You've hardly seen such delight, she was so overjoyed. Then the client told me that she had wanted to be a member of some particular club back home and that among the membership requirements was that one had to have been charged by a lion. That was all this had been about! Can you believe it? Hell, she was such a dedicated, tough person that had she been obliged to walk barefoot backward up Everest to gain admittance, she'd have had a damn good try, I'll tell you that. There is hardly a male client I've ever had on safari who could have matched her tenacity and general ability.

"Well, she killed the lion before it got much into its charge, but I have no doubt she obtained her membership. The important thing is that nobody was hurt and that we finally caught up with the wounded lion, which was probably more tired of this rigmarole than I was. The client flew home delighted, having stuck it out in conditions that would have quite frankly daunted most men and landed several in the hospital with exhaustion, blisters, and exposure.

"But before I leave this phenomenal lady, let me tell you a bit about her skill at shooting buffalo.

"She was carrying a pipsqueak 7×57mm Mauser and had two buffalo licenses. I thought the rifle a bit light in the hands of an amateur.

"'Not to worry, Mr. Johnson. I've shot a lot of buffalo in Chad and Sudan. I see a buffalo and I just give it one shot. That's that.'

"'Well, you'll find the buff here quite a bit different. The ones you're used to shooting are a hell of a lot smaller. Our buffalo are a great deal bigger and tougher. But if you insist, we'll see what you can do. Still, I think a 7mm is mighty small for this business.'

"'Don't worry about that. I know just how to shoot a buffalo, Mr. Johnson. *Nur ein Schuss.* Just one shot. Always just one shot.'

"I was now worried. I thought she was just bragging, and a cocksure client can be a danger to everyone in the African bush. But we went out and found some buff and I pointed out a decent bull to her.

"'If I were you, I'd take either a heart or neck shot. He's broadside on.' She raised her rifle, squeezed off—and the damned thing went down in a heap! What a shot!

"'I told you that I always kill a buffalo with one shot, Mr. Johnson.'

"I just shook my head. She then decided that was rather fun and that she would like to go out the next day for her second buff. So, next morning, we went out, found buffalo, and singled out a good bull which was looking right at us. Before I could say anything, she took aim and dropped this one as dead as a can of spaghetti!

"I was astonished! If you don't hit a Cape buffalo exactly right, you'll have to put another five or six shots into the bugger. Hell, I've seen some people put in fourteen shots. And not with a dinky little 7mm either. Now that's shooting.

"'I keep telling you, Mr. Johnson, I always kill a buffalo with one shot. Do you believe me now?'

"I was a believer.

"I wish I had had more people like her out over the decades I spent hunting. She was a *real* hunter, and although she was in her fifties, she never said she was tired and she never gave in. She was really something for a woman alone and with her own ideas. A member of the European aristocracy, she was truly in a class by herself when it came to perseverance, skill, and bravery."

"As I mentioned earlier, you get the bum ones too. I had a couple out from Switzerland to hunt in the early seventies in Mozambique. We were hunting elephant, and the spoor of a good bull seemed to lead behind a termite heap which was quite tall. We couldn't see the elephant and it couldn't see us, so I wanted a good look at its ivory before deciding to okay a kill.

"We got to within twenty-five or thirty feet of the heap and I was just about to sneak around it when that damned elephant charged, full speed. It must have sensed or smelled us, because it really meant trouble.

"'Christ, man, *shoot!*' I yelled. The client did, with his wife, right behind us, filming the whole thing. She turned out to have a lot better nerves than did her husband.

"At his shot, absolutely nothing happened with the elephant. If anything, it picked up speed. It was almost on us and I thought to myself, hell, I'd better kill this thing before it's in our laps!

"I took a brain shot and dropped it no more than a couple of feet away, where it skidded to a halt in a huge cloud of dirt, blood pouring from its ears. I looked around, as the clouds of dust began to settle, but the guy was nowhere in sight. But his wife was still right there with the camera going. After a few minutes, when he was sure it was dead, this chap came rushing out of the bush, up to us and the jumbo.

"'I didn't run! I didn't run!'

"'I didn't say you ran,' I told him.

"'No. I saw all the men running away but I was with you all the time.'

"His wife was listening to this lot and said, 'What? What? You damned liar! Look here, when we get home, I've got all this on film. When we show it, then you can tell me you didn't run!' Then they started a terrible argument in Swiss German. Man, it got nasty. I just cut in and stopped the bickering, saying that they still had very good ivory to take home.

"We had a look at the elephant and you could see where I had given it the frontal brain shot. But when the men examined the body, there was no other bullet mark anywhere. I couldn't imagine how the client had completely missed it at only a few yards. Then one of the trackers discovered where the bullet was—right between two of its front toes! No wonder the bull was literally, hopping mad.

"On departing, the wife turned to me and said, 'Wait until you come to Switzerland. You'll be able to see the film.'

"I never went to Switzerland, but you can bet your life that that film somehow found its way into a Swiss fireplace in a hell of a hurry upon the couple's return."

Wally has been host to many hundreds of safari clients over the years—from medical doctors and business tycoons to family groups and loners—each with a unique story of African hunting. A book twice this size would be needed to do justice to the many fine people Wally got to know on safari, and with whom he has remained in touch to this day.

Now for the Africans. . . .

9

AFRICANS

Before Wally starts on one of his favorite subjects, the rural Africans—a group of which he considers himself a member—let me, as his chronicler, offer a quick capsule of his qualifications to make the observations that follow.

Wally arrived in Africa as a baby, having been born aboard ship from Australia. Later he arrived in Lourenço Marques at fourteen. It was not long that he was out in the bush, learning to hunt in the company of skilled African trackers and tribesmen. After nearly five decades, first as a professional ivory hunter and then as a safari operator of note when unrestricted elephant hunting closed down in Mozambique, Wally has known and lived among the rural Africans more so than among fellow whites. He speaks fluent Portuguese and Fanagalo, as well as being able to make his way without a paddle in Shangaan and a number of other Mozambican dialects. He has lived for nearly a year at a time in the bush without seeing another human of his pigmentation.

Wally is *an African, and has a passport to prove it. And he has been for nearly three-quarters of a century.*

After having taken some thirteen hundred bull elephants as a commercial ivory hunter and having been a gold miner, farmer, prospector, and general entrepreneur, Wally entered the new field of sport safaris with Baron Werner von Alvensleben in Mozambique. Wally was recruited and made south from his home in Vila de Manica to help set things up for the new company, Safarilandia.

Wow! What a difference in life-style! Now, after years of hardship, he was in heaven in his beloved bush. No more half-starvation, polluted water, and sleeping on the ground. No more fending for yourself and battling with all kinds of problems with no backup.

"It was so different from the ivory-hunting days," Wally said. "Everything was laid on for you. Never had to bother about ordering food or equipment, as everything was handled by the head office. You didn't have to worry about paying the staff, there was no need to struggle for clients, the food and drink were great, and there were comfortable beds with clean linen as well as hot-water showers. It was like going to a bloody hotel for me. There was even somebody to look after your safari car! You just hunted around with clients for different species, and we had slathers of game. It sure was a different life from the one I had endured.

"All the camps, before Camp Ruark was built on the Save River, were of the 'fly' type in the early days. They were erected wherever there happened to be plenty of game in the concession Werner held. Despite their temporary nature, they were damn well run and comfortable."

Wally must have liked it as he stayed with the Baron from 1959 until 1970, when he got a crack at some top concessions and left to start his own safari operation. He began to understand what the Baron had gone through in setting up Safarilandia *as he now had to provide everything from food and refrigerators to vehicles and staff. But Wally had a solid core of loyal clients from past years who kept coming back. He also had his staff of outstanding Africans whom he took with him.*

"I always enjoyed the Africans," Wally told me with Lew and Dale Games on the Mupamadzi of Zambia. "I learned so much from them—and, especially *about* them. It's fascinating what a culture gap there is between our worlds, but we always got on extremely well. In fact, I owe my life to a few of them, and they to me. I had the advantage of being comfortable in another culture too, so I had a better perspective of what made up the world of the rural African of Mozambique, and, indeed, of Botswana and other places, like the Central African Republic, where I have hunted.

"But sometimes the difference in cultures was impossible to fathom. They weren't lesser people, of course—just different from their white fellow countrymen when it came to way of life and values. Much in the way that a Japanese businessman differs from a Finn in how he views the world and what he considers important.

"A good example was my head gunbearer and tracker, Luis, whom I probably knew better than any man on earth. He was also the same man who refused to come with me to save my life after I had been bitten by the Gaboon viper. He just saw that bite in a very different light than I did. He was very loyal, but there are some things beyond my understanding in terms of bush logic.

"Let me give you a few illustrations of what a non-rural African—American or Swede, for example—would consider odd logic, although such behavior makes sense to the bush black.

"One day my wife came to me and said that Luis had been working really hard in the off-safari season and that he deserved a raise in salary. I agreed with her and spoke to Luis, saying that he would now get several pounds more a month, as he'd been doing such a good job. He just shrugged and walked off, actually leaving my employ without a word of warning after years and years together.

"After a few days, I asked one of the other men what had happened to him."

"'Oh, Baas, didn't he tell you? He's gone to work in Rhodesia at that sawmill.'

"I was floored! I give him a raise and he quits! After twenty years!

"I got in my car and drove over the border to the sawmill, where I spoke to the head and explained the problem. He told me Luis' salary, which was less than one third of what he'd earned from me! Figure that one out! I asked him if I could speak with Luis and, provided Luis wanted to, if my companion of so many years could be released. The head of the sawmill agreed, as there was an abundance of labor.

"It turned out that the problem was, again, bush logic. If I had decided to pay him more money, said Luis, that meant he was worth more than he'd been paid the previous years. So, as mad as a snake, he wanted to know why he hadn't gotten this salary twenty years ago, when I first hired him.

"It took me hours to talk him back, but he never saw that working for a third of his usual wages wasn't pure logic. Hell, he had never even come to tell me that he was unhappy, and I was known as an employer everyone could approach to discuss anything that was troubling him.

"In any case, he did return with me and resumed his duties. He was by no means a particularly strange bird among the Shangaans or other tribes, as I shall amply demonstrate later. Their thinking was different and that was all there was to it. Luis did suffer a great tragedy later in his life, though, and it certainly affected me.

"Many times, he would come to me in the off-season, and, if we weren't hunting, request permission to visit his family in a place called Cheline, near the Mozambique Channel port of Vilanculos, some distance to the south. Invariably, I'd tell him it was fine. He'd normally ask a few months ahead and I would give him his money and a bonus. He'd take the train, try to make the best connection, and then walk the rest of the way.

"The last time he had seen his family was some eight months before this incident. I asked Luis several times if he didn't want to go home. No, he reckoned, not now. I asked him why not. He wouldn't say.

"'I'll go a little bit later,' he told me.

"A month later I asked him again if he was going and he said that he was, but he didn't. I was hunting again after another month and Luis asked me where I was going. I told him I was off to the Save River and he asked if I would drop him off at a place called Nova Mambone, which was one hell of a long walk. I figured there were usually elephant near the Save River, so off we went, with the rest of the crew, as I'd have to do without Luis on this trip. I agreed to take him to Nova Mambone rather than go directly to the hunting area I had in mind.

"There were some villages thirty or forty miles from Luis' home and everybody knew him. Nearer his home, we stopped at a village where we ate and rested. Cheline was now within walking distance. While there, a really mean-looking old crone called Luis aside, saying that she wanted to talk to him. She took him aside, sat him on the ground, and they spoke for half an hour. I had no idea what was up. Luis finally rose, looking very sad.

"'What's the matter?' I asked. No answer.

"Then Luis told me that he wanted to leave. One of my other men asked him what was wrong and Luis told him that his entire family, consisting of his mother, two sisters, and heaven knows how many nieces and nephews, had been dying of starvation during a terrible drought that was still not quite over in the region. The family had waited for Luis to return and somehow help them, but he had not shown at the usual time of year he had always visited them. They just lost hope, hanging themselves. And there I was, asking why he didn't want to go home for an extended holiday during our slack period.

"I suggested we visit his home but he told me he never wanted to see the place again. As we left that village, we passed a shallow *pan* or pond with a sandy bottom. Luis said to me, 'Carry on. I just want to do something.'

"I watched him sitting at the water's edge, looking at his face as if it were a mirror. I watched him for a long time as he just sat there crying. Then he got up, walked to the car and simply said, 'I never want to see this place again.'

"He never spoke another word of the tragedy and couldn't be drawn out over it by anyone. How do you explain such behavior as his not going home when he must have known of the drought in his home area? It was the first time he'd ever changed his holiday routine.

"Tell you what I think: He knew they were dead. How he knew this, I have no idea, except, after all these years among tribesmen, I recognize that they are capable of premonitions far beyond our reckoning. Luis was an apprentice witch doctor, for the record, and was held in some esteem by the other men on my staff. As I'll tell you shortly, the role of black magic in rural and even urban black African society is not to be dismissed. And if you call it pure trash, you haven't spent seventy-four years in Africa.

"Luis was with me through thick and thin, mostly rather skinny, for a straight twenty-five years. One day, he was gone. No good-byes, nothing. Gone. The others wouldn't divulge what had happened, so I just bided my time, eventually finding out months later that he'd gone to work for another safari operator. I felt very hurt. I thought we had been friends after all we'd been through together. I was a just employer and tried to be decent to all. Well, he just walked out and I never saw him again. That behavior is not uncommon."

"Africa really is a place of the unexpected. Weird things happen and one meets some exceedingly strange people.

"I was out professionally hunting for ivory in a new area once, and was asking the locals about the elephant in their district. Now this was a remote place and, as is custom, they referred me to the head chief of the district. It would have been rude for them to give such information on their own. There could have been a jumbo standing under the next tree and they wouldn't have told me. Breach of etiquette. Those chiefs ruled with an iron fist, I tell you. Something Westerners seem incapable of accepting is that the black man, especially the rural black man, does not come from a democratic tradition. The chief is the law. There is no such thing as a free-for-all by any tribesman, and opposition to the chief is not tolerated, not for a moment. Opposition is equated with enmity. Period. And misbehavior in terms of tribal law is swiftly and savagely dealt with.

"But let me get back to that day. Luis and I were taken to the chief's village to request his help in locating elephant, in return for meat for his people. It was an ordinary-enough village in appearance, but there was one especially nicely made hut that stood out from the other, shaggier dwellings. This one was neat as a knife.

"I saw a man sitting by a small fire and was surprised to see how much fatter he was than his brethren. I walked up to him, squatted down, and started asking him in Shangaan how he was and how his crops and cattle were doing. To come straight to the point would have been extremely rude. I would later get around to asking about elephant and request his cooperation. Not now. Black Africans have a different perception of the pace at which life should be lived. They are never in a hurry, hence the greeting rituals, the delays.

"Imagine my absolute astonishment when this huge man cut me short in accentless British English, asking, 'I *do* say, old chap, don't you speak English? I think we'll be more comfortable conversing in that tongue, what?'

"I thought I was dreaming a bad novel. Completely taken aback, the only thing I could say was that we certainly could chat in English, as my Shangaan was not remotely at the same level."

"How may I be of assistance?" the chief inquired. Wally didn't believe it. He explained the reason for his presence in the chief's area and requested his help in locating elephant.

"Oh, by all means. I'll get my men to gather some information for the nonce and then we shall see what transpires."

Wally was floored by the Oxfordian English and couldn't resist asking where the chief had learned it.

"London. I was there for some years. The Mission Society sent me there on scholarship to study medicine. I was rather a bright scholar, you know."

Wally asked him how he'd liked London.

"Oh, it was fine. A great country, but I'll tell you what happened. I was doing my housemanship, or what the Americans call the period an intern serves, and I was living in a rather pricey flat. Every morning I had to get up at half past six to catch a bus and then I would spend the day living by my watch. I was also mostly broke after I'd paid for everything, especially at month's end.

"One day, I began wondering how my aged parents were faring

back in Mozambique. I hadn't seen them for many years and was longing to visit. So I managed to save up some money and a couple of chums helped me out. I bought a ticket home to see my parents.

"I was so surprised to see the way they were living. Of course, I had left when I was young, but I had forgotten a great deal. Anyway, I stayed for a while and began wondering what I was doing, by Jove, in a place like London with its revolting climate, high cost of living, and very few fellow countrymen to whom I could, indeed, relate.

"Mr. Johnson, I never returned to complete my housemanship after the summer recess. Look at me! This *is the life, by gad! I belong here. I have four wives and can have more if I so wish, but I know women and four is enough. I am lord of this entire area and have all the people under me, as I am a hereditary chief. I don't do a stroke of work; I sit and drink beer all day and my wives also make all the palm wine I can possibly consume. They tend the cattle and goats, they nurture the crops, and give me children. I am living the perfect life, Mr. Johnson. I can hunt whenever I please and I am surrounded by friends and loyal fellow tribesmen. My word is law. You could give me all the British pounds in the world, I would never return to live in Britain, or anywhere else, for that matter. There, I was always cold, wet, and alienated as a doctor among a sea of whites in that dreadful city. Here, I am warm all the time and I am king. I am also nicely plump now, a mark of my prestige. Now what of a good cup of tea?"*

Wally was quite thunderstruck. He thought about what he'd just heard and said, "Man, you made the right decision!"

"This man was quite fantastic. After he had arranged for some guides to help us hunt elephant, we had tea on a proper silver service, do you mind, and when we went into his hut, *by God,* what do I see but a grand piano! A bloody Steinway! And he could play it well, giving a pretty good rendering of a Chopin piece, much to my delight.

"How he got a grand piano into the middle of the bush is quite beyond me, but he was that sort of exceptional man. Over the years we became close friends and stayed that way."

* * *

"There are many seemingly inexplicable facets concerning the outlook of the bush African as he relates to his fellows and his environment. His sense of humor is, in general, so different from that of the foreigner as to be beyond understanding. I have thought about this for a long time and have decided that it's just another way by another people of looking at the world. But there is a lack of compassion, a streak of cruelty in their humor that defies understanding. For a Westerner, Bob Ruark had an unusual degree of insight into the soul of the black African. After a few gins he would loosen up and tell of incidents where the sight of a creature's suffering or the misfortune of a fellow human being would arouse laughter and outright hilarity among the blacks.

"He once told me of his early experience of black Africans' humor where the sight of a man with his face or testicles or both bitten off by a hyena was the essence of humor to them. This was comedy in its purest form.

"I remember once coming around a bend in the road, near camp, and seeing a dead dog in the road. It had obviously been hit by a vehicle. The six or seven men I had with me broke up into uncontrollable laughter, so I asked them what was so funny.

"'We're laughing about that dead dog, Baas. Did you never see anything funnier in your life, *patrão?*'

"And the same day, on the edge of a small village, sure enough, there lay another dead dog. I thought these men would wet themselves. If a dead dog was funny, imagine the humor of two dead dogs. I never figured it out. Now, after all these years, I have stopped trying to fathom the Africans' sense of humor.

"Another time a client wounded a wart hog, and before he could shoot it and finish it off, Luis shouted to stop. He pulled his small hatchet and threw it, embedding it into the skull of the pig. These guys are damn handy with their little tomahawks. Anyway, the blade hit the pig right between the eyes and stuck, probably damaging the brain as the pig started running around in tight circles. My men were hysterical with laughter. I shot the pig straightaway to end its misery. I didn't think it was funny. Neither did the client. He wanted to belt the lot of them to shut them up.

"And in Botswana a rip-roaringly funny incident, by bush African standards, occurred one day when another wart hog was wounded. My head gunbearer, a Masarwa tribesman named Benai, pulled the same ax-throwing act, but he wasn't as good as Luis. The hog caught the ax in the head and immediately charged him, biting Benai's right kneecap clean off before I could shoot. The rest of the crew screamed with mirth at Benai's agony. *That* made their day!

"He was very clever, Benai. We got him to medical aid and somebody was able to stick the kneecap back in and graft it or whatever one does to replace kneecaps. Benai now qualified for one year's financial compensation from the Botswana Government. He had the most awful limp and mostly couldn't walk—except to the bank—for exactly 365 days. When the compensation ran out, he had a miraculous recovery and discovered that he could not only walk but run! That was in 1981 in the Okavango Swamps—a long, long way from any bank, by the way.

"By tradition, in rural Africa marriage is considered a business transaction. Also by tradition, the woman tills the soil, carries water, and is the bearer of numerous children, usually having one or more before tribal marriage arrangements to prove fertility. They're subservient to the menfolk, and wife-beating is condoned. I didn't like what I saw, so we'll leave it right there."

A most interesting angle on the bush African, as Wally and I discussed, is his perception of time. He lives on a completely different level from those of us who slave by the clock and whose lives in Western cities run on timetables, schedules, and deadlines. Many bush blacks probably have wristwatches now, but they serve more as symbols of consumer prestige than a vital part of daily life. I can well remember passing a young man on an isolated bush road in Zambia. He was waiting for the rattly old country bus to come by. Hours later, on passing the same spot again, I noticed the young man still in the same position, passively biding his time, scratching designs over and over in the dusty road with a twig. He had what looked like a bundle of food with him and something to drink. Despite the lack of company, he seemed unperturbed, contented—suspended, as it were. I have sometimes wondered that a touch of the bush African's patience and ability to wait uncomplainingly in circumstances where he hasn't a choice wouldn't be a good thing in our pressured existences, where looking idle is often interpreted as sloth, as lack of involvement, as failure to keep up, produce, excel, and rise. I wonder what the ulcer/hypertension rate is among rural blacks. Later, my old gunbearer, Silent, had a conversation with that young man. The fellow had been there three days! The bus service was erratic—often off by as much as a week. *How many of us could have handled that?*

Anyway, Wally and I swapped observations and he told me of the time when he and Baron Werner von Alvensleben were building the original camps in 1959.

"Although the camps were not permanent, we had the problem of furniture. We discussed the matter and decided that, with the beautiful hardwoods growing about, we'd be crazy to truck in new chairs, tables, and such from L.M. It was much more economical, we figured, to hire a good local woodworker to make the stuff we needed. So we got a local guy who'd been to a mission school and had learned carpentry. At least he said he had.

"We got him the lumber and bought a complete set of tools for him to use. We even got him an assistant and he swore he'd have the first chair ready in three days. We waited three days and there was no chair.

"In ten days, two legs of one chair were ready. After twenty-five, there still wasn't one completed chair. Turned out he was flying on high-octane local palm wine. We fired him and bought the stuff, as we were now running out of time. We ate the expense and realized that whatever the missions taught, they had not implanted our idea of time and keeping to agreements. We were careful not to engage in such arrangements ever again. They don't work.

"Now I don't think the bush African is purposely more cruel than anybody else, but he seems to be far less unthinking about somebody's pain, never mind the suffering of animals. The idea of pets, such as we know, was something I never encountered in all my years in the African bush. An animal had to have a function—food, a labor tool, a symbol of status, or, as with dogs, an aid in hunting. The idea of animals serving as objects of affection and companionship is alien. In any case, dogs, for example, eat meat, and meat of any cut is a valuable commodity in the rural African's life and diet. Hence the poaching.

"My son, Walter, had an experience that is not for the weak-stomached. He was driving along a bush track near Camp Ruark and saw a local coming along on a bicycle. On the back of the bike was a sack, tied to the carrier part behind the seat. Walter thought this guy was poaching meat, so he asked him what was in the sack.

"'Oh, it's just my little son in there,' said the Shangaan.

"'Your son??? In a sack??? What the bloody hell are you talking about?'

"'Well, he's sick and I'm taking him to your camp because I know you have medicine there.' We kept a dispensary there for simple injuries and illnesses.

"Walter asked what the problem was and the man said, '*Ndzilo.* Fire. He got burned.'

"Walter was horrified to open the sack and see a child of about seven whose whole arm was actually charred. When he got him out of the sack, he saw that the boy's chest was *moving!* Crawling maggots!

"'My God, what happened? When did this happen?'

"'Ummm, about a week ago,' said the tribesman.

"'Why the hell didn't you bring him sooner?'

"'Well, I thought I'd wait awhile because it didn't look like he would get better. Now I see he is still alive, so I am bringing him to you.'"

Walter told me, "Hell, this little chap had fallen into a campfire and was nearly burned to death, then he became badly infected. Luckily, we had an aircraft going to Beira, so we patched him up and sent him there. They had to amputate his arm, but they managed to save his life with antibiotics, which they still had in those days. The little chap was sent back after four months and we kept him at camp for the rest of the season so he could eat properly and receive some decent care afterward. His own father wasn't to be trusted. Man, talk about callous toward your own kids. But then, this guy figured he had plenty of them anyway and lots of women to make more."

"There was another purely horrifying case," Wally told me over a cold beer one twilight. "It was the early seventies when I walked into a Shangaan village and saw a small boy with his eye hanging out of the socket and down onto his cheek. Of course, his face was coated with pus and flies, but he was somehow smiling, although he must have been in a lot of pain.

"I thought, what the hell's this business, and had his father called out. The mother, being a mere woman, didn't count. Only the men could be consulted, especially by another man, an outsider.

"I asked the father what had happened.

"'A stick or something got in his eye and pulled it out. Two weeks ago.'

"'*Two weeks ago!!!*' I raised perdition with him and asked why he hadn't taken him to our dispensary at camp, why he hadn't taken his child for immediate help.

"'Ah, yes. My bicycle had a flat tire and I had nothing to fix it with.'

"'You take this boy right now to my camp. I will fix your bloody bike so you can leave right away. It's quite far, but it's also your son's eye. What's the matter with you, you swine?'

"Well, he just shrugged. I happened to return from my hunt past the same village a couple of weeks later and called to see how the little chap was. That poor little bugger was still there, the eye covered in flies and hanging down his cheek. He was still smiling. I grabbed the father and kicked his tail properly. I really lost my temper with that unfeeling bastard. I grabbed the boy, put him in the vehicle, and immediately drove back to camp. We could do nothing for him, so I flew him out at my own expense to Beira, where the eye had to be removed. I had asked the father why he had waited another two weeks when I had fixed his bicycle. He simply said he had been too busy. 'I just did not have the time.'

"After seventy-four years in Africa, I have learned that attitudes do not change easily, if at all. Dying is much more important in the bush African's life than the celebration of a birth. Only when somebody is beyond aid does anybody often bother to try to get the poor bloke help. Then it's usually too late, but the wakes are great reasons to get stoned for a couple of days. Life was very cheap in the bush. Today, it is even cheaper and death as common as a scorpion."

This is not a happy chapter, but Wally and Walter speak the truth as I have seen it myself. Africa is a very difficult place to live, but it is clear that although Wally and his son were bush-hardened professionals, they've never been anything but compassionate.

"I very much hope nobody thinks that I have been unfair or somehow degrading in what I have told you here. It's *not* meant that way. It's merely to point out that different parts of the world and different peoples are no more than that: different. If you speak of Africa, adapt or move. I adapted."

10

CUCHUCUCHU

This book would be incomplete without a reference to Wally's incredible experiences with the dark arts of Africa. They have influenced his life. What I knew as tagati *in other African countries where I have lived and hunted is known as* cuchucuchu *in Mozambique when one speaks of black magic, of witchcraft, of the supernatural. Pronounced "kush-kush," as in "cushion," this is a pure Mozambicanism of obscure origin. Appropriate when you think of the mystery enveloping the extremely strange occurrences in Wally Johnson's life in the bush. He will tell you of the powers of the* cuchucucheiro, *the witch doctor, in the rural Mozambique he knew, powers that defy any logical analysis.*

Of course, you may scoff. I used to, until I lived in Africa. It is only then that you begin to realize that things aren't quite so pristine and rational there as they appear to be in New York or Manchester.

Is there something to it? Well, after about twenty years in Africa, I would say that the answer is unquestionably affirmative. Far too much for coincidence or convenience. How does it work? Autosuggestion? I can tell you that if you tell a bush African that he's been "hexed" by someone with reputed powers in this domain, he'll lie down and actually die on you after three or four days. I have seen this happen twice. Of course, the potential victim can consult a rival witch doctor to remove the curse, and it usually works if the witch doctor enjoys a greater reputation than the one who placed the curse. I have seen some bloody strange things myself, and although I am college-educated in the United States, I simply can't explain them. They defy explanation.

Let's also remember the superstition, the stranglehold of one or other kind of belief that we see in so-called sophisticated industrialized nations like the States. Every society has such phenomena, but there is something about supernatural occurrences in the African bush that unnerves the outsider. And rightly so.

Wally tells of weird experiences related to, for example, his elephant hunting. . . .

"I was hunting one time down on the Save River and we cut the spoor of two big bulls. My God! We followed them for four days. Finally, one of my men came to me and said, 'Look, Baas. We must tie these elephant down.'

"'What the hell are you talking about? These elephant are moving. We'll have to walk like mad to catch them, even though they've gone in a circle and brought us near our camp.'

"'No,' the man said. 'Here's what we do. To tie them down is easy. Hey, Baas, we spent twelve hours walking yesterday, so let's not do it again today. We'll just tie them down and get them tomorrow.'

"'Now, what is this trash you're talking? Tie them down? Don't be a damned fool! How are you going to tie down two bull elephants?'

"'I'll show you, *patrão.*'

"'By all means. This I'd like to see.'

"'Well, you take your rifle, stamp the butt into the biggest track, scrape off the dirt, and tie it into a knot in your handkerchief. Tomorrow, we'll find those two bulls sleeping on an anthill. They will be so asleep we'll have to wake them up.'

"I thought it was damned funny, but, with the luck we'd been having, I reckoned it couldn't hurt. So I ground the butt of my .375 into the biggest track, having put some saliva onto the rubber pad, and I dropped the earth that came off into my handkerchief. I made a knot and put it in my breast pocket.

"'Okay,' said this guy—who was not one of my regulars, by the way—'now we have tied them down.'

"We tracked for two hours the next day, sort of half-heartedly after all this time on their trail, and, by God, all of a sudden the lead tracker stopped and pointed. It almost gave me a chill as I saw two big bulls asleep on an anthill, or termite heap, actually snoring! But as I came up, I saw a troop of baboons which I was afraid might scare the elephants, so we decided to sit down quietly until they had passed. One of the buggers came up to within ten feet of me but it never saw or winded me. But that baboon had some premonition and gave a screech of surprise.

"Both elephants stood up, wondering what in hell was going on. I dropped one on the spot and got a chest shot into the other. I ran after it and killed it within a hundred yards.

"The man who had arranged the 'tying down' came up to me and said, 'See, Baas, it's just like I told you. They were sound asleep and couldn't move.'

"Hell, I was astonished, as just what this man had said came true. The elephant were exactly as he said they would be. But that proved nothing about *cuchucuchu,* as it might have been raw coincidence."

I agreed with Wally in his original skepticism. This sort of thing is not readily accepted or believed, depending on the individual's exposure to the black arts. . . .

"Those, incidentally, were good elephants, one going seventy-five pounds a side and the other seventy. Man, if I could get results like that every time, I'd learn witch-doctoring myself," said Wally.

After years in Africa, one would only need the perception of a newt to start wondering just what it is that explains the inexplicable. To say that there is no genuine black magic in Africa simply indicates that you don't know the place very well. I have had many odd, even alarming experiences related to witch doctors and their powers but I'll keep those stories for a couple of years. I'd rather charge you a few bucks to hear them.

Wally and Werner von Alvensleben with the results of their poaching raid—bows and arrows.

Madica, a Shangaan witch doctor or chuchucucheiro of some repute.

Wally in the Central African Republic in 1979 with an unbelievably big tigerfish.

Wally with an incredible greater kudu.

Wally in one of the dugouts used to transport the broken-down Land Rover to the far side of the Save River.

Wally and Gerry Knight (the man who saved Wally's life when the buffalo had him down) with a kudu.

"Pushing" a herd of buff to see if there was anything worthwhile following up on foot. Game is not shot from a car.

Making do: a pontoon made from oil drums to get across the river.

The author, left, and Wally recording this book.

The Last Ivory Hunter.

* * *

"The 'tying down' of the elephants wasn't by any means the extent of my experiences with *cuchucuchu.* I remember two others related to hunting that were quite similar.

"I was at a small village called Nlazi and was asking about elephant. I was assured that the crops were being ravaged, and the chief pleaded with me to please shoot them. Most of these men had old muzzle-loaders and such, but the elephant were damned smart. Anyway, the chief came to me and said, 'Listen, *patrão,* to be sure we get elephant tomorrow, I'll pray to the gods and everything will come right.'

"'Well, that's very nice of you.'

"'No, I'll pray to our forefathers. I shall go to the tree.'

"In nearly every village, there was a piece of white cloth nailed to a prominent tree. Sometimes the cloth was colored, but it was usually white. It was known as the praying tree, where anybody needing advice or whatever went to speak with the forefathers. But you had to give an offering, so I immediately smelled a bucket of rodents. It didn't turn out that way, however.

"'Could you give me some of your tobacco?' asked the chief.

"'Sure,' I said. I gave him a couple of pipefuls. He asked me if I had any food, and I gave him some cornmeal. Then he asked for some spirits of any kind, and I figured, what the hell, and gave him a cup of the Portuguese red wine I used to carry on safari, the stuff in a big bottle wrapped in split cane.

"'Ah, yes, that is very good, *patrão,*' he told me. 'You will kill an elephant tomorrow and we will feast on the meat.'

"I knew of the custom of paying frequent homage to dead relatives, to the forefathers. I saw that in other African countries too. Well, as I was spreading out my groundsheet of canvas to sleep on, the chief came over. There had been chanting, and a lot of people were busy praying for us. There was a great clapping of hands to arouse the forefathers' attention. All the villagers were bowing and variously carrying on at quite a pace.

"The chief told me, 'Oh, yes, we prayed most effectively. The forefathers will keep an elephant for you.'

"'What do you mean when you say they will keep an elephant for me?'

"'Oh, it's no problem. I spoke with them and they spoke back. They will keep an elephant for you. It will be fast asleep. It cannot run away, as the forefathers told me so. You will find it when the sun is high.'

"I went to sleep on my canvas sheet, not having paid a lot of attention to all this business, and rose at first light to start tracking. At eleven-thirty that morning we came to a water hole where the bull we were tracking had had a drink and we did too.

"I figured it would take all day if we were lucky, but suddenly, my men froze! They had heard some noise I hadn't caught.

"Then I got it too. It sounded like the drone of an aircraft going overhead. The men looked at one another and Luis took off into the bush.

"He came back at a trot and said in a whisper, '*Vamos, vamos, patrão. O elefante está perto. Está dormir no chão.* Let's move it, Baas. The elephant is close by. It's asleep on the ground!'

"By God, if there wasn't a bull elephant lying dead asleep on the bloody ground not a hundred and fifty yards away! The trouble was that I didn't have a decent angle for a heart or brain shot. What the hell do I do now? I can remember thinking.

"We were now only twenty yards from the bull and I whispered to one of the men to throw a stick at the bull. He hit it and it lifted its head but then went right back to sleep. Can you believe such a scene!

"Then I had two men throw some *masalas,* the local bush oranges, at the jumbo. Hell, it picked up its head again, looked around, and went back to sleep again! Pretty potent, those forefathers!

"Finally, a guy hit it in the ear with one of those fruit and it got to its feet, whereupon I immediately dropped it. And that elephant too was a seventy-pounder. Everything came off exactly as predicted by the chief. You should have been in the village that night. The feasting, the dancing, the drums, the singing and shouting, the foot-stomping abandon of those people as they gorged on elephant meat. I'll never forget it. I felt like General Patton at the Battle of the Bulge. Bloody marvelous night!"

"You know, if something extremely strange occurs out in the bush for which you have no rational explanation, you can call it coincidence. But when odd occurrences recur, you begin to wonder. You start having second thoughts. You look at the beliefs of the bush blacks with a little more caution.

"I'm thinking, for example, of a recurrence of that praying-tree incident. Let me tell you about it.

"I had been walking for five days with Luis and a couple of other men, but, dammit, we never cut a fresh spoor. I stopped at every bush and tree, every village, and asked every black if they knew of elephant. '*E-e, tatana.*' 'No, sir.' The answer was always negative. In five days, I never saw a track that wasn't months old.

"I don't know, but it was well over a hundred miles through the thickest stuff you ever saw, and we never found anything worth following. It was the hot season, which, believe me, is not misnamed. We had a lot of rain, so tracks would have shown had they been there.

"We were near the Save River that fifth day. I asked Luis how far away the river actually was and he said it was somewhere between a mile and maybe half again. I remember looking at my wristwatch and saw it was half past two in the afternoon when we bumped into a little village Luis knew and where they knew him. Hell, you could smelt copper in the sun. We made camp across the Save. And I bought a watermelon from the tribesmen. There was nothing I recall being more delicious, as I was parched.

"I was sitting there, eating this great thing when Luis came up to me and said, 'Hey, Baas, the chief says that if you'll give him some tobacco and some mealiemeal, he'll pray for you and you'll positively get a good elephant.'

"I remembered the previous incident with the praying and put it down to pure coincidence. But I figured that I couldn't do any worse by having another try. 'Luis,' I said, 'I think all this chief wants is some tobacco and food. That's all he's after, isn't it? He can't help us find elephant.'

"'No, *patrão,* he wants elephant meat. He'll talk to the praying tree.'

"'Hell, man, we've been walking hard for five days now. There are no bloody elephant here at this time. There just aren't any. Have you seen a fresh track anywhere? Of course not. And now you tell me the chief's prayers will bring me an elephant? That's ridiculous!'

"'Well, Baas, you never know. Some of these men have powers, which I am starting to learn. Anyway, what do you have to lose by it? A little *fole* and *mugayo.* Some tobacco and mealiemeal. That's all, Baas.'

"I figured the hell with it and gave him what he asked for. At least with this chief, there was no booze involved. He took the tobacco and ground corn down to the sacred tree and hung it from the branches, a bit different from the other routine. He then called up about fifteen women and five men, who all squatted or hunkered around the chief. I spoke the language and their chief was telling the tree that the white man, the *mulungu,* had come and he wanted to kill an elephant. He continued with the tree: 'You know the elephant have been attacking our farms and we have been dying of hunger in the past. So we beg you to give this white man an elephant so we may avenge ourselves of these animals. They're always coming here, eating our crops and killing our people.'

"As he was sort of chanting this, all the other people were clapping their hands and chanting *avuma* in agreement. After half an hour of talking to the tree, the ceremony broke up and I asked Luis what would now happen.

"'He's gone to get a man to show us a good elephant. He will go with us now.'

"'Now? Are you crazy? It's nearly dark! Where the hell are you going to find an elephant now when we've walked for five days looking for one and not even seeing fairly fresh spoor?'

"'I don't know, Baas, but the chief's man will find one. He is very powerful in these matters.'

"I saw the chief call over one of these men and tell him to go and find me an elephant. African conversation is hardly soft. The man said to the chief, 'How can I find this white man an elephant when there aren't any here now?'

"'Just do what I tell you and go and find an elephant. A good bull.'

"I spoke with Luis and said that this was going far enough. We had combed the area. There were no elephants.

"'Baas,' he told me, 'listen to these people. Many times they've found elephant for us where there were none. Give them a chance.'

"'Well, Luis, maybe there's something in it. We haven't much time as we have to cross the river back to camp before it's dark. But we'll take a little walk with this guy, even if it's just around the village.'

"I practically fell over with astonishment when, without any tracking, just zigzagging through the bush, we almost walked into a big bull elephant. Oddly enough, it was also standing on a termite heap!

"I killed it with a brain shot and commented to Luis that this chief was pretty slick, that he had known all along that there was an elephant there and had sent the guide with us, although the man seemed as completely astonished as the rest of us. Luis spoke with him and was personally convinced that this man had absolutely no idea there was an elephant within a thousand miles.

"'Okay, Luis,' I said, 'let me make my point. Let's backtrack this elephant and see how long it's been hanging around.'

"We did. And it went a long way toward my belief in witchcraft. That bloody thing hadn't been there for twenty minutes. I just couldn't believe it. It just walked out of the bush, stood on that anthill for a few minutes, and I killed it!

"When I got back to the village, the chief asked me if I had killed a good bull. Still almost in shock, I told him I had.

"'Yes, I knew you would'" was all he said.

"Well, that's Africa for you. . . ."

"*Cuchucuchu* did not by any means extend just to hunting. I had many fascinating experiences in other spheres of African life that really, to this day, leave me baffled.

"One day, I had instance to speak quite casually with Luis about the coming rains and how heavy he thought they'd be.

"'No, *patrão,* they will be light this year. Not enough lightning eggs.'

"'Lightning eggs?'

"'Of course! The lightning from the year before lays eggs which bring the rain the next year. They are laid in the sand by the riverbank like the crocodiles. Have you never seen them in all your years, *patrão?*'

"'No, what are they?'

"Well, Luis told me that where you saw lightning strike the earth, you would find these so-called eggs. He told me that if there were only a few, a dry year would come.

"'Come, *patrão.* I have several in my *ntsonga* and will show them to you.' We went to his hut.

"He brought out two or three globules of fused quartz sand, most obviously melted by the lightning strikes. They were smooth and did rather look like odd-shaped eggs.

"'Oh, yes, if there are a lot of them, it will be very wet, but the lightning did not lay well this year. It will be dry.'

"My God, it was, too. A bad year. Scant rain, poor crops. I started thinking about this further and questioned Luis, as this whole *cuchucuchu* business had aroused my interest. Most obviously, when lightning would hit the riverbank, which was silica sand, it would melt it into these balls. I used to have some, but lost them in the 1975 revolution. All the locals believed that the lightning eggs caused the rain. In much the same way that a welding iron throws off small round balls of metal, so it is with the tremendous power of lightning. If you dig a bit into the riverbank where there has been a strike, you'll find these 'eggs.'

"The really weird thing about these eggs was that my men were invariably right about the rains, according to the number of eggs found!"

"Another very odd thing happened in the late 1930s, when I was out hunting with Harry Manners, my good friend and, at the time, my financial man in the tire-retreading business.

"Man, we'd walked all day before coming up on a small herd

of good bulls. We killed four and one of the locals said, 'Baas, you've done a thing that will cause something to happen.'

"'What are you talking about?'

"'You don't know? It's going to rain very, very hard. And soon.'

"'Oh, come on! There's a clear sky. It's the dry season. How can you say that?'

"'Ah, Baas, if you shoot four elephants, one after the other, on the same day, there's going to be one terrible storm!'

"Harry and I just laughed it off as the sky was pure blue, not a hint of a storm. We walked back to camp and settled down, finally having dinner. Then, out of nowhere, lightning started and it began to pour as I've rarely seen it, and Mozambique storms are nothing to fool with. In retrospect I wished I'd had this guy on hand when I had so much money into bananas and was flooded out three years in a row.

"Christ, the water was two feet high in the bloody tent! We had to put everything on the beds and the beds on stones to save our gear!

"The next morning, the trackers just laughed and said, 'Well, we told you it was true. You shoot four elephants and you get a big storm. The white man makes a mistake when he laughs at our magic and at our forefathers' power.'

"Well, maybe it's just one of their superstitions and huge coincidence combined. But their warning of a storm proved correct!"

"One of the truly inexplicable experiences I had with *cuchucuchu* involved a man I had working for me at my home in Vila de Manica. This guy had his life savings of forty pounds—no small amount—hidden somewhere, and he was robbed of the entire amount. I was off hunting at the time and he asked my wife if he could have permission to consult a witch doctor some sixty miles away, a man of great repute.

"Lilly gave him the okay and he went off on foot to this *cuchucucheiro.* He threw the bones, actually coming up with part of the thief's name, which my man recognized, and told him where the money was.

"'He has spent ten pounds on a cow but has buried the other thirty pounds not far from your hut. You will find it by a certain tree.' Which he then described.

"Sure as hell, it was there. Not only that, the thief had spent ten pounds on a cow. How could the witch doctor conceivably have known that? The thief was collared and spent some time on the inside looking out.

"How could a man sixty miles away immediately identify the thief and where the money had been buried? I don't know. But this is a tiny example of what the *cuchucucheiro* accomplishes. He is a feared man when it comes to the sniffing out of wrong-doers, the unraveling of crimes in the community. The consequences can be pretty drastic by our standards, but then we must not try to impose our values and ideas of justice on a totally alien culture and people where different norms prevail from start to finish. Maybe that's where some of the missions went wrong in the African bush."

"*Cuchucuchu* is, then, an integral part of life in Mozambique, and indeed, under one or another label, in many other black countries. It can get nasty, though. In several places where I have hunted, the work force would not show up until full light unless I picked them up at their villages. The reason? Fear of being skinned alive.

"There was an Arab ring reputed to be waylaying people and doing just that. Somehow, it seemed important that the victims be alive when skinned, but it was real enough. Whole districts lived in terror of this threat. The skins were then sold to various *muti* or black-magic dealers, and I have seen physical evidence of this nicety."

I, too, have gathered a great deal of information on this business and have spoken to hunters in, for example, Botswana, where they verify such ghoulish goings-on in the recent past.

"Other strange things occurred in Mozambique. Maybe they're not strictly part of *cuchucuchu,* but let's call them phenomena.

"Conversation with the locals often reveals very odd happenings. Once, I was about thirty miles from the Save River, hunting for ivory, and I'd picked up a couple of locals who knew that place well. I heard them in the back of the vehicle speaking of a big fire in their fathers' time, a fire that went on burning for a whole year. I turned and asked them what it was all about.

"'No, *Nyampandla* (my other African name, meaning "baldheaded"). We are speaking of what our fathers told us many years ago.'

"'Well, you were speaking of a great fire. What happened?'

"'*Ina*, yes, my father told me,' said one of the men, 'that there was a terrible noise one night and a fire that burned for a year. It was so bright nobody could stand to look at it! My father said this was a sign the forefathers were unhappy with them. It was a warning! The people were going to suffer and the cattle die.'

"'When did this happen?' I asked."

The bush African has little concept of the Gregorian calendar under which the whites run their affairs, so the man couldn't give a date. Wally worked out it was around the turn of the century, at the time of the rinderpest epidemic.

"'And where was this?'

"'Just over here. Not far. There's a great big hole in the earth. Come and we'll show you.'

"'Good Lord! There was a circular crater at least two hundred yards across, quite deep and cone-shaped. The bush had overgrown it, but it was still most recognizable. Apparently a meteorite of no small size!'

"I got a hold of an old safari client, Dave Dawson, of one of the major American oil companies, and asked him to have a look at this thing, as he knew about such matters. I never really followed it up—but what a whopper!"

Such events live on in the collective memory, largely on oral memory, of the tribal black, much as we tend to recall great tragedies such as the sinking of the Titanic, *and those few souls who survived. The bush black sets great store by omens and interprets natural occurrences according to his world and values, not according to the "learned" attitudes of outsiders from other cultures who do not fit in anyway.*

Wally had many narrow escapes from death during those long years in the African bush, and some of his escapes were the result of timely warnings and hunches from his black hunting companions. He escaped a fiery death in Nevada when an aircraft crashed in the Sierras because he had to rebook onto another flight as that one couldn't accommodate him at the last moment. How many other passengers had hunches that day? Cuchucuchu *in one or another form is sometimes seen in other parts of the world, but never so dramatically as in rural Africa, where it can truly be said to permeate life.*

Wally's men had all kinds of superstitions concerning the world in which they lived and the animals which shared it. Perhaps nothing scared them more than lions. They feared them out of various tribal beliefs, and they feared them out of raw experience. As the following chapter will reveal, these were not idle fears—and Wally was to share them all too frequently.

11

NGHALA

Wally made no bones about it. He told me that had he known right at the beginning what he now knows about lions—the much feared nghala *of the Shangaan people among whom he hunted most of his life—he would have stayed a shipping clerk!*

He and I swapped stories about Panthera leo, *and I constantly marveled at the fact that Wally survived so many lion hunts, using, as he did, only the suicidally light caliber he had in those early days.*

"I told you," Wally said, "that I had obtained a Winchester .30-30 lever action when I was quite young (about seventeen) from my brother-in-law, August Wood. So I decided to start hunting lions, and a pal joined me in one of my first experiences with them. We were in a camp, if you want to call it that, in a wild area northwest of Lourenço Marques. I don't recall its name, but I shall never forget what happened that first night out.

"We had shot a reedbuck, and as it was getting quite late by then, we decided to turn in on a canvas tarpaulin in our blankets. We had a couple of locals with us, mostly along for the meat, but also to help us with the finer points of tracking, general bushcraft, and skinning.

"Suddenly, one of them woke me. 'Hey, Baas, a big lion has just come and taken the reedbuck away.'

"'No,' I told him. "'Must have been a hyena.'

"'No, Baas. I saw the lion. I had a torch.'

"I grabbed mine . . . and there was the bastard, not twenty yards away! It was so close I got a fright, but I grabbed the old Winchester and the lion ran off into the blackness. It'd only pulled this reedbuck a few yards out of camp and was eating it, and it came back after about ten minutes to resume feeding. Before I could fire, everybody else did so first, and again the lion was off.

"Damned if it wasn't back in twenty minutes! Brazen as could be. There was a fusillade and somebody hit it in the leg, so I knew I would have my hands full come the morning.

"Dawn broke. Not fifty yards from the damned blankets, the wounded lion was lying in a depression. We found it and it charged. It took three shots to stop it. That was my first experience of lion, and, pal, I wanted to hunt nothing else!

"I used to go out every Saturday after work, leaving at midday, and I'd drive into the bush, often accompanied by friends. The pavement cafés in L.M., with their distinctly southern European atmosphere, the dusty streets, quaint trams, and horse-drawn carriages one still saw, held little charm for me. I wanted the wilds, the bush, the challenge of hunting. Even the comings and goings of a seaport left me cold. My ambition was to get out as soon as I could find a way to survive in the bush and hunt for a living. In the meantime, I acquired skills. And every weekend, I would return to L.M., often leaving a place called Nuanetsi in the late afternoon on Sunday, arriving back in time for work on Monday. I did this every weekend.

"Eventually, I expanded my weekend excursions into different areas, and ran across a farmer near the border with the Kruger Park in South Africa. He was unmentionably scared of lions, but he had a lot of cattle that were being taken and he was most upset, asking me if I wouldn't thin out the lion population for him. Well, I spent two nights with nothing but a hangover. But on the third night, the cattle were raising hell and so were the lions, roaring and growling as if they were under your armpit.

"I got into my car, and heaven help me if I didn't see and count ten of them in the headlights. To be perfectly honest, at that point I was completely inexperienced and had no idea which one to shoot with that old .30-30. But I did kill three before the rest buggered off. I wasn't about to follow them at night and decided to leave it for morning.

"The next day, I found one of the lions eaten by the others. This was a revelation to me; I had heard of such things but never seen them. I examined the other carcasses and tried to see where my shots had hit so effectively. I already understood that if your bullet placement was poor, you'd wind up with lost animals and impossible amounts of time spent in trying to recover them—a daunting task for an inexperienced tracker.

"When I returned the following weekend, I found that these cattle-killing lions had smartened up. If they killed a cow and had to leave it, they wouldn't return to the carcass but would often go on and kill another. Then they would drag it away as far as half a mile before starting to feed on it. Amazing.

"This particular night, after so much trouble, I decided to take my blanket and stake down the freshly killed cow's carcass so the lions couldn't carry it off. That is a night I shall never forget. I was still in my teens and very impressionable.

"I had a man with me, a local, and we both fell asleep after a whole day chasing these things through the bush with no joy. And then I felt this guy's horny hand on me, shaking me instantly awake. I could hear him whisper, 'Baas! Baas! *Leão!* Lion!'

"I grabbed the .30-30 and the flashlight and *Jesus!* A lion—a big male—wasn't one foot from the man's head! I was looking right into its bloody face! I could literally touch it, those terrible eyes gleaming in the light, and big, rasped red tongue slavering over its muzzle. Never did my mundane little job as shipping clerk in L.M., with the constant jangling of telephones and the mounds of paper infesting my cramped, dingy desk, seem so attractive as at that chilling moment. I was done for. My companion, for sure.

"Before I could shoot, the lion was gone and my companion got up. He was shivering as if frozen. It wasn't a cold night, but my knees were shaking and I then saw that the poor man was now going into shock. I was really afraid I might lose him through heart attack."

"'Please, please, Baas. Let's get up a tree! These lions want to eat us! They will come back tonight! Please!'

"He was correct. Well, we sat on those blankets the whole night with my rifle cradled in my arms. To get to a suitable tree meant moving a bit too far into the dark bush surrounding us—and we were afraid to twitch. Luckily I had a flask of brandy, which I shared with the poor man. He was in tears from shock and fear the whole night, although the brandy eventually steadied him a bit.

"In retrospect, I do believe those lions would have taken one or both of us, they were that brazen. I later learned that that area was notorious for man-eating."

"On later occasions, things got hairier, for sure, but I was steadily building good nerves and gaining more and more experience with lions.

"Anyway, I was out with Harry Manners when a *chefe de polícia,* a police chief, came to me and said that one of the locals had snared a cattle-killing lion, and would I please come along and dispatch it with my new .375.

"Of course I agreed, and Harry joined me. The two of us were becoming known for our effective hunting forays and were quite often approached like this. Well, we found this damned angry lion, the cable from his snare attached to a large log. We felt pretty secure, so we went in close and took some pictures with Harry's Number 2 Brownie Kodak camera.

"This animal was carrying on something ferocious. When we were less than seven yards from it, I figured it was high time to take the bloody pictures. Harry did, but, my God, suddenly the snare cable came off the log! The lion was already so angry at us, it was on us in a second. It doesn't take much time for a lion to cover seven paces.

"Christ! It took a swipe at Harry before I could fire, so quick was the whole thing, and it actually knocked Harry's pith helmet off with a stroke that would have removed his head, had it been a shade lower! At the same instant, I got a round off from the .375 from the hip at *less than one yard!* I wouldn't be here to tell you that story if I had been using a lighter rifle, like my old .30-30. It hit the lion in the brain and killed it instantly, and it fell on Harry. We were both considerably shaken."

"One of the most fascinating and humorous lion incidents happened to me and a good friend of mine, a Greek by the name of Kitsos Perros. He used to come out with me sometimes and was very fine company for a lonely ivory hunter.

"In the good old days, the boundaries of Kruger Park were unmarked. There was no fence, and you were never quite sure when you were, in fact, trespassing. We probably did quite a bit of hunting together in the park itself, but it's impossible to say.

"Perros had one flaming desire; to shoot lions. He suggested to me that we go out for a couple of weeks, but stipulated that he'd be damned if he was going to risk his life doing it. He had it all figured out. 'You can't see in the dark,' he said, 'but a lion can see you when you can't see him. Hey, you're going to be eaten. I'm going to shoot a lion, but you'll be surprised how I'm going to do it.'

"We went out a week later in quite a big truck, and boy, was it loaded. He had brought along a complete mattress and bedstead. I asked him what in hell this was, and he showed me that he'd had a steel ring welded to each corner of the frame. His idea was that he'd hoist himself up on a set of pulleys into a big tree about thirty feet over a bait. When the lion came, Perros would pop it.

"He asked me why I wouldn't come with him. I told him, hell no, and that his idea was suicide.

"The next day, we shot a zebra for bait, and Perros asked me if we could divide it between ourselves. I agreed, and we put half of the zebra under his tree, where a big branch stuck out. One of my men hooked up the pulleys, raising the bed, and I tied the knots tight. I also got one of my men to sit with him on the mattress. Talk about ready for a world war! Perros had a knife, an ax, a rifle, ammo, and a flashlight. I had decided to sleep on the ground about four hundred yards away.

"In those days, it was legal to shoot lions at night; not quite so simple as you would think today. Came darkness, we hoisted the Greek into his tree and tied the ropes around the base of it. There was a night wind and the fool bed was twisting fit to make you seasick. I was laughing to beat hell as I knew at that time of year there would be a wind all night long, and this Greek pal would never be able to shoot a lion from that platform.

"I had my men drag the other half of the zebra several hundred yards away where I was going to sleep. As I put my blankets on the ground, I heard lions in the distance. They were so far I didn't think they'd show up.

"I had dozed off, leaving Luis on watch, when, at about ten that night, a regular firefight erupted. There were shots going off all over. My men said, 'Hey, he's having a busy time, but none of those lions has come over to us. He's screaming and shouting—hear him? Must be all excited because he's shot a lion!'

"The shouting continued awhile, then stopped. We expected the lions, but nothing showed up, and I wasn't about to go wandering around through that stuff with a flashlight. When dawn came, we walked to the Greek's tree with the utmost caution; with all the shouting, we didn't know whether or not there was a wounded lion between him and us. What I didn't need for breakfast was a couple of wounded lions.

"I had one man ahead, whom I was covering. He was throwing sticks and clods of earth into the long grass in case of wounded lions. Then, from about forty yards, I saw the damned bed just above the bait and the ground, not more than a few feet! I reckoned that he must be taking pictures or something, but when the Greek saw us, he started screaming at me.

"'You did it on purpose!' shrieked Perros.

"What had happened was that during the night the knots I had tied had become slack because of the swinging in the wind and the pulley ropes had slid up the bark, dropping his bed platform to about six feet above the lion bait—of which he and the man effectively became part. So the shots had been simply to attract attention.

"All night long he had been frozen with fear that the

damned things would eat him. Probably would have, too. He had told the man with him to get down and rehoist the bed, but the guy was no idiot and flatly refused to wander around lion baits in the middle of the night.

"At last, after a few brandies, Perros calmed down. Thereafter, he would trust nobody to tie those ropes. He worked out a system to wedge the bed into a crotch of the tree where it would not swing in the wind. After many tries, Perros finally got a good male and gave up the game, much to my relief."

"This man Perros was quite a character. Previous to the bed incident, he had invited two South Africans, who were quite good shots, to join him for a lion hunt, although he'd never even seen one before. Sure enough, one day they bumped into a decent male. One of the men shot and the thing went for the long grass.

"It disappeared, and they were all afraid to follow it up. Perros, as the resident 'expert,' decided the thing to do was shoot a zebra, drag it around, and wait for night, when they'd all go back and have a look.

"The men had dinner, waited for dark, and went up to the zebra carcass. There was nothing feeding—as if a wounded lion would come to a bait immediately! On their way back to camp, the Greek turned on his flashlight . . . and saw eyes.

"'Shoot! Shoot!'

"Hell, all three opened up, but the eyes didn't waver.

"Perros and his pals found they were shooting up their own truck! The 'eyes' were the front reflectors. Fortunately, there was just one hole in the radiator and a few more in the mudguards. The men were able to patch the radiator, but until he started with me, this was the end of the Greek's night hunting."

"I killed something like thirty to forty lions with that .30-30, and now that the years have sifted by, I realize what a wonder it is that I'm still around to tell my tale. I didn't know at the time, being a kid, that I was most dangerously undergunned. You just can't use too much gun on a charging lion, as

Capstick will tell you—especially after his very close call in Botswana in 1985. You shouldn't use more gun than you can handle, but *enough,* as Bob Ruark wrote.

"In later years, I marveled that I survived as so often a lion would require six or eight .375s or .458s to stop a charge, unless you got lucky and hit the brain. The spine wasn't a good bet on a charging lion, because it gives you only a longitudinal shot, which is hard to make. The brain is low and is protected by the entire face. Use as much gun as you can handle with dangerous game, but don't ever forget that it's bullet *placement* that counts.

"Take the case of Ken Fubbs, my good friend and a professional hunter in Mozambique. Back when my mother died, I was called across the border into Rhodesia. I asked Ken if he would take over my clients and safari until I could make it back, and he agreed—much to his later regret.

"I was notified of my mother's death on the second day out on safari with a somewhat elderly client. I had to see to funeral arrangements and spent three days in Rhodesia before I could get back to the Save River. I took the cable pontoon to cross. On the pontoon, I asked these guys, who usually never volunteer any information, how things were going with Ken and my client.

"'*Patrão, muito mal.* Very bad, Baas.'

"'What's the matter?'

"'Oh, *Senhor* Ken was eaten by a lion.'

"'*What????*' I thought, oh, God! Then I remembered an incident I experienced in camp just the day before I had to leave for Rhodesia. I was sound asleep (I generally sleep with my tent wide open) and, oddly enough, I woke up just when my mother died, not knowing why.

"One yard away from my bed was a set of fresh lion tracks. It had most obviously looked inside and seen me sleeping, but had done nothing. I grabbed my torch and rifle and saw that there had been three or four other lions and lionesses lying just outside the tent. When I was getting up, the men said to me, 'Baas, you were lucky. Those lions were right next to where your bed is.'

"What horrified me was that, with the shock of hearing about my mother's death, I hadn't told Ken about this lot. Finally, the pontoon reached the other bank and I made my way to camp and asked what had happened. I was feeling just awful. I was afraid it was my fault that Ken Fubbs had been eaten.

"The first thing I asked Luis was whether they'd buried Ken or what.

"'No, *patrão;* he's not dead.'

"'Great God! I was told he had been eaten! How can he not be dead?'

"'Ah, well. The *senhor* is a little bit eaten. His arm and shoulder. But he lives. He is in hospital.'

"I finally found out what had happened to Ken from the men who were on the spot. It wasn't the same lions that had so recently visited me. Ken had taken the client and his wife out the day I left, and the husband had wounded a zebra which ran off into a very thick bunch of bush.

"Ken told Luis, who was there acting as his chief gunbearer and tracker, to take an extra rifle and go in to chase the zebra out so Ken could have a whack at it. To their astonishment, waiting outside the patch of bush were a lion and lioness. The lion had a nice mane indeed, and Ken told the client to take it. The client hit and it ran off, the accompanying female going in the opposite direction. Ken told the elderly man to stay put and he'd go in and sort matters out.

"Well, he walked and tracked for about an hour before he saw it, a hundred yards away. It saw Ken too. The animal crouched down, stiffened its tail, and came for Ken like a lightning bolt.

"Ken had a bolt-action .458 Winchester Magnum caliber, stuffed with 510-grain soft points. Over the five or so seconds the lion took to reach him, he actually shot it through the heart three times! The last shot was at five or six yards. It grabbed Ken by the shoulder, sunk its claws into his back and thighs, and forced him onto his back.

"Suddenly, the lion dropped dead from the effect of the three heart shots. Luis, who told me this, had been standing at Ken's side. He tried to get the lion off Ken, who was clearly badly hurt, but the jaws were locked in a death grip. He eventually had to use his ax handle to pry them open. Ken was a real mess and was bleeding very badly from the shoulder, back, legs, and especially from one arm. Luis had the good sense to rip off Ken's shirt and jam it into the wounds. Luis then raced back to the car and got the clients to drive back to Ken, whereupon they all returned to the main camp, and an aircraft was radioed in to airlift Ken to the hospital.

"This catastrophe happened the day before I returned. I asked Luis if we couldn't still skin out the lion as a trophy. Most happily, the lion was still in heavy bush and was okay. We skinned it out, and that's when I was astounded to see that Ken had hit it three times right through the heart, which was nonexistent. Tatters. I really don't know how it managed, but it sure took Ken Fubbs apart. Thank goodness he recovered. . . ."

"I never had another accident with lions and feel I wasn't to blame for Ken's accident. He was just unlucky and had an especially stroppy lion. But that didn't mean I didn't have some close calls and bad frights with lions.

"In the early 1970s, I had a strange thing happen with a client and his young son of about fifteen. The client was really hot to get a lion and I was ready to accommodate.

"Hell, we spent a week trying to find a good lion. One day, we came to a water hole in the late afternoon where a lion had just killed a sable antelope—no easy trick. We were in business! We quickly headed back to camp, got some blankets and stuff, and returned to sleep near the natural kill where the lion would return to feed.

"We put the blankets down about fifty feet from the kill—probably somewhat rash—and sacked in. The problem was the teenager. He was afraid to sleep on the outside of his father and me, so he nestled in the middle.

"Something, I don't know what, awoke me. It was brilliant moonlight, and the entire bush and water hole were silvered over. Then I realized with a shocking jolt that the kid wasn't there! I really didn't look around too much as I figured that I had probably been snoring and that the kid had moved to the far side of his father. But no sign of the youngster.

"Oh, man, I thought. Where is this little bugger? In the brilliant moonlight, I saw an indistinct white thing about twenty yards off and I wondered what the devil it was. I grabbed a flashlight and went to investigate, my rifle at the ready.

"Sure enough, it was the boy. He was lying on his blanket, not twenty feet from the kill!

"'What the hell is going on?' I yelled at him. 'My God, that's a lion kill right there, next to you! The lion could have returned and bloody well eaten you! Don't you realize where you are, you idiot? This is not Central Park. This is the African bush! Get up! Get back to where you were! And if you move again, I'll thump you! Move it!'

"'But you and my father snore so much, I couldn't sleep. I just had to get away,' said the kid.

"Well, I was awake before false dawn and heard feeding sounds on the sable. It was about five in the morning and I could just make out a beautiful big lion chowing down. I woke the father, placing my hand over his mouth. He decided that the boy should shoot this lion.

"That bloody kid flatly refused. I was, quite frankly, relieved, as that cocky little bastard couldn't kick his way out of a wet paper bag. He would have buggered it up, and I'd have had an angry lion with a bullet in its guts.

"In any case, the father shot it dead as international peace, and we then proceeded to backtrack this big lion to within a couple of feet from where this boy had gone to sleep the night before! He got a terrific fright when he saw the spoor and he listened to me after that.

"Some parents I have known have truly wasted money on bringing their kids along on safari. Badly behaved teenagers are a real danger in the bush, as are self-assured amateurs who think hunting a piece of cake they can share anytime with their pals, taking mad risks, shooting badly and breaking all those rules which go into the ethic of a professional hunter's life.

Nobody appreciates what's involved until they are exposed to a few realities—like that kid was that day with the lion."

"But this wasn't the only time we got close to lions with clients. I had another client after lion and we were sitting over a bait in a blind. I knew from the spoor that there was a big chap who might show at dawn, so the client and I shared a tin of corned beef and spent the night in the blind. All evening we could hear lions roaring in the distance. We just sat, eating, when Luis whispered to me that he had heard something.

"I whispered to the client that there was something nearby. We weren't yet sure what it was, even though Luis had excellent night vision. I was damned if I could make out a thing in the murk. Then Luis pointed straight ahead, right in front of me.

"I was less than a yard from the side of the blind, made of grass and branches. Jesus! There was the head of a big male lion two lousy feet away! When I turned on the flashlight full onto its face, grabbing my rifle at the same time, I saw that the lion had stuck its head right through the wall of the blind and was damned near in my lap!

"I didn't want to shoot this cheeky bastard, as it didn't have much of a mane. Despite our being right there, it went straight to the bait and began to feed. I slipped out the back and grabbed a jack handle, pegging it over the blind. It must have hit the lion square as it gave one helluva roar and went off a few yards.

"I was on top of the cab of the car and saw it about twenty yards off, its tail lashing like a bullwhip. It had lain down and was just watching us. Then, just to the right of us, two more lions began to roar. At that range the volume was incredible. It was enough to shake your bones. To be honest, we were now all as scared as hell. The lions were beginning to gang up. They weren't thirty feet away when, dear God, two more started the same act ten yards to the left! We really thought they were going to rush the blind and come in and take us. I was frightened. These were not shy lions. They seemed to have that man-eater contempt for humans.

"The client said: 'Look, Wally, I can't take any more of this! Let's get out now. No lion is worth this!'

"Boy, but did I agree with him! I got the client and Luis into the vehicle, windows rolled up, doors locked, and we drove right through the blind. In the headlights we saw perhaps ten lions, crowded right round the blind like a bunch of street thugs around a victim. They completely ignored the bait. We had now become the bait! When we got back to camp, the client said he'd never do that again. That was enough of that!"

"I recall another time in Mozambique in the old days. I used to take friends down to the same area where I was later bitten by that Gaboon viper. There was a lot of good fishing around, mostly bream and tigerfish. I was, for the most part, shooting meat for the men on the mines while my friends relaxed and fished.

"One day I shot a buffalo, and we soon loaded it up and brought it into camp. I dropped it off a distance from the tent and told my men to butcher it. They did so, taking most of the meat but leaving the carcass.

"Later that day, I had to drive about twenty-five miles to pick up some supplies, and I left these men in camp. When I got back at around nine that night, I heard a hysterical story being told in high-speed Shangaan.

"What the hell happened? Turned out they were sitting around the fire and heard a noise. A bunch of lions had come and grabbed what was left of the carcass, pulling it over a little rise. The men had taken a flashlight but couldn't see over the rise, but they could hear a lot of eating and crunching.

"I don't know how they got their nerve up, but the men took a flashlight and a spare rifle and went over this little rise for a closer look. They immediately saw four lions and fired one shot, which missed but scared off the lions. The men—three in all—then dragged the carcass back over the rise onto their side where, if the lions came back, they could see them. They didn't have long to wait.

"The lions came back, and the men actually killed one! I arrived about ten minutes later. I got the story, and we went out to bring in this lion. I covered the men with the lights of the car, my rifle ready. They had been afraid to pull the dead lion back to camp but were huddled around a fire in the highly mistaken belief that the flames would protect them; that all animals fear fire and stay away from it.

"I told them not to be such fools, that lions were *not* afraid of fire. No animal is. Hell, the bush is full of fire much of the dry season. There are always bush fires, and it is a dangerous fallacy to believe that fire will chase away or scare off *any* animal."

Listening to Wally at that point reminded me of a real roarer of a fire at Gordon Cundill's camp, King's Pool, on the Chobe River in Botswana one evening. I got a peculiar sensation that night as I sat by the fire. I felt a presence, something behind me. I swung around and there, not five feet away, was a huge hyena. Fire or no, it was there. Whether it wanted to grab a chunk of author, perhaps preferring imported delicacies, I don't know. But the hyena wasn't there for the view!

In any case, the lions luckily decided to decamp that night and Wally, together with the rest of the people, could spend the night in peace. He had dozens of close shaves with lions and it is indeed strange that he never got nailed by one, using that .30-30.

He was not nearly so lucky with buffalo, however. . . .

12

GORED

The buff, an extremely dangerous animal which is mighty hard to kill straight off, is the only one of the Big Five that actually got Wally in all his hunting life. That's if you black ball the Gaboon viper from the Big Five club (elephant, buff, lion, leopard, rhino . . . the classic man–killers).

Wally has no idea exactly how many buffalo he has shot, but he knows that he killed a great many more buffalo than he did elephant. With some thirteen hundred bulls to his credit, that would mean something like two thousand buff, what with meat hunting for the mine staff and actual safari work. Now, with so much exposure for so long to such dangerous animals, the odds are outstanding that the pro hunter will eventually get caught.

Wally was.

"A pretty terrible incident occurred once with some Shangaans who were in the habit of distilling a real stump-blower called *nipa* which was made from sugar cane: whew! It would really pick you up and feed you to its young! I was out hunting with an American doctor at the time when I got word that one of these Shangaans had been badly gored in the groin by a buffalo. It had come to eat the sugar cane, as buff often did. I asked the doctor if we could try and help the victim, who was in a nearby village headed up by Chief Kanjaan. The doctor readily agreed and we headed straight for the village, together with the messenger who had brought the news.

"We reached the village. There was no electricity, and it was already dusk. By the light of my flashlight, the doctor examined the poor guy; he had one hell of a hole in his guts and was in terrible pain. We got one of my gas lamps off the car and the doctor did what he could. He organized hot water and sewed the man up, putting a drain in the wound. He instructed the chief as to what the womenfolk had to do if the man was to have any chance at all of surviving. After powerful shots of this and that and a painkiller that knocked the man right out, we left. The doc confided in me that if ever he had seen a goner, that man was it. Hell, I personally had seen what looked like part of his bloody stomach hanging out of a huge hole in his lower chest!

"Well, ten days later this man walked into my camp from his village a few miles away! He told me that he felt just fine, had taken out the stitches and the drain himself, and was completely okay. He thanked us, the doctor in particular, and went on his way to get more cane to brew up more hooch. The doctor just couldn't believe his eyes. 'My colleagues back home will never believe this one,' he said. 'Never!'

"While in the area of Chief Kanjaan, I got word on a different occasion of a very bad bull buff near his village that had already killed several people. It may have been the one that gored the man we had fixed up some time before, but I could not be certain. Well, this big bull used to hang out in the long stuff along the riverbank. Chief Kanjaan himself—not an underling—came to me to ask that I cancel this buff's career, as it was really becoming a menace to his people.

"The chief came with us when we went after it, through grass that was easily fifteen feet high. I took the hunting vehicle, as I wasn't about to get stuck into a rogue on its turf if I could possibly help it. After a while, we heard what seemed to be the sound of the buff running away, and so I tried to catch up.

"Unfortunately, I did.

"This thing was huge! It swung around and charged the car, hitting it with a tooth-grinding slam. The client got a shot into it, but I knew I had to put it down before it disappeared, wounded, back into the *bundu.* I did this and the bull collapsed. But that son of a bitch had hit that car with such force, it had actually lifted the front end well off the ground, meaning that I had something of a patch job before we could get out of there. Anyway, Chief Kanjaan was delighted and I could always count on his cooperation whenever I was in his area and needed any sort of help or advice.

"I always loved hunting buffalo and enjoyed taking out Walter, Jr., in the mid-1950s. He was at boarding school in Umtali, Rhodesia, at the time, just across the border from our home at Vila de Manica. He used to bring some of his chums from school if they had a long weekend, and I daresay the kids had the time of their lives in the bush.

"One of these youngsters had a little .22 Hornet, which only fired a 45-grain bullet but at decent velocities. Most Americans I had out thought that it was even too light for woodchucks or groundhogs. Well, I reckoned the kid could take a duiker or a steinbuck with that gun, so I told him to bring it along. We all went on a real 'picnic safari' to Moribane, the closest good hunting area to home.

"Once there, we settled in and soon ran into a big herd of buffalo. I took Walter, Jr., on a one-hour stalk with his .30-'06. I was carrying a .375 with 300-grain bullets. We found a pretty good one and I dropped it, but the whole damned herd started running in our direction; they hadn't caught the wind and were confused by the location of the shot.

"Lord above, but the kid with the .22 Hornet took a shot at a buff and astounded the lot of us when it fell stone-dead! He'd hit it, whether by accident or design, right behind the ear, flattening it. Well, maybe it was just a lucky shot, but this story shows how dangerous even a tiny gun can be. Remember, Karamojo Bell killed buff with hyped-up .22s.

"On another 'picnic safari' down at Moribane, I took my wife, Lilly, my son and daughter, as well as another family friend and her two children. The kids were keen to take a couple of antelope for *biltong*, dried meat, to eat back at school. I knew the area very well and we camped by a murky water hole about twenty-five by thirty yards across. Elephant had been drinking there and had really stirred it up. I decided we needed some meat and went out to swat a buffalo, taking Walter, Jr., with me as well as two of his school pals. I nailed one with the .375 and we had to go back to the car to bring in the meat.

"Now this was a very hot day and the kids all wanted a swim in this water. In the meanwhile, my men were cutting up the buff on a big canvas sheet, which became so bloody that they soaked it in the water overnight. At dawn, the damn thing was gone! We couldn't figure out who in hell had taken it so we shrugged our shoulders as there was no spoor. When we returned from hunting at around eleven that morning, my wife showed me a huge croc she'd shot just after we'd left. Lilly had used the spare .30-'06. It was tremendous! Obviously, this was where the tarpaulin had gone. I should have known better.

"That night, I plugged a big spotlight into the cigar lighter and picked out the eyes, glowing ruby red in the water, of at least fifteen big crocs. My god, but we had been lucky. You can bet that nobody else went swimming in that water hole afterward."

A really unusual thing happened to Wally, Walter, Jr., and, by the strangest of coincidences, Steve Liversedge, with whom I have hunted twice in the recent past.

The incident happened on some agricultural land Wally was farming in Mozambique before the revolution. He had put in quite a bit of coffee, as the ivory hunting and gold mining were both doing well and he was inching his way back up the ladder of prosperity, which has some pretty slippery rungs.

"We were going along in the late afternoon on this tractor with heavy cast-iron counterweights in the front, past a stand of bush, when a really big bull buff boiled out, looked at us, and charged. Walter, Jr., was driving, with Steve and me balancing on the back of the tractor. Walter had the sense to turn directly head-on. The bull slammed with sickening force into the pig iron and apparently got quite a headache, judging by the way he staggered off.

"This encouraged a second buffalo. It went into overdrive and came for us, too! I yelled to Walter to try and run it over, which he actually did. But the damned tractor stalled smack on top of that buffalo, leaving it pinned under the chassis. (Bear in mind that none of us was armed.) We couldn't shoot him, and he wasn't nearly as stunned as the first one—which was still standing off a bit with a dazed look!

"That buffalo under the tractor was putting on a deafening performance. It nearly turned it over twice. We had a council of war and somebody remembered that he had a Japanese copy of a Swiss Army knife. We couldn't get the tractor off the buff and figured the only thing to do was to cut the damned thing's throat with the biggest blade, which was only a couple of inches long.

"Walter or Steve produced this penknife and we took it in actual relays to try and cut the buff's jugular. Naturally, it wasn't very fond of these proceedings and let us know it. Remember that a buffalo's neck hide is over an inch thick; in fact, many of the warrior tribes made their shields from it. It would turn most spears, even thrown from a close range. Besides that, the blade wasn't very sharp, and the buff wasn't exactly holding still for this lot. After a full hour, we finally got through and the buff stopped its struggles. The other wandered off. Helluva thing."

"Like all the dangerous species, there are hundreds of personal stories I could tell you about buffalo; but there is one story in particular that I most definitely will never forget. It sticks in my mind as if it had happened yesterday. One of the buggers, in fact, got stuck into me. Literally.

"I had two Americans with their wives out to hunt in Mozambique. One of the men was named Gerry Knight, to whom I owe my life. His companion, who may be equally culpable for my survival, was a veterinarian, Al Plechner. The entire party was from the Los Angeles area.

"We were out one day very early in the safari, and found a very good buff in a herd. One of the men hit it, and the buff went off on its own. Although it was losing a lot of blood, we followed it for over an hour into some of Capstick's famous long grass.

"At twenty yards, it jumped up, half invisible. I yelled for the men to fire and both did, as the animal began an immediate charge. I also shot. Now dream of this: One man's magazine floor-plate sprang open, dumping all his cartridges over his shoes, and the other guy had a lock-tight jam! I shot twice more but the buff never faltered, even though I could see my bullets were going into the right spot.

"The bull chose me as a target. In an instant, it was on top of me. I stuck the muzzle of my rifle in the crease between the horns and pulled the trigger. Nothing happened!

"The next I knew, I was upside down, with my rifle spinning away from the impact. Then, somehow, I was under this damned great belly. I managed to crawl out, as this thing was pretty sick—or should have been—and found myself, through some reflex action, hanging on top of its bloody back!

"I can clearly remember looking over his horns and seeing my clients and trackers white with fear. One of the trackers had a spare .458 Winchester Magnum caliber and I knew it was stoked with solid 500-grain bullets. One of the clients was shouting for the black with the rifle to shoot. Instantly, I realized that the solid would go right through the buffalo and kill me in the process.

"'For God's sake, don't shoot!' I screamed over and over.

"But Gerry Knight grabbed the rifle from the man and shot anyway. Rapture of raptures, he hit it in the spine and killed it instantly. The bullet did pass through the bull, missing me by inches. I was able to pull myself off, as everybody else was more in shock than I was.

"At that point, I didn't know the extent of my injuries, except that my leg felt odd. I looked down and damned near passed out. There was nothing in my thigh but raw meat with blood pouring over it. It was a hole I could have actually stuck my fist through!

"I said, 'Oh, hell,' and quickly sat down as the men got their act together and came over to help. They saw what had happened and did what they could for me. We put a tourniquet on the leg and tied it up, slowing down the terrific bleeding. Gerry Knight, the man who shot the buff out from under me, managed to get me on his back. We headed for the car, which was a good hour away at a brisk walk without the impediment of having to carry me. From there, it was another two hours back to camp. By the greatest luck, the buff had missed the femoral artery by a fraction of an inch, or I might have been a goner right there.

"Hell, I was incredibly fortunate that Gerry had been able to kill the buff, as it surely would have gored and maybe stomped me again. I really owe my life to Gerry. He was a brave man and was practically on top of that buffalo when he shot and killed it.

"Anyway, by the time we got back to the vehicle, I was really in severe pain, as the shock of the wound had worn off. The horn had actually gone through the back of my left leg and come out the front of the thigh. Gerry or Al drove the vehicle back to camp and I faithfully promise you that every bump was perfect agony.

"It happened to be a Sunday, and as soon as we got to camp, they put me to bed and did all they could for me. The veterinarian had some *muti* with him and poured some stuff into the hole to try and stop infection. It largely poured out the far side. I was in such pain that I drank half a bottle of Scotch neat but certainly didn't get any sleep that night.

"The next morning, one of the men figured out the radio and got in a charter that flew me to Umtali, Rhodesia. Brother, there the doctors stitched and patched like on a quilting bee and I lay there for twelve days.

"I was an idiot and left too early, despite protests by the doctors. It was early in the safari, and I felt that I had a responsibility to give my clients a good hunt. Anyway, I got back to camp and took them out after elephant, not a good choice at that stage, as it entailed so much walking. I had more stitches than a damned parachute and was still weak from loss of blood. Nevertheless, I went back.

"So, off we went for a tusker, my leg heavily bandaged. But after a mile or so, the fool thing tore loose and I could feel the meat squishing in my leg against the bandages as the blood began to seep through. I wanted to go on despite this, but Gerry Knight saw my agony. 'Hell, no,' he said. 'That's it. You must go back to the hospital and get retacked!'

"I took his advice and went back until the leg had healed up a bit. When I got out, a tight bandage helped a great deal. Nonetheless, it was many, many months before I could walk properly again, and I was damned lucky at that.

"Gerry Knight, who was an amateur gunsmith, had a look at my rifle, recovered after the goring, and went over it thoroughly to determine why it wouldn't fire when I stuck it in the buff's face and was backpedaling as it poured down on me. Gerry thoroughly cleaned it and found it quite dirty. The primer of the cartridge was indeed dented but the round did not go off. Who knows? It worked fine after that, but can you imagine the odds on a triple breakdown of rifles during a buffalo charge? Impossible.

"But it happened. Africa."

I understood Wally's anguish only too well. When you read Peter Capstick's Africa: A Return to the Long Grass, *you'll see what happened with misfires and duds in the middle of a lion charge. A nightmare come true, one all hunters hope they never have to experience but which sometimes happens, despite all precautions taken beforehand.*

Wally told me he just couldn't imagine how an animal as big as that buff could shove a horn thicker than an American baseball bat right through his leg without him noticing it at the time.

"Neural or muscular shock, I guess. Still, it was the only time I ever really got nailed, despite many very close incidents. That scar has been a reminder ever since that, in the African hunting situation, death is only a hair's breadth away.

"After Gerry finished polishing up the rifle, I took that same lot of ammo and tried it out. It wouldn't fire, even though the primer was properly indented by the firing pin. Just old, perhaps. I never could figure it out, as the action and barrel were as clean as a mirror after Gerry had finished with them. Maybe just *kismet.* Why I never went into real shock with that goring, I just can't figure. Maybe I'm just an overboiled hyena!"

Africa, as I have seen for myself after years of residence, is a mighty odd place. Things that are supposed to happen don't, and quite the opposite frequently prevails. And there is the tendency for us to remember the unusual and to forget the commonplace. If a witch doctor says that you will kill two elephants on one day and you don't, you forget about it. But when you only have a license for one and his prediction comes true, you tend to remember the incident, forgetting the mispredictions.

On a recent safari, I asked a witch doctor to bless my rifles, a superstitious custom of mine. He flatly refused, although I offered a fair amount of money for the doings. We had trouble with buff that day!

It wasn't from dangerous game alone, however, that Wally was at risk in all those tough hunting years. He and Werner von Alvensleben still cannot believe their luck at having survived a run-in with a huge gang of heavily armed poachers. . . .

13

POACHING

Baron Werner von Alvensleben paid me a visit in the mid-sixties at the offices of the company I owned in New York, and I well remember his Heidelberg dueling scars and the grand conversation we enjoyed about hunting in Mozambique. Wally worked for years in von Alvensleben's company, Safarilandia, *and got to know the Baron as a person of great courage, strength, luck, and resolution. An experienced hunter, the Baron had shot quite a few elephant and was pretty well proof against surprises in the bush.*

One thing he never got used to or tolerated in any way, however, was poaching. Wally agreed: "Man, they were taking the bread out of our mouths, these poaching swine. And you just never knew what you were up against when dealing with poachers. These were mighty aggressive chaps."

Around 1970, Werner and Wally had a gap in between clients, so they decided to take off on a human hunt in an effort to track down a poaching ring that was really doing wholesale business in that government-granted tract of land—their hunting concession. Wally rounded up two policemen and the party of four men set out in one vehicle, looking for poachers in the thick African bush.

"Eventually, we came across an area where everything was dead-quiet—until we ran across a path leading into the deep bush. The path was eight inches deep, with bicycle tracks, indicating heavy poacher activity there. We followed the track until we came to a big water hole.

"After a little while on this bicycle path, we came to a ton of camps and shelters and fires, but the only people around were a few small children. As soon as they saw the car, they tried to run, but the police chaps were pretty swift and caught one of them.

"We asked what was going on, and the child said that everybody was out hunting meat. Now there were at least fifty or sixty fires and thousands of pounds of meat already hanging up to dry. Bikes were all over the place. There were no adults at all, so we told the policemen to grab every damned bike they could find and stack them in a heap. It turned out that there were over one hundred and fifty bikes, so we had some idea of what the four of us were up against. Plenty.

"The interesting thing was that I had forgotten my ammunition and, but for the few rounds in my rifle, I was effectively unarmed! That's a hell of a lot of poachers to confront with your bare hands. Werner and the policemen had ammo, but nothing like what would be needed if things really got ugly with that mob. The African bush is a wonderful place in which to 'disappear,' and news doesn't always reach the authorities quickly enough for search parties to be organized in time and for criminals to be caught what would have been literally red-handed.

"Werner and I chatted it over and decided in the end to wait for these guys. Certainly, it seemed there were at least one hundred and fifty of them. Maybe more. My second guess was more accurate.

"We hid on the outskirts of the water hole, and just as we got into position, we saw a man come in with an impala on his back. I watched him secrete the impala and march into camp with his bow and arrows.

"I sprang from our hiding place and grabbed the man, telling him to get the impala and leave it by the fire, which he did. The man got a devil of a fright when he saw me. Werner was doing the same thing on the other side of the water hole—he had moved with the police.

"Before it was remotely dark, we had thirty to forty of these poachers under guard, but they were still coming in. We could hear them singing in the distance, and one hellish chilly sound it was. When they arrived, there were fully two hundred of them, heavily armed.

"Then we had a stroke of luck—African style.

"I immediately recognized one of the men as wearing the regalia of a senior witch doctor, or *xingomatandza.* I nabbed his tail immediately and stuck the .375 in his ear, advising him that if it was most adequate for elephant, it would do nicely for him, unless he had a quick homey chat with the assembled throng and told them to do exactly as we said.

"Ah, we had a lovely talk with the rifle in his ear! Being something of a holy man, the others would not jeopardize his safety, although they could have taken us any time they wanted. But such is the status of the witch doctor, and in the fear of running afoul of him, the people listened.

"Hey, we were four against two hundred! Both Werner and I knew that we had chewed off a lot bigger chunk than we could gag down, and we had to make the best of it and take any and every advantage if we wanted to come out of this little lot alive. The witch doctor was the key, and everybody knew it.

"Clearly, there was no way on earth to bring these men in. They held all the cards except the ace of spades. But we kept up a brave front and told them that we were there to stop the poaching, and that we'd return with thousands of army troops if they didn't quit. That seemed to impress them as much as did our audacity.

"I told the witch doctor to inform the crowd that, provided they did what we told them, we would not call in troops and we would not arrest them. As if we could! But if they refused, we had a wonderful pile of bicycles which would be burned instantly. That really got their attention.

"I practically pushed the barrel of that .375 through the *xingomatandza*'s skull. He cooperated. Whenever a hunting party came in, he would harangue them and they would deposit their weapons and the game in a growing pile. They didn't know we only had a handful of cartridges among us. Had things turned ugly, there would have been one dead witch doctor, with us four tacked on.

"As this pile of weapons grew, I took the witch doctor to each little subcamp and had him explain that all would be fine if they did what we told them. My God! We had a small mountain of guns, bows, arrows, and spears. Trouble was, these poachers were becoming surly as they started to realize their strength and our numerical weakness.

"While lying by this pile of bikes, weapons, and game, I noticed that it was now pitch dark. Suddenly, a shot went off! I rolled out of the light, only to discover that the shot had come from one of the policemen who had confiscated a muzzle-loader. He knew it was loaded as the percussion cap was still on, and he just fired it into the air. He then threw it onto the pile of confiscated weapons.

"I was back by the pile of bikes, weapons, and game when I noticed a crowd of about one hundred and fifty men beginning to gang around me. This is it, I thought. It was truly strange. They just formed a line and passed me, all shooting me evil looks as they filed by, not six feet from me. Nobody made any overt move. I quit counting at sixty-five but my finger was now right on the trigger. One wrong move and I would have opened up.

"In retrospect, had we not grabbed that witch doctor and held him hostage to control the crowd's behavior, I know my bones and those of my companions would be bleaching there now, after the hyenas and ants had finished. I looked at these men closely. I know the bush Africans and their expressions. There was no doubt what they were thinking: Tonight, when these people are asleep, we'll put arrows and spears into them and go happily on our way.

"Werner had gone to get the vehicle and I was most pleased when he returned, as these chaps could easily have killed us. We could have done nothing about it. Hell, even if the authorities had found our bodies, who could possibly say who had done the deed? There were a couple of hundred of these poachers, maybe more, and they would never have betrayed their fellow poachers to outsiders.

"Still, we were facing a very long night ahead. We had to wait until daylight, when we would attempt to force the huge band to leave. Werner and I decided to take twenty blankets from these brigands and wrap ourselves in them for protection against arrows. You really must try draping yourself in ten blankets in the Mozambique heat, should you desire an experience you won't forget. Sitting well back from a small fire so we wouldn't make very good targets, I discussed the matter with Werner. We decided to take relays at watch. I took the shift to midnight and he the next. To be perfectly honest, through nervous exhaustion I fell into a stupor. I'd have been shot in the front lines in the last war for that.

"Nothing happened, probably because one of the police had his rifle at the head of the witch doctor, whom we had so thoughtfully brought along to share the accommodations. I really must hand it to those black rural police. They did their job. They, together with the crack troops in the army, faced a terrible fate after the 1975 revolution. They were hated by the new masters and they were butchered. But that's a story on its own.

"At dawn, the whole crowd assembled. It looked like something out of a Cecil B. De Mille movie. I was covering the witch doctor again. My God! We thought there had been a lot of prisoners the night before. By daylight, they had either been reinforced, or more poachers had come out of the bush.

"Big trouble came up again as some of the men accused us of stealing their blankets the previous night. I almost had to stifle a laugh, as it was quite true, of course.

"Werner gave a haymaker right in the chops of the first man who came up and accused us, physically pitching him back into the crowd. If we had let up control for one second, we would have been overrun and killed. I still had the .375 in the ear of the witch doctor, who managed to keep the mob cowed.

"We dragged the witch doctor up and told him to tell his people they could take their bikes back to their villages. In fact, we let some of the peacemakers keep some meat on the strict understanding that we would shoot them stone-cold dead if we ever caught them poaching on our concession again. We kept rigid control in our area and the devils stayed away.

"Well, they packed and buggered off. Still, I often lie awake at night, thinking about the lack of ammo and the sheer wonder that there are not four clean skeletons shallowly dug into the soil of Mozambique.

"One of them could have been mine."

"I can assure you that poaching is the greatest threat to all wildlife in Africa, no matter where it is, no matter what form the poaching takes—shooting, poisoned arrows, or snares. That's where the game has gone, albeit there are areas such as South Africa where wise game management and strictly controlled hunting have resulted in a fine increase in the game population over the last couple of decades.

"But this does not make up for the mindless depredations going on in some African states, where there is no concept whatsoever of the value or place of game as a foreign-currency earner and employer. Civil wars and hunger have added to the chaos, creating an intolerable situation for wildlife. The sad thing is that this topic has become politically untouchable in certain countries, where officials are terrified to stick their necks out and plead for sanity in an effort to conserve the wildlife heritage for the benefit of all.

"The answer is not to prohibit the importing of highly selected trophies into other countries but to kill the weed at the root, keeping game departments and hunting concessions open and well-staffed so that game areas can be policed and the ordinary people can derive benefit from game-generated revenue for jobs and food."

Wally and I agree, as do all those who know the African hunting scene from the inside: So long as the huge profits for poached products are there, it will take more sophistication and adjustment on the part of officials and far greater foresight than is being shown in most African game areas today before the tide even beings to turn. It's that simple. And the ignorant activities of the antihunters elsewhere in the world have, ironically, only hastened the deadly decline in viable game populations in Africa. This affects the safari industry and the livelihoods of untold numbers of local employees. Wally has been there. I've been there. We've seen it. The poacher is now king. Visit the Luangwa Valley, once home to teeming herds of elephant. You'll kick over the occasional immature skull, long, long bleached by the African sun. The elephants are gone and the poachers have moved on.

14

AFTERTHOUGHTS BEFORE ARMAGEDDON

The hunting life is one of huge variety. As Wally and I chewed the fat and dug up his experiences in the field, we shared notes on anything from encounters with deadly army ants to elephants, from capers with crocs to those with leopards and snakes, with a liberal sprinkling of stories about clients and their quirks.

"One narrow escape that especially sticks in my mind happened in Botswana. Some clients and I once found a big herd of elephant on an open plain. I closed up with the vehicle to about sixty yards, when the last elephant in this bunch, a bull, stopped and started walking toward the vehicle.

"The clients were happily filming away when I noticed that this bloody thing was picking up speed at rather an alarming rate. Elephants can't really run as other game does, but they can sure cover a long distance in a very short time, especially if you happen to be the object of their charge.

"I quickly turned the car to get the hell out of the way, when I heard the trackers in the back start screaming at me, 'Baas, go as fast as you can! This thing is nearly on us!'

"I glanced around and found there wasn't a liar among them. The bull was almost in the back of the car. The trouble was that there were so many holes in the plain I couldn't drive very fast, and the damned thing kept gaining on us all the time. Soon it was right behind the vehicle. I glanced behind my shoulder and thought it was going to grab somebody with its trunk!

"I'd never run into an elephant that had come this far in a real charge—at this point, over four hundred yards. Still, the trackers were screaming that it was almost on them, and they were right. In front of us was thick bush and I knew this would just slow us up, and allow the elephant to get us at last.

"I slammed on the brakes to the point where I could jump out with my rifle and cool this bugger. I don't know how fast we were going, but I rolled, got to my feet, and dropped the elephant dead with a single shot. It couldn't have been nine feet behind us when I shot, but I knew that the light bush would stop the car gently—and it did.

"It was a strange end to a very strange incident."

It's amazing the kind of people who come on safari. You don't always get the practiced shot, the lifelong hunter, as Wally's next story will demonstrate.

"I had a call from a fellow pro in Mozambique, Carlos Arujo, who had a concession in the Gorongosa region, northeast of my home in Vila de Manica. He had no professional hunters assisting him, and up to this point had managed well. But now he had accepted a booking for four medical doctors coming out from New York for a month, and he just had to have another pro along in order to cope. I wasn't so sure I wanted to take on the extra work, but Carlos convinced me to take part of the safari for a month. After he'd come all the way to persuade me in person, I really couldn't turn him down.

"We picked up the party at the airstrip and loaded all their gear into a big truck. We then headed for camp, where the first thing I asked them was what species they wanted.

"'*Everything!*' came the response.

"I asked what rifles they had and they said, 'Oh, we didn't bring any. None of us owns a gun. In fact, none of us has ever shot a thing in our lives. Perhaps you can give a tip or two and we can borrow some guns.'

"Oh, dear God! My heart nearly stopped. I not only had to hold their hands, but had to teach them how to shoot, too!

"I stuck up a helluva big target, taught them how to load and carry their rifles, grilled them on safety procedures, taught them the principles of aiming, hold-off, squeeze, and trigger follow-through. I couldn't teach them ice-cool nerves, presence of mind, and quick reactions. That only comes with exposure, experience, time. These guys had four weeks, and, like all clients, expected some return for their money in the form of trophies. I felt like packing it in right then.

"Well, it took two full days to get these doctors to hit anything at all, let alone the target. But we really couldn't waste more time on training, as the hunting time was evaporating.

"I decided to take them out and just see how things went. So, what's the first thing we bump into? A very fine sable antelope. I asked who wanted a sable and two men said they did, tossing a coin for the shot. The guy who won killed it deader than lard with his first shot! I don't know who was more astounded, he or I. I had just told them what I had been trying to teach them: Be calm, squeeze, and watch the sight picture. Of course the group was tickled: it was the first time they had taken a trophy.

"A few miles on, we saw a damned good eland and the other doctor elected to take it, or at least to try. We went through the same drill, and *he* dropped it cold! Arujo was doing as well with his two, and I was starting to reckon that these guys were naturals.

"At this point, everybody thought themselves primed for Cape buffalo, so Arujo and I agreed, with the clients' consent, each to take two men on this hunt. The idea was for me to have my clients shoot first, while Arujo and his group would go ahead and take their buff a bit later. After all, we couldn't have four men shooting at the same time.

"When we neared a potential trophy, my two asked if I minded whether they shot together. I agreed and I took a look at the cover. The bush was very thick, and with two rifles trained on the buff, the odds were better of flattening the animal before it had a chance to flatten any of us. We only had to walk thirty yards to get within range, and I told the men which one to take. I advised them that I would count to three, whereupon they were to squeeze off together.

"The buff hit the ground like a ton of ore.

"'Jeez,' I said, 'that's *great*!'

"Unfortunately, the herd turned, confused by the sound of the shot, and came straight for us. One doctor panicked and fired wildly into the group. They turned, but I saw that he had wounded one and it was limping.

"It went straight into the long grass and just carried on. I told them to wait right there with my trackers and not to move. When I found the buff, I'd whistle for them, and the gunbearers would bring the men in to finish the buff off.

"Didn't quite work out that way.

"While moving toward where I thought the buff would be, I had to pass the dead one. When Capstick talks about long grass, he's not putting you on. I found a sort of corridor and could just make out the horns sticking up as I passed it. Ahead, the wounded buff was facing me. I figured he'd charge any second from now, so I quickly calculated where to shoot it, even though I couldn't see the vitals and ran the risk of deflection. I took a shot. Thank heavens it dropped.

"The next second, I heard screaming and shouting! It was behind me and I wondered what in hell was going on now. I ran like mad toward the sound. It was coming from the place where the first buff, which I figured was stone-dead, had been lying.

"When I got there, I couldn't see anybody. But I did see a menacing dark shape. In a blurred, black flash, the bastard was on me. The buff caught me under the right armpit and tossed me a distance you wouldn't believe if I told you. The son of a bitch was instantly on top of me but was pretty obviously sick, as it couldn't seem to gauge the distance between us and was tearing the earth and bush to pieces right in front of me. I rolled over and the thing passed.

"I thought I could get up, but I'd been hit so hard I just couldn't. The goddamn thing turned around and came for me again as I rolled. It made that bush and earth look as if a dozen hand grenades had gone off around me!

"All this time, I had kept a death grip on my rifle. Now I shot the buff in the chest from the ground. I emptied the full magazine of the .375 Magnum into the buff until it was bloody well kneeling right in front of me, blood pumping from the nose. I aimed at it again and heard that most frightening of all sounds: *click!*

"My God! When I was a second away from cashing my chips, one of the gunbearers arrived with a rifle he'd snatched from an understandably terrified client and banged the buff, which fell over. I looked and saw all these people rushing up to me. One of the doctors had a camera around his neck and the other had a tripod.

"'Hell's bells! Hot damn! You killed a charging buffalo!'

"'Of course, you photographed the whole thing,' I said.

"'Well, not exactly. We saw when he had you down the first time and we were afraid to shoot because we were scared we'd kill you. We figured he'd put a hole right through you when he tossed you. Then we heard shots and saw you on the ground wrestling with the buffalo. We saw all the shots you fired. Lucky you and the gunbearer got him down and you're not hurt.'

"'No, I'm not hurt. But how do you think your pictures came out?'

"'What?'

"'Your pictures, man. I do this all the time for my clients. Just to put on a decent show.'

"They looked at me in thunderstruck amazement. 'Good heavens, man, you were nearly killed and ten minutes later you can joke about it!'

"'All part of the business,' I told them. I found out exactly what had happened after I had started the follow-up on the wounded buffalo. One of the clients said to the trackers that he'd like a look at the 'dead' buffalo. They got their cameras all ready and one told the other, 'Right, George, you sit there and I'll get your picture and then you take mine.'

"George was sitting in the middle of the buffalo with his rifle in a suitably heroic pose when he felt a movement, looked down and saw the ear of the buff flicking! Of course, he realized that it was still very much alive! He jumped up about the same instant as the buffalo and hightailed it for way yonder. Happily, so did the buffalo, but into the grass. That was the point where it caught me as I was running back to see what was going on.

"Sure, I put on a brave front for the doctors, but an hour later, when I was back in my tent, my knees were actually knocking, and I was shivering with shock."

Wally doesn't say it in so many words, but, as I have written in previous books and have said on hunting videos, don't ever forget the old dictum of East Africa: "It's the dead ones that get up and kill you." Pay *the insurance. No cartridge or trophy is worth your life or, at the least, massive hospital bills and possible maiming.*

Talking about his bad luck on the horns of that buff reminded Wally of how his pal, Werner von Alvensleben, used to put himself in harm's way, taking buffalo with dogs and a long spear.

"I take my hat off to him. There aren't many people who would do that. He never got caught, either."

I know the feeling, as I have killed two buff with a spear but without the benefit of dogs. Also a man-eating lion with a broken spear as it was busy dissecting my gunbearer of those Luangwa days, Silent.

Wally tells of an experience he had with buffalo and dogs in Mozambique. "A client had wounded a buff and it went off into the long stuff, leaving lots of blood. I was with Walter, Jr., and realized that it would charge from a few feet in that stuff, so I thought that dogs might be able to root the animal out and give us a bit of shooting room.

* * *

"Now the natives kept dogs for hunting, and I got some from a nearby village in exchange for the promise of some meat. These bloody things were useless. They would walk behind you and wanted to know nothing about buff. But among this half-starving pack were two with real heart. They saved my life.

"As we followed the blood spoor, these two dogs kept up with me. In a flash, the buff charged and the dogs bravely ran straight at it. But as the wounded one charged, so did another buff I hadn't seen. One of the dogs kept on the first bull and the other went for the second bull. I dropped the first and was able to cash in the second. Those two little mangy mutts were lion-hearted but far from the normal village dog. I was bloody lucky they were along. I have taken out dogs many times before, but found that these village curs were terrified of even a whiff of lion or buffalo."

"On another occasion, Harry Manners and I had a damned scary thing happen to us in the early days. We were on our way to an elephant area and were looking for a place to camp, when we came across a little village which had, by heaven, a neon sign which read *cantina.* It was only a small native trading store, but we stopped. I asked if they had any food and they said they had only some tinned bully beef. Well, that was okay. But they also had a couple of circular huts, rondavels, where travelers could spend the night; hence the glorious name of *cantina,* tavern.

"We ate the tins of canned beef and went to sleep at half past eight. Hell, the beds had clean sheets! We had one flashlight between us, and there was also a kerosene lamp. Harry took one hut and I the other, he keeping the flashlight.

"Well, I hadn't been in bed fifteen minutes when I felt something funny on my stomach. Felt like bugs of some sort. I got out of bed and went over to Harry's rondavel to get his flashlight. When I came back, I found the place aswarm with *siafu,* or army ants!

"As Peter can tell you from his own experience, these boys you don't fool with. I escaped their fate by a hair's breadth.

"You see, had I not got out of that bed when I did, I would

have died. They have mighty interesting behavior insomuch as they will first gang you and then bite with tremendous pincers. They wait until they are all in position and then they bite at the same time on a chemical signal from the leader. They will then strip your carcass like a pack of hyenas. Their formic-acid toxin has a paralyzing effect, and there are some stories about them from Mozambique I know to be true as rain. One concerns three prisoners who had been jailed by a *Chefe de Poste*, chained together and locked in a small hut. In the morning, there were but three skeletons. Army ants.

"Luckily, there was another bed in Harry's hut, but I didn't sleep that night. I kept recalling army-ant stories. Like the time a client of mine stepped on a column of the creatures near camp. Although he was bitten only twice, his leg was paralyzed for a full day. They're very bad news."

As Wally spoke, I thought back on two instances I knew about in which women had left their babies in the shade while they hoed their crops. The babies were eaten clean. Actually, Africans tend to welcome an invasion of these ants, which march with flankers and sentries in a column about six inches wide. They will clean the huts of any vermin, including rats, then pass on. No spider or bug has a chance against the siafu.

"I got mixed up with plenty of leopards in my safari career. One incident I especially remember involved a Japanese client who came out to Mozambique and wanted absolutely everything. He was a youngster of about twenty and a good shot. We had already taken a lot of stuff but were still looking for leopard. One afternoon, we spotted a leopard lying under a bush. I told the client to take it.

"He shot and hit the leopard, but it ran off. I followed it for half an hour but it was now getting late and the light was fading. I went back and told the client and my son, who was along, that we'd best leave the follow-up until first light.

"Walter, Jr., and two of my men told me they'd like to keep after the leopard, despite nightfall and the great danger. There is nothing funny about a wounded leopard in heavy cover at night, as Capstick has written in *Peter Capstick's Africa.* I was with him in Zambia when he stalked a badly wounded leopard at night through grass some sixteen feet tall and over rough terrain smothered in undergrowth. We must have been mad that night!

"Anyway, I was talked into following up the client's leopard, so the four of us went in, leaving the Japanese on the road. Now and again, we'd pick up blood in the beams of the flashlights, then we'd lose it again and separate to find more tracks or blood. Not my idea of a good time.

"I was bending over, looking at a track, when suddenly Luis gave a screech. Right behind him, actually in the air, was the leopard! Just by reflex, I got the .375 up and hit this thing smack in the ear! It brushed Luis's heels as it dropped.

"Luis nearly died of fright. He said that he was following some blood, happened to look up, and here was the damned thing crouched not six feet away, staring at him. As Luis turned his back to run, the leopard charged him. It was just luck that I was able to smack it in the brain."

"There are a hell of a lot of crocs in Mozambique—big ones. Years ago I met a man named Dunn who had a most strange and terrifying experience: He was taken by a croc but was alive to tell me the tale:

"'I was fishing from the bank of a small river,' Dunn explained, 'when, like a rocket, a big croc actually leaped out of the water, grabbed me on a booted leg, and pulled me under. It then started swimming away with me.

"'I held my breath as long as I could, trying to figure what to do; the pain in my leg was terrible. The river wasn't very deep, and we came to a sand bar where I managed to get my head out of the water for a moment to draw some fresh air. Then I could just hang on again as the croc started off with me.

"'Just as I was out of air the second time, the croc surfaced and went up onto the bank. For some incredible reason, it left me and went back into the water again! But as I dragged myself away from the water, I could see the croc was coming back! I couldn't walk but got far enough away from the river where my men found me. What luck! But people don't believe me until I show them these scars!'

"Man, how Dunn didn't lose that leg to gangrene, nobody knows. He was very very ill for a long time and his nerves took a terrible bashing. You can't be too careful around some rivers. I once saw a small herd of impala rushing into a river, chased by wild dogs. As one male impala was soaring through the air, a big croc actually caught it in midleap in its jaws and pulled the creature under. I wouldn't have believed it, had I not seen it."

I've mentioned before that Walter always had pals keen to come over to Mozambique for holidays and do a bit of shooting. One year, we went out to the Pungoé River, which reaches the Indian Ocean at Beira. There was a lot of game and good fishing in the particular spot we chose. I found a small village nearby and had the idea of perhaps supplementing the ivory hunting with croc skins, there being a superabundance of crocs in the remote rivers. I asked the people if there were any crocs about and they assured me that there were but plenty, and that they would welcome my thinning them out a bit.

"I made a deal for a dugout, since, after having had a look in daylight, I could see no sign of croc activity. Yet these tribesmen said that every year they had not a few people taken by them. They pointed out the best places and I decided to go out the first night with a big flashlight and a couple of locals.

"Lord above, crocs were all over the place, eyes gleaming like hot embers in the light. But before I could work out a drill to shoot some of the bigger ones, one of the men shouted that water was pouring into the boat!

"Sure as hell, water was gushing in. A hole in the boat had been plugged with some sort of stopper and, in the dark, somebody had kicked it out! We paddled like mad toward the bank, but we just couldn't make it. The dugout sank on the spot and we had to swim for the bank through those crocs in total blackness.

"I was hanging on to the .375, and one of the others also had a rifle. But it was our rifles or our lives. I let go of mine and he did the same with his. Somehow, we made it. Everybody was scared as hell—and with good reason—as we scampered over the greasy mud of the bank. I felt we were bloody lucky to *get* to the bank. But I sure hated to lose that rifle. It was a tough walk back to camp in that dark, I'll tell you.

"The next morning, I asked these people how we could get my rifle back. Nobody had any ideas. No ideas at all.

"They were deadly afraid of those crocs, and the water was some fifteen to twenty feet deep. I don't blame them. They just wouldn't go in. Besides, we weren't exactly certain where the dugout had sunk and how far the current had carried us before we reached shore.

"Then I got a brain wave. I always kept a huge and powerful magnet in the back of the car, because when I had to carry out the odd repair in the field, nuts and bolts and stuff would fall into the grass. Boy, one sweep with that thing and nothing was ever lost. So I got another dugout and some paddlers and tied the magnet to a long length of strong cord. We went to where I figured the canoe had sunk and where our tracks showed where we had clambered up the bank.

"I dragged that magnet around the bottom for days; it was most certainly powerful enough to lift the rifle. But we never hit anything.

"Finally, time ran out and the kids had to go back to school. I mentally wrote off that favorite rifle but decided to leave the magnet and some cord with the chief, offering him a very handsome reward if he could find it. He understood what to do and gave me his solemn promise that he would try.

"Two months later, at my home—which was one hell of a walk from the Pungoé River—one of my staff came to me and said that there was a man with a big bundle of grass who wanted to see me. I wondered what this was all about and told him to send the man along. I looked at him and he seemed to ring a bell, but I couldn't remember from where.

"'Don't you remember me?' he asked.

"'Yes,' I answered in dialect, 'but I can't remember from where you come.'

"'Don't you remember when you lost your rifle near my village on the Pungoé, and you left me the magic metal to find it?'

"'Aha! Of course!'

"'Well, I have it here, in this carrying of grass.'

"He opened it and there was my rifle, still in very good shape, no rust and no warping of the stock. I couldn't credit what I was seeing. That elderly chief had gone out every day until he lucked into it. So I got my beloved rifle back under circumstances that almost smack of science fiction. I gave the chief a whopping great tip and took a few days off so that I could drive him home to his village. I shall never forget that old man.

"I was deeply touched by this event. The chief had taken a hell of a chance walking that far with a rifle in a grass bundle, since, in those days, it was forbidden for a tribesman to have a gun of any sort. He would have automatically attracted suspicion, too, since the carrying of grass is strictly the work of women in this culture."

"This being a chapter of afterthoughts and miscellaneous reminiscences, I must tell you of my experience with a bicycle and how it helped me out in a real jam.

"I had a flat battery a thousand miles east of nowhere around 1972 or 1973. My hunting vehicle had an alternator, rather than a generator, so if it was really dead, you couldn't just jump-start it, as it required a slight electric impulse. My client and I waited two hours before a local came along on a bike with one of these generators that rubbed against the front wheel and powered his headlamp as he pedaled.

"Heaven-sent! I put the bike on a makeshift stand, free of the ground, and had this guy start pedaling after I had wired the alternator to this tiny rig, which threw about two volts.

"Other people came by and I paid them all to spell this chap and my gunbearers. They pumped for about three hours and we had a good spark. A short push and she started. That's why we're not still there now.

"In another, similar, incident, I used a five-cell flashlight to provide that start. I put one wire into the positive and the other into the negative, leading from the flashlight. After that, I knew that as long as I had a flashlight, I'd never be stuck with the battery. Just remember that when you're in the bush, you just have to make do, as it's a long walk home. Use your head."

"The first time I caught malaria, I was in my twenties, and it later developed into the dreaded blackwater fever. You must understand that it is so named because severe and prolonged bouts of malaria break down the kidneys and cause the sufferer to pass black water, discolored with blood. It was an automatic death sentence in early African hunting.

"The cure in those days was most interesting: champagne!

"I was put in a little clinic run by nuns and given champagne to drink—by the gallon. I lost a great deal of weight, and the cure was expensive, but it worked. My kidneys kept functioning and I have had little trouble from malaria attacks since that treatment.

"Several friends without access to genuine French bubbly beat blackwater by staying stoned on the local native beer. They're convinced of its effectiveness, and so am I.

"Quinine, the old standby, wasn't much good, I believe. Besides making you deaf, it tended to aggravate rather than alleviate blackwater. I base this simply on what I saw. I'm no doctor but I am a survivor."

"I must sadly end this part of my story with a short account of the death of my good friend and companion on many an ivory safari, the Italian, Bellino. One day I received a telegram simply saying that he had been killed in a Jeep when he rolled it after missing a detour on the road to the Rhodesian border.

"That little Italian was a grand chap. He had been a prisoner of war and was being brought to Durban on a British ship, as the South Africans absorbed many Italian prisoners. The boat was torpedoed by the Germans, and of the nearly six hundred prisoners, Bellino was one of about five survivors.

"I had originally met him in Lourenço Marques during the war and liked him so much that I bought him a truck later and gave him a job. He got onto his feet and was soon doing well with his own transport company.

"Sadly, his truck caught fire in the bush one day and was a complete write-off. He had no insurance, and the bloody thing was worth tens and tens of thousands of U.S. dollars in those days. He didn't have the money to get a new one, so he stayed with Lilly and me, helping out with the mines, hunting, and general fare. I had gotten into the banana disaster and couldn't refinance him, since my credit was thinner than my wallet.

"I shall always miss that cheery little bloke. I was very sorry to see him go."

Safari work and hunting naturally involve risks, and the pro hunter is often unprotected against the sort of disasters few insurance companies would be interested in covering. Wally had lost a good friend in Bellino, as he had in others who died in hunting accidents or who became ill in the African bush and never recovered. It was one thing to say good-bye to good friends. But nothing could have prepared Wally for the losses he eventually suffered in Mozambique. A rough road lay ahead.

15

AMBUSH

The Portuguese authorities had been aware from the mid-1960s of the growing Communist agitation and guerrilla presence in Mozambique. Wally witnessed the swelling struggle to quell it. There is no way anyone who has not lived in Mozambique—or had Mozambican friends and followed the political turmoil of that part of the world in the last couple of decades—can begin to understand the horror that was about to shatter Wally's life. That horror swept through Mozambique, affecting the lives of absolutely everybody, and caused Wally's home of some fifty years to become a Communist revolutionary playground. There is a particular chill to his words when he says:

"I cannot help but be grateful that my wife, Lilly, died several years before that terrible day in 1975, because the shock and horror of what happened to me after she worked decades to secure our lives together would have surely killed her.

"The Portuguese had been in Mozambique since 1505, long before settlement in a place like America was even a remote thought. With Ghana's independence from Britain in 1957, the so-called winds of change—I think of them as the gales of chaos—began blowing, with increasing aid from places like

China, the Soviet Union, East Germany, North Korea, and other radical, Communist/socialist revolutionary states whose aim was and remains anything but the true freedom and peaceful development of the peoples of Africa. Now anyone who doubts this doesn't know Africa, and as my old friend and hunting companion, Bob Ruark, so often said, hasn't any experience of the realities of 'Uhuru-ed' Africa. Many Western countries are guilty of amazing ignorance, gullibility, and outright collusion in their support of the 'freedom movements' which have ruined Africa for indigenous Africans and brought a new kind of subjugation to its peoples.

"Mozambique's tragedy was not the simple anticolonial black-white struggle which has so conveniently been touted by the disinformation services of the world. This was a remarkably nonracial society where many white Mozambicans supported the idea of a more independent Mozambique that would be less reliant on a distant Portugal for decision-making and administration and where a truly Mozambican identity could emerge. Many whites also chafed under the Salazar/Caetano yoke of distant colonial dictatorship.

"With Tanganyika becoming independent in 1961, Tanzania was born, providing a huge, convenient base for Communist-backed rebels, who were intent on the collapse of Portugal in Africa, in this case, Mozambique. The leader of the terrorist movement from 1962 was one Dr. Eduardo Mondlane, a Shangaan who had been educated at university in Johannesburg before going on to Harvard and the United Nations, finally becoming a professor at Syracuse University. He and his white American wife, Janet, lived in Dar-es-Salaam, where he headed the FRENTE DE LIBERTAÇÃO DE MOÇAMBIQUE (FRELIMO) terrorist movement, the Liberation Front of Mozambique, the ruling body of present-day, one-party Marxist Mozambique. Dr. Mondlane was killed by a parcel bomb in 1969 and a certain Samora Machel took over.

"In the meantime, communist weapons poured into Dar-es-Salaam, as did newly returned, trained guerrillas, ready for a war in Mozambique, which got underway in October 1964 when a Portuguese priest was ambushed in the far north of the country; his head was cut off and stuck in a tree. Soon afterward, several innocent black tribesmen in the same area were murdered, their genitals stuffed in their mouths and revolutionary slogans stuck on their mutilated bodies to intimidate others.

"For years the Mozambique guerrilla activity was confined to the far northern province of Cabo Delgado, where the fierce Maconde tribe straddles the border with Tanzania, and to the province of Niassa in the far northwest, where the Nianja tribe straddles that border with Malawi. Both tribes were actively recruited to the guerrilla movement of what became FRELIMO, the Liberation Force of Mozambique.

"The Portuguese Army, which was two-thirds black in Mozambique and totally integrated, with many blacks serving in the elite commando/paratrooper units, became more and more heavily involved in quelling the revolutionary warfare in its several overseas provinces. The thing the world would not believe or accept was the terrible atrocities inflicted by black upon black to intimidate compliance. The hospitals in Tete and Nampula in Mozambique, for example, were filled with armless and legless blacks, many of them children, who had run foul of Kalashnikovs, Siminovs, Russian mortars, and Chinese hand grenades. Surgeons from South Africa used to fly in on gratis mercy missions to try and patch up these guerrilla victims, and all kinds of lay and religious organizations tried to help the people. The escalating contagion infected and affected every tribe in all ten provinces of Mozambique. Soon, the simple tribesmen were being regrouped in protected villages called *aldeamentos* in an effort to protect them and enable them to grow crops and live in relative peace, separated from the plague of terrorism. The cost to the impoverished Portuguese Government in Lisbon was staggering beyond belief. All part of the communist plan, as you will see.

"By about 1973, there were 'red' zones in former favorite hunting haunts of mine such as the Gorongosa region. The war had spread way south from those early atrocities just over the Rovuma River border with Tanzania. But I experienced no direct personal problems of any kind. I enjoyed excellent relations with one and all and felt that as long as I was left in peace at my home in Vila de Manica, I would live out my days in Mozambique. I had never been politically involved and had worked hard and long for all I owned. Mozambique was my home, with everything that word implies and which we all use so casually until it no longer exists.

"Then something amazing happened in Portugal itself. Sapped and drained by the mounting guerrilla war, there was felt indeed growing concern and outright antagonism by many continental Portuguese, particularly by young men of army age, concerning the heavy military burden of its African provinces. This, of course, was exploited by leftists everywhere to corrode the fighting morale of the nation and to implant the deadly seeds of guilt and military impotence. We Mozambicans, black, white, and brown, waited. Although we all knew it in our bones, none of us wanted to admit that we were about to be sold out, abandoned.

"There was increasing talk in, among others, Portuguese military circles, of the impossibility of a purely military solution to the guerrilla wars in Africa. Then a certain General Antonio de Spinola, the deputy chief of staff of the Portuguese armed forces at the time, published a book in early 1974 entitled *Portugal e o Futuro,* Portugal and the Future. In it he advocated the creation of a Federal Republic of Portugal in which each of the overseas provinces such as Mozambique would become independent but would be part of a federal assembly in Lisbon with a common head of state. That was the spark.

"On April 25, 1974, a coup took place in Portugal. Diplomatic relations were suddenly restored with the Soviet Union, which was directly responsible for the victims of guerrilla atrocities who languished in hospitals in Mozambique. Leftist leaders returned as heroes in Lisbon, and many top-ranking conservative officials were sacked and replaced by more compliant people, including the then Governor of Mozambique, a string of generals, some Cabinet ministers, and university professors. Portugal and her overseas provinces were now under what was supposed to be a provisional military junta.

"Within only four weeks of the coup, General de Spinola was already alarmed at the growing anarchy. His pacification politics were backfiring in May, 1974, and the Communist propaganda machine had a ball as it played on emotions, churning out atrocity stories, about those who opposed the Communists. Of course the world did not hear one word of the years of terror and bloodletting by these same Soviet-backed terrorists, whose violent campaign was unleashed throughout Portugal's African provinces, where instant death was the reward for questioning the 'new order.'

"The next thing we saw was emissaries being sent out to Mozambique after May, 1974, to negotiate with the powerful Marxist FRELIMO movement. A kiss-and-make up deal. As if you can ever negotiate with a crocodile. The murder gangs of FRELIMO 'freedom fighters' stepped up their activities, which now included active participation by children of thirteen and younger. Spinola's vision of a united federal Portugal was in tatters. It never had a chance, and we, who lived close to the action and who knew Africa from the inside, knew he was doomed. Trouble is, he took us along with him. FRELIMO continued to burn, pillage, rape, intimidate, and murder at will.

"We in Mozambique also saw the active collaboration with the terrorists of 'peace priests,' something I can never forgive. These priests and, indeed, nuns, were also active in neighboring Rhodesia, but that is another story.

"The Portuguese lost control very rapidly in Mozambique after the 1974 Lisbon coup. The will to resist, to fight was gone. The young troops from Portugal wanted to go home, while the gallant blacks in the army, all entitled to Portuguese passports, found themselves with whites who were talking appeasement with the very people who had, in numerous cases, murdered members of their own families, abducted children to guerrilla training camps, and committed unspeakable atrocities.

"Came June 25, 1975, and Mozambique became 'independent' from Portugal. The winds of chaos were now at gale force and I was soon engulfed, despite a clean track record of fair dealing in a country where I gave infinitely better than I ever received. I saw planeloads of people leave the country as it became increasingly clear that the new masters, under Samora

Machel, were intent on the total destruction of all we had built up, nurtured, and paid for over the decades.

"All of a sudden there were FRELIMO people with Soviet-bloc weapons all over the place, from small kids to old men, in their war against the Portuguese. I found out the hard way that these people weren't fooling around with their new toys.

"Very soon after that day in June, I had to go east from my home at Vila de Manica to Beira, some one hundred and sixty miles away. I took a pickup truck, as I needed to load on some spare parts. I was on my way back when I heard screaming and shouting. About six uniformed soldiers started pouring automatic fire into my truck and the attached trailer!

"Jesus! I couldn't believe it! Three RPG-7 rockets came right across the windscreen, missing the cab by inches! I slammed my foot to the firewall and somehow got away, although the vehicle as well as the trailer was shot to chunks. I wasn't hit. The RPG-7 is a formidable weapon, rather like a super bazooka, which, had one connected, would have had me one gone goose. Unless you've ever had the experience of being shot at, you cannot possibly know the shocked state I was in when I got home. I was nauseous, shaking, sweating, sick with shock and fear. I was sixty-three years old, and all of a sudden I saw blackness and doom ahead. Turned out I was nearly dead right.

"I later figured out that these gentlemen had just arrived and had not had a chance to place their ordnance in position. They took me for a Portuguese, since I am white, and that, pal, was quite enough for them. I think I surprised them, but the funny thing was that they held an overlead with those RPGs, whereas most of the Kalashnikov AK-47 assault rifle fire was behind me. I didn't know if there were more of these fellows farther along the road. The dust track seemed interminable. I reached home in a bad state.

"Yes, I had met FRELIMO roadblocks on the way down to Beira every few miles, but when I told them I was 'English,' everybody seemed to relax and I was waved through. I was afraid to pass myself off as an Aussie, as I figured they wouldn't have the first idea what that was. Most of those Africans didn't know themselves where they were in relation to the rest of the world. And it was this ignorance that was so exploited by the new masters. They didn't have the slightest idea of geography, except to know where the next shebeen was. They also had a fine knowledge of AK-47s, as some had been trained in eastern Europe—the part of the world that talks peace and exports murder.

"At these roadblocks the troops would search me and look over the car pretty carefully, then give me leave to push on. Now I didn't know how much of this I was going to be able to take. A little time went by, maybe a couple of weeks, and I had to head north to Vila Gouveia. I passed through several of these roadblocks.

"Then I was really nailed. The adult soldiers didn't touch me, although they were armed to their molars. It was the kids, all toting AK-47s and grenades, kids—some of them no older than eight years of age—with bloody machine pistols! Assault rifles! RPG-7s. These little bastards really got mean. It was like the former Belgian Congo and the *jeunesse* in 1960. Twelve-year-old generals, and the like. Something like six-year-olds packing nail bombs in Northern Ireland 'because mom told me to.'

"These animals swarmed the pickup and almost tore it apart in their enthusiasm to catch a white spy. By God, after all these roadblocks, what do these creatures find in my toolbox? Five .375 H & H cartridges, that's what! Oh, they were delighted! Never mind that the cartridges had been placed there by accident years previously and were green with age. The kids had found an armed enemy of the state! I was done for.

"Before I caught the first rifle butt in the stomach, one of them said to me, '*Somos os vigilantes!* We are the vigilant ones. You want to kill our president!' That was it. They got stuck into me and the men present took no notice until a new FRELIMO district administrator happened by and asked what the hell was going on. Why were they beating me to death?

"He stopped the swine as the soldiers sat by yawning. One of the kids brought out the cartridges.

"'Children, leave this man alone. Those are very old cartridges. They probably wouldn't even fire.'

"'No,' said the ringleader of this bunch, 'if he has cartridges, then he has a rifle. We, the vigilant, shall find it.'

"Of course I wasn't that stupid, but they dragged me off to a prison camp nearby with a high barbed-wire entanglement surrounding some huts and other dwellings, probably barracks. I spent the afternoon watching the 'vigilant ones' taking my car apart in their search for the miraculously concealed rifle. They then grabbed me and locked me in one of the huts.

"I slept fitfully through the night, as I was pretty ragged around the edges, thanks to their rifle butts. I asked one of the guards what they were going to do with me.

"'Well, you'll have to see the commandant.'

"'Where is he?'

"'Not here.'

"It came to lunchtime and I was getting pretty hungry. They had grabbed me a full day ago, and had not as yet fed me anything. I said to one of the soldiers, 'Look, there's a little store just down the road there. Can't you send somebody to cover me so I can buy some food?'

"The guy was reasonable enough to assign a couple of chaps to walk me down the road with AKs in my back to the store. There I chanced to bump into a Portuguese I knew."

"'What the hell are you doing here?' he asked.

"I told him and he said, 'Christ, Johnson, if that commandant catches you with those cartridges, you've really had it.'

"'Yes, but they tell me he's not here.'

"'Don't worry, he'll be back. He's really a bad guy. You know, the other day in one of these little stores, a terrorist took out a hand grenade from his pocket and put in some food and forgot the grenade on the counter. The storekeeper was arrested and put in a concentration camp and I hear he was shot. Hell, I really feel sorry for you. Let's see what happens.'

"I hung around the little store, having bought these guards some food which they ate while one man poked a hole in my ribs with the muzzle of his assault rifle. Then two Jeeps pulled up. One was absolutely loaded with machine-gunned impala.

One guard walked over to the Jeep and spoke with an officer, who turned to study me and gave me a wicked look. I figured that this was the commandant I had been warned against. The soldier came back, gave me a prod with his rifle, and told me that I now had to go to headquarters.

"They took me up there but, oddly, didn't let me inside the enclosure. After half an hour in the roasting sun, one of the soldiers told me that the commandant would see me just now.

"I saw this man, who could have had me shot with a snap of his fingers. Then another officer came by, and he also gave me a filthy look. Oh, man, here it comes, I thought.

"This second officer walked past two or three times, studying me. Hell, this went on for two to three hours, my waiting to see the commandant.

"Finally, the guard opened the gate and ordered me in. He said, 'Look, all the things we have taken out of your truck are lying there. Load them all back up again.'

"This practically meant reassembling the truck. It was one hell of a job. I finished, wondering all the time what was about to happen.

"The guard turned to me and said, 'Okay, you can go home now.'

"'But doesn't the commandant want to see me?'

"'No! Go!'

"I was so happy to get away from this lot! I was positive they were getting ready to shoot me. But as I got in the truck, the guard said he had a message for me: 'The commandant says he is also a hunter and has heard of you. He sometimes makes the same mistake you did. Sometimes he leaves cartridges in his car. It was a mistake. Now, go!'

"On the way home, I was stopped at several other roadblocks but there were no brutalized, crazed children or problems, other than the usual searches. I got through the whole lot without further incident."

"The handwriting was clearly on the wall and it would have taken an idiot not to see that it was scrawled in blood. I had goods to protect, but I had no idea to what degree this thing was going to escalate.

"I then began to make my plans. I had quite a few rifles, twenty very fine tusks which I had taken in the Central African Republic as a guest—really good stuff—and quite a bit of gold I had smelted down into three-ounce ingots. But what the blazes was I going to do with all of it? What was I going to do with my big house, all my possessions, my land, the little mine?

"Obviously I had to hide what I could against the possibility of receiving 'visitors.' But where?

"I took all my guns and ammo, protected them in some grease, carefully wrapped them, and on a moonlit night, took my headman, whom we shall call João, to bury them in the garden. I don't know if my man is still in detention, and I don't want to compromise him if he is still alive. Anyway, I had a grand frangipani plant and decided to dig it up and stick the stuff under it. João dug a deep hole. We removed the excess earth and watered it down so it looked natural. João understood what all this was about. He was an older man and had become alarmed at how his life and the order of his culture were being demolished, with little children now shouting the odds in a society where the adult's word had always been rigid law and kids towed the line. I could trust him.

"When I was satisfied, I thought about all that lovely ivory and decided to stash it way back in one of the ancient mines on the property mentioned by Dr. Karl Peters. We carried this ivory between us in relays, João and I, until it was all pretty well hidden.

"I still had the problem of the gold ingots.

"I seem to remember that I had made twenty-four of them, which, at three ounces per ingot, was a tidy sum of money. It was pure gold. I didn't want anybody to know where those were, so I told my men that I had sold the gold in Beira.

"At this point, I still figured I would be able to cross the border. I took that gold and, without anybody else knowing, I cut out pockets in a case of butter I had, one ingot to a slab. I then carefully smoothed over the butter, rewrapped each slab, and stuck the whole lot back in the deep freeze.

"I thought I was being pretty bright as I knew that my staff would never pinch food from me. Nobody knew about this gold, not even the kitchen staff.

"Yet the best-laid plans often backfire in the most curious manner."

"Not long after the June independence, I had to go to Umtali in Rhodesia for some mine piping and what not. I took my hunting car, drove the eighteen or so miles to the border, and crossed over with no trouble. I bought what I needed and headed back home within a few hours. When I reached the border post, the gate was closed.

"A man I knew very well asked me where I thought I was going. '*Vou para a minha casa.* Home, of course,' I replied.

"'Oh, no, you're not!'

"'What the hell are you talking about? I've lived here for fifty years! You know me. What do you mean, I can't go home?'

"'Yes, I know you well, Mr. Johnson, and you used to live in Mozambique. You no longer do. You can't come back.'

"'Why?'

"'We have your name here on this list. You are never allowed to come back to Mozambique.'

"'Are you crazy? Everything I own in the world is in Vila de Manica, my home!'

"'Sorry, orders.'

"Then four goons came up and pointed AK-47s at my belly. They constituted a convincing argument. I backed off."

"Jesus. Half a century! And these 'freedom fighters' take everything I own except the clothes on my back, my car, and a few bills in my wallet. I was dazed with shock and bewilderment. And I was angrier than I have ever been. What now?

"I went back to friends in Umtali and spent six months writing to the authorities in what was now Maputo rather than Lourenço Marques. To my great surprise, they answered one of my numerous letters in which I had pointed out that I was known for square dealing and fair treatment of all in Mozambique. No go. I was an officially declared 'prohibited immigrant.' And, in the Marxist state of Mozambique, that is that. I was also told in writing that if I ever tried to reenter the country, I would be shot on sight. I shall never know the reason for such hatred.

"My son Walter was working in Botswana as a pro hunter, so, since I already had a license there, I went over and joined him. I became a Botswana citizen, and did my best to start life all over at sixty-three. I also had my married daughter and her family in the Los Angeles area, where I could spend off-seasons. California is now my home for part of the year, when I am not in Africa with my friends in hunting camps. My son eventually also settled in California. So, in a way, I am luckier than many other people pitched out of their African homes and left utterly destitute."

"One thing that especially worried me was that I had a German chap working for me in the mine as well as general overseer of my small farm and property. His name was Herbert. I tried everything to get a message through to him as to what had happened, but with no success.

"After a year, he somehow found me and wrote a long letter, telling me what had happened at my place. I had previously tried to get a note through to him via some border guard 'friends' but they were far too afraid to help.

"I remember reading and rereading that letter a hundred times. In all, I lost my valuables, a good bank account, because it was frozen, the ivory, the gold, the weapons, several vehicles, implements, my home, all the furnishings, my books, personal papers, a lifetime of photographs, and everything else that made up the very fabric of my existence on earth. The photographs you see in this book are the lucky few copies my daughter had in America. Otherwise, we would not even have these."

"The German wrote:

> Shortly after you were shut out at the border, a bunch of these FRELIMO goons arrived at your home. I was there. The

party included a Bulgarian, an East German, a Russian, two blacks, and a couple of Cubans. All spoke excellent English and Portuguese.

It was lunchtime and these men demanded that we kill six of your chickens and have the staff make lunch, which I ordered them to do. I was frightened and had no appetite after these men grilled me about the location of your gold. I told them that, as far as I knew, you had sold it in Beira. I don't think they believed me. I did not eat with them and the Russian said, 'Why don't you eat with us? I know why. It is because we are Marxists, no?'

I told them that I just didn't have any appetite and they became rather surly but they left me alone.

In the middle of lunch, the Russian said to me that he greatly admired that frangipani shrub in your garden and he asked me if I would like to make a gift of it to his wife in Maputo. What could I say? While this lunch was going on, he had me get several of the new 'comrades' to dig it out. The Russian then told the men in perfect Shangaan to dig a bit deeper. He was interested in the soil composition.

They hauled up all your guns and ammunition. I knew *nothing* about this, Wally. But the FRELIMO people did not believe me and started asking me about your ivory. The Bulgarian said he believed that there were some interesting old mines on the place and he would like to have a look at them for archaeological reasons. Obviously, he knew the location of the ivory, as had the Russian about the guns. After lunch, they went directly to the ivory, but not before a terrible thing happened at the lunch table. It was the longest day of my life, Wally.

I did not know you had hidden your gold in the butter. Well, these men demanded bread and butter at lunch. The cook got a frozen chunk out of the freezer and served it up, not knowing any more than any of us as to what was hidden. The butter softened pretty quickly and the men began to scrape the butter when one of them hit something hard.

'And what's this?' the East German asked.

I told him I didn't know. Well, the gold was discovered and the freezer torn apart. I and all your staff were then arrested and transported to a FRELIMO concentration camp at Vila Pery, about eighty miles east. Your headman was missing, though. We were kept there in terrible conditions for eleven months before, for some reason, being transferred to a camp in Maputo.

"Herbert then went on to write that he was marched, together with some other prisoners, in the streets of Maputo. An Indian whom he had known very well in the old L.M. happened to recognize Herbert and went to another German friend to explain what he had seen. The other German then went to the FRELIMO authorities and demanded to know why Herbert was in detention.

"He was told Herbert had been a war criminal and that he had killed hundreds of people. That's funny, coming from the likes of FRELIMO. The second German then went straight away to the West German consul in Maputo and pointed out that Herbert was only five years old at the end of World War II! So how could he have killed hundreds of people?

"Pressure was exerted and Herbert was freed and deported to West Germany. It was from there that he eventually contacted me."

Wally told me this tragic story one evening on the banks of the Mupamadzi River. When he had finished, I asked him how this bunch at lunch had known where the guns and ivory had been cached.

"Ah, it had to be João. I have never blamed him. Those bastards probably put a blowtorch to his feet until he admitted where all the stuff was. They probably shot him after that so as not to take chances. You can bet that none of my valuables, especially the gold, ever found their way into the Communist coffers for the good of the 'people.'

Wally, understandably, has never been able to shrug off what happened to him at the hands of those "comrades." It happened too late in his life for him to start anew. But this did not deter him from trying to find out one last time the final fate of his home and possessions at Vila de Manica. He reckoned he'd been through so much already that a few more shocks would be quite bearable. His chance came in 1986.

16

AFTERMATH-THE STRUGGLE CONTINUES

Wally and I discussed at great length the most appropriate end to this story. We wondered if the standard "epilogue" would really be the correct term. Then we thought that the word "aftermath" was more apt. It indicates the remains of a battlefield, which Mozambique has become, like many other places in Africa where safari hunting once flourished and game abounded. In Wally's old home, there are, indeed, as Shakespeare put it in Julius Caesar *"carrion men groaning for burial," as the dogs of war have most surely been slipped.*

This chapter rounds out Wally's story and is a eulogy to the grand hunting world Mozambique once was where men such as Wally upheld the traditions and shared the magic with clients from all over the world. The quality of African safari hunting is diminishing by the day, as conditions quite beyond the control of the pro hunter encroach upon his world and threaten what remains of the game. We shall all be the poorer should the safari industry elsewhere in Africa share Mozambique's fate.

Probably the most widely heard communist slogan in the Mozam-

bican bush war was A Luta Continua, *the struggle continues. You will not fail to notice the deep irony of those words as you read of Wally's attempt in 1986 to revisit Mozambique with his son in an effort to see his old home again and to learn just what had happened in Mozambique in the intervening years. Let Wally tell you himself.*

"Walter, Jr., came over to join me after I'd spent months on safari in Zambia in 1986. We did a marathon stretch through most of southern Africa, reliving old dreams and exhuming old memories with friends. In Zimbabwe, formerly Rhodesia, we made a point of trying to get back to Vila de Manica through the old border post I knew so well and for so long.

"My God! Some of the chaps from the old days were still on duty there. They greeted me warmly, and I finally got around to asking whether I could come in for a few hours so that I could go down the road and see what had happened to my home. After all, I do carry a Botswana passport, a country friendly to Mozambique.

"They were courteous, but the AK-47s were still there. 'No,' came the answer. 'You remain a prohibited immigrant.'

"I saw the waste of time this would be as I looked up the road that led to my real home. As I gazed, I was further informed that antigovernment 'bandits' in Mozambique were in the region and that I could not travel safely anyway.

"I just turned my back on those border guards and their 'workers' paradise' and walked away. This time, I did not look back."

"Mozambique has been devastated by its communist-led and -financed bush war, which replaced a remarkably integrated and peaceful country, whatever the faults, injustices, and oppression of the past era, with a way of life that makes me think of an impala in the jaws of a hyena. The rest of the world hasn't a clue as to the price that has been paid for this 'freedom.' The Mozambicans do, particularly the rural folk.

"I am not interested in the political claims and counterclaims as to who is supporting what faction in my old home. All I know is that a huge, effective anti-FRELIMO rebel force exists in Mozambique. Ironically, it is widely supported by people who at first supported FRELIMO but turned to supporting RENAMO when they saw and suffered the consequences of FRELIMO rule. I also know that this rebel force, known as RENAMO—the Mozambican National Resistance—has been locked in vicious combat with FRELIMO since soon after independence in 1975, when we were handed over to the wolves. I also know that RENAMO now effectively controls 85 percent of the country, the FRELIMO forces maintaining control only in the towns, as was the case in the end with the Portuguese. Civil war is raging in Mozambique, and hundreds and thousands of desperate people—black people—have fled their homeland as famine sweeps the country.

"I regard myself as a refugee from Mozambique. I shall always feel bereaved at the loss of my home and my way of life. I lie awake wondering what happened to it all. Is my house still standing? Is it pockmarked with bullets? Who lives in it now or on the grounds? Where did my books go, especially my autographed collection from Bob Ruark? It is like having a death in the family—but the body is missing, so there is always the insane hope that maybe the bad news is not true; that things will return to what they were.

"Understandably, I read everything I can on Mozambique. I have pages of harsh facts from irrefutable sources as to what Marxist rule and brutal civil war have done for my old country. Here's a sampling, and as you skim through the items, ask yourself if Mozambique will ever be a safari country again. It is finished as far as foreign hunting clients go. Finished forever. My story is now history, and the following bears me out":

- In a country of some fourteen million, enough food for only five million people was predicted as the harvest in 1986, scheduled to last exactly one month. This from Pierre Serge Bolduc, the Swiss adviser to the World Food Program. The 1985/1986 harvest was scheduled to be the worst in thirty years, drought, floods, and civil war adding to the misery. So, Mozambique is existing on international handouts as never before in its long history.

* * *

- The late President Samora Machel admitted that his socialist economic policies were not working. Yet foreign nationals can buy pretty well what they want, from French champagne to color television sets, from a special supermarket in Maputo—as long as they pay in hard currency, not the Mickey Mouse money of Mozambique called *meticais.* As a result of economic mismanagement and years of brutal civil war the ordinary people of the country struggle for such basics as cooking oil and soap and have to exist on draconian rationing, and the people of the countryside are dying like flies from sheer starvation.

- The country's infrastructure has broken down and the blame lies with rebel activity, administrative incompetence, and ideological madness. At the height of the Portuguese struggle against Communist insurgency, the people never knew such suffering and hunger as is now the case in Mozambique.

- Oxfam, the British-based relief agency, stated in December 1986 that Mozambique is facing outright famine in 1987 and that over four million Mozambicans have been displaced by the civil war. There is now talk of a new Ethiopia and of desperate calls for airlifts of basic foodstuffs and clothing, never mind medical supplies.

- The Mozambican Red Cross has told of rural folk in my old area eating roots from wild trees and wearing bark for clothing. The Save the Children Fund, together with Oxfam, have declared Mozambique an emergency area as refugees continue to stream into Zambia, Malawi, Zimbabwe, and South Africa.

- RENAMO has gained control in many areas of Mozambique's ten provinces and the FRELIMO government is facing a foreign debt which is three times its annual GNP. In turn, this GNP is a mere quarter of what it was at independence, these harsh facts being given by Professor André Thomashausen of West Germany, an acknowledged authority on post-independence Mozambique.

- To round out this picture of human misery and economic collapse, I quote Randolph Schmid, reporting from Washington, D.C., on the findings of Joseph Speidel, vice-president of the Population Crisis Committee, a group that monitors the quality of life in countries all over the world. Basing its findings on elements such as the infant mortality rate, access to clean water, literacy, per-capita calorie consumption, inflation rate, increase in urbanization, the gross national product per capita, and general personal freedom, Mozambique recorded a massive ninety-five points out of a hundred on the scale used to measure the level of human misery in a country. Mozambique leads the world now in human suffering on all fronts. This report is dated March 1987, so nothing much can possibly have improved by the time you read my story.

Despite the shiploads of Russian weaponry and the presence of thousands of troops from Tanzania, Zimbabwe, Ethiopia, and Cuba, my old country is more strife-torn than ever. It is perhaps the most catastrophic example of political mismanagement and the effects of war. The misery of the Mozambicans seems now boundless, and I am deeply affected by every report of war and devastation I read as I realize more and more clearly that I have indeed lost my home and the way of life that went with it.

"Perhaps my fate would have been worse had I been allowed back that day in 1975. I would almost certainly have been killed by the '*camaradas,*' the 'comrades.' The harassment had already started. At least I managed to survive and record my story with Peter concerning a world nobody else can now know. It is buried, together with the remains of a hunting country that stood with the best, and which will be remembered by many as having given them a safari experience that no money on earth can now bring back or even remotely duplicate."

INDEX